JOSEPH CONRAD
Achievement and Decline

Joseph Conrad

Achievement and Decline

by Thomas Moser

ARCHON BOOKS-Hamden, Connecticut
nineteen hundred and sixty-six

© 1957 by the President and Fellows of Harvard College

Reprinted 1966 with permission
with minor corrections

Library of Congress Catalog Card Number 66–12321

Printed in the United States of America

For *MARY CHURCHILL MOSER*

ACKNOWLEDGMENTS

A small portion of this book appeared, in different form, in the *Harvard Library Bulletin*, Autumn, 1956.

J. M. Dent and Sons Ltd., have kindly permitted me to quote extensively from Conrad's manuscript, "The Rescuer," to which they hold the copyright.

I wish to thank two officers of the Radcliffe College Library, Miss Ruth Porritt, Head Librarian, and Miss Mary Howard, Archivist, for special assistance during the writing of this book.

A grant from Wellesley College paid part of the typing costs.

I am grateful to members of Professor Albert J. Guerard's 1950 and 1953 Harvard-Radcliffe graduate seminars in the modern novel, who will no doubt see some of their ideas reflected here.

Several persons read this book in manuscript. I wish to thank Professor Douglas Bush of Harvard University for both his tolerance and his valuable suggestions. Miss Ellen Rogers, Wellesley, Class of 1955, contributed a number of useful comments. Mr. John Hawkes of Harvard helped significantly with the introduction. Mr. Peter Davison, formerly of the Harvard University Press, read several versions, showed me how to rearrange and condense some especially unmanageable material, and pointed out an important matter of style.

One person deserves particular thanks. For nearly a decade Albert J. Guerard has been sharing with me his ever-deepening perceptions into Conrad. (These will shortly become

viii　　　　　*ACKNOWLEDGMENTS*

generally available with the publication of his new book on Conrad.) Even more important for me, however, has been the pervasive influence of the attitude toward fiction which informs all his criticism. Mr. Guerard sees the relationship between the novelist and his work as extremely complex and sees the novel as the often imperfect product of the novelist's conflicting inner impulses. Finally, he has wrestled with my book from its earliest rough draft through to the present version with a devotion beyond the call of duty and, even, of friendship.

Let me conclude by thanking my wife, who did much more than merely type manuscripts and protect the author from son and dog. She participated vigorously in the revision of every sentence and succeeded in removing at least some of the faults. Her presence, moreover, gave encouragement to the whole effort.

THOMAS MOSER

November, 1956
Stanford University

CONTENTS

JOSEPH CONRAD
Achievement and Decline

Introduction

As England's most complex novelist, Joseph Conrad requires and deserves the most discriminating study. In the last decade or so he has begun to receive such perceptive reading. It is my hope that this book, although concentrating upon Conrad's less successful productions, will contribute to an appreciation of his best work and give insight into a great writer's creative strengths and weaknesses. This study grew out of a chronological reading of Conrad's works, and it would perhaps be well to state specifically the prejudices with which the first complete reading was begun some six years ago. I was already acquainted with *The Nigger of the "Narcissus," "Youth," "Heart of Darkness," Lord Jim, Typhoon,* and "The Secret Sharer," but not with *Nostromo* or *Victory.* This introduction had engendered two general ideas: that Conrad is as great as M. C. Bradbrook[1] and F. R. Leavis[2] believe him to be, and as serious and subtle as Morton D. Zabel and Albert J. Guerard show him to be. I have been particularly influenced by these last two critics, by Mr. Zabel's perceptions into the "test" in Conrad,[3] and Mr. Guerard's awareness of Conrad's classical pessimism and of "his simultaneous achievement of intimacy and detachment, his power to sympathize with his victims without losing clear sight of their deficiencies." [4]

A complete reading of Conrad produced several surprises. *Nostromo* proved to be even better than I had dared hope, and *Victory* seemed, in comparison with the early novels, an utterly inferior work. A scanty knowledge of Conrad criticism made me eager to read *The Secret Agent* and *Under Western Eyes, Chance* and *The Shadow Line*. The first two, while clearly serious, respectable novels, seemed to lack that particular magic one thinks of as "Conradian." *Chance* proved to be as unsatisfactory as *Victory*. The first reading of *The Shadow Line*, following, as it did, my disappointment in *Victory*, produced feelings of approval, but subsequent readings have considerably altered that evaluation. On the other hand, subsequent readings of *Chance* and *Victory* have revealed a few hidden virtues that were missed in the depths of the first disappointment.

Mr. Guerard's account of Conrad's "anticlimax" [5] had inspired suspicions about the novels after *The Shadow Line*, suspicions which were more than justified. I was particularly struck by the degeneration of Conrad's prose style. In 1899, Conrad was writing sentences like this:

Jim would glance at the compass, would glance around the unattainable horizon, would stretch himself till his joints cracked with a leisurely twist of the body, in the very excess of well-being; and, as if made audacious by the invincible aspect of the peace, he felt he cared for nothing that could happen to him to the end of his days.

In 1918, he was writing sentences like this:

My emotions and sensations were childlike and chaotic inasmuch that they were very intense and primitive, and that I lay very helpless in their unrelaxing grasp.

What I found to be major Conrad was confined, then, to the work of about one half of his career (from *The Nigger of the "Narcissus,"* first published in book form in 1897, through "The Secret Sharer," 1912).

This reading of Conrad is not at all a new intuition. At the time of Conrad's death in 1924, John Galsworthy plotted a curve of his friend's career much like the one I have just sketched.

Chance, in 1914 — an indifferent Conrad — at last brought him fortune. From that year on to the end his books sold well; yet, with the exception of *The Secret Sharer* and some parts of *Victory,* none of his work in that late period was up to his own exalted mark . . . It does disservice to Conrad's memory to be indiscriminate in praise of his work. Already, in reaction from this wholesale laudation, one notices a tendency in the younger generation to tilt the nose skyward and talk of his "parade." The shining work of his great period was before their time; it places him among the finest writers of all ages. Conrad's work from *An Outcast of the Islands* to *The Secret Agent,* his work in *The Secret Sharer,* in the first chapters of *The Rescue* (written in 1898), and of some portions of *Victory,* are to his work in *The Arrow of Gold* and the last part of *The Rescue* as the value of pearl to that of mother-of-pearl.[6]

Although most recent critics have tended to disparage some of the work that Galsworthy calls Conrad's best and praise some that he disparages, Mr. Guerard and Douglas Hewitt,[7] whose excellent book on Conrad appeared while the present work was in progress, seem to be in considerable agreement with Galsworthy.

In undertaking this study, I have had in mind two questions: why did a writer of Conrad's calibre write so unevenly and why is his later work so inferior to his earlier? The plan of the study follows, in a sense, the sequence of one common reader's response to a chronological reading of Conrad's works. The first chapter tries to define what is "Conradian"; to measure the height, in Galsworthy's phrase, of Conrad's "own exalted mark." It studies the early period in terms of key ideas and typical characters and of the complex structures and symbolic style which express these ideas. The first part of Chapter II tries to account for the marked unevenness of Conrad's writing even in the early period. It finds "love" to be the lowest common denominator of the apprentice work of *Almayer's Folly, An Outcast of the Islands,* and *Tales of Unrest;* of the inferior short novels "Falk" and "Freya of the Seven Isles"; of the weak portions of "Heart of Darkness,"

Lord Jim, and *Nostromo.* The second part of Chapter II examines the subject of love as it dominates the later period, where it is central to six of the seven novels. Chapter III deals with Conrad's work after 1912, concentrating on *Chance, Victory, The Shadow Line,* and *The Rescue.* It contrasts to the early the later Conrad's view of man and the world as revealed in key ideas, types of characters, and technique. The last chapter discusses Conrad's fatigue, his loss of invention and creative energy in the novels after *The Shadow Line.*

To some, this study may seem incomplete. It has already been called a "limited sort of pathography" [8] because, while it discusses the mind revealed in the novels, it eschews biographical materials. I do not intend to apologize for studying the quality of Conrad's mind. Henry James long ago made that his chief criterion for judging a writer. Moreover, to study any writer's *development* (the common reader instinctively compares works by the same author) surely means presupposing a living mind behind those works. The question of biography cannot, however, be so summarily dismissed; certain aspects of Conrad's life do appear relevant to a study of his decline.

Since the validity of this study virtually hinges upon my analysis of Conrad's difficulties in writing about love, the reader may well wonder why I have not discussed Conrad's own marriage. The material available seems to merit investigation. It is certainly curious, for example, that Conrad did not marry until he was thirty-nine years old. And the circumstances of that marriage, as recounted by Mrs. Conrad, are even more curious. He prefaced his proposal with the announcement "that he had not very long to live and no intention of having children." [9] When Jessie George accepted him, his face wore an "expression of acute suffering." [10] They parted almost immediately, and she heard nothing from him for three days. Just before their wedding he demanded that she burn all his letters to her. He revealed later that within two hours of the marriage ceremony "he perceived what he had done, and got into a panic at the thought that he didn't know what it was to live with a woman." [11] Moreover, Mrs. Conrad's books, goodhumored as they are, reveal that her life with her husband was something less than idyllic; frequently irritable, Conrad must often have seemed an unreasonable husband and father.

But, not being an expert psychoanalytical biographer, I would be most hesitant in deducing "fear of sex" from the recorded events of Conrad's life. I would always be uneasy about the context of those events. Conrad had, after all, compelling practical reasons for being terrified about marriage in 1896; just then he was trying to decide whether he should, after twenty years of merchant service, give up the sea for the unpromising career of a writer: *"Le vrai métier de chien!"* [12] Later, he had motives other than misogyny for being an irascible husband. Conscious of his great gifts as a writer, he suffered countless frustrations from the outset of his career. Despite a favorable press, his books did not sell, and the Conrads were in financial straits until 1914. The "jungle gout" which he caught in the Congo sporadically inflicted on him severe pain; an accident rendered his wife a virtual cripple after 1903; acute illnesses almost took the lives of both his sons. Despite all this, much evidence indicates that Conrad remained most of the time an affectionate, vivacious human being, genuinely fond of his wife and children.

Perhaps a full psychoanalytical biography could find sources in the life of the historical Conrad for the evasiveness which the writer Conrad reveals when dealing with sexual situations. But I am not sure that the explanation would be relevant to the purposes of this study. As readers of Conrad's fiction, are we not primarily interested in the ways in which his ambivalent feelings about sex, whatever their sources or their expressions in "real life," affect the novels as novels?

Again, Conrad's relations with his publishers and his public may seem germane to a study of his decline. Certainly, Conrad's last popularity was due more to the clever publicity of Alfred A. Knopf, the young reader for Doubleday, than to a belated recognition of his true worth.[13] Moreover, the subject matter of his last, inferior novels does seem potentially much more "popular" than that of the early, great works. Yet we shall see that the early Conrad tried to write popular fiction at the suggestion of his publisher and simply could not do it; the problem is, then, more complex than one of external pressure. Even if one can demonstrate that the later Conrad tried deliberately to be popular, the pertinent question for this study remains: what was the effect upon the novels?

Finally, Conrad's extreme ill health in the last years may appear to be worth more detailed consideration than it receives in Chapter IV. No doubt the fact that he had to dictate his last novels after having composed with pen for over twenty years altered his prose style. But this fact tells us nothing about the nature of that alteration. Henry James dictated his last, most complicated novels and in a style quite different from his early prose. Yet it is hardly a settled matter that James's fiction declined then; it is certainly clear that his last novels far outshine Conrad's. Thus, to point to dictation still begs the question: what was the effect upon the style itself? Only a close examination of Conrad's novels can lead us to an understanding of the decline of his creative powers.

As the reader will discover, I have made some use of biographical material. It has established the dating of his works — most important in an analysis of development and decline. G. Jean-Aubry and John Dozier Gordan, as well as Conrad in his autobiographical works, have provided excellent accounts of the real-life sources of his fiction. This information proved invaluable in determining how heavily

Conrad drew upon certain experiences and whether he had written himself out. Finally, Conrad's letters to his closest friends in the last years of his life give us a picture of his final efforts different from and more human than that sketched by some of his critics.

It may be correctly guessed from this summary that no single answer is found to the question: "Why Conrad's anti-climax?" I must confess that from the first I did not expect to find an answer, that I felt about explaining Conrad's decline much as Lionel Trilling feels about explanations of Wordsworth's:

> Given the fact of the great power, the desire to explain its relative deterioration will no doubt always be irresistible. But we must be aware, in any attempt to make this explanation, that an account of why Wordsworth ceased to write great poetry must at the same time be an account of how he once did write great poetry. And this latter account, in our present state of knowledge, we cannot begin to furnish.[14]

It seemed, however, that several partial answers might come closer to hinting at the truth than one neat but perhaps utterly wrong answer. There have been so many attempts to discover the figure in Conrad's carpet that I resolved *not* to find one. Mr. Hewitt shows the dangers inherent in settling upon one interpretation by attacking Gustav Morf's reading of Conrad: "The practitioners of the [psychoanalytical] method do not, by it, discriminate between the qualities" of the novels.[15] Yet Mr. Hewitt makes the same mistake in trying to justify at all costs his own very plausible bias that Conrad's best period is 1898–1909. Trapped by his thesis, he discusses "The End of the Tether" in the same chapter as "Heart of Darkness" and "Youth," and makes "Falk" an important connecting link between Conrad's two greatest novels, *Lord Jim* and *Nostromo*.[16] He gives no hint that "Falk" and "The End of the Tether" are seriously inferior to the other works of the period.

The method of this study is (or would like to be) exegetical. Two considerations made close attention to the text seem the only way to approach the problem of Conrad's decline. The first was the conviction that the essence of Conrad is his complexity and that this complexity can best be conveyed by a detailed examination of his work. Just as important as the figure in Conrad's carpet is its color, texture, richness, depth. Conrad vibrates with correspondences; yet only Dorothy Van Ghent, in her analysis of *Lord Jim*,[17] has begun to demonstrate how complex his attitude is and how close-textured his prose. The exegetical method is employed, secondly, because of my belief that Conrad's decline is in some degree implicit in his creative temperament, and that the possibility of such a later decline is present in his earliest work. This accounts for the close attention paid to the unknown early fragments, *The Sisters* and "The Rescuer," and it accounts for the repeated references to early work during examination of the later novels. The year 1912 should not be thought of as a definite watershed. It is simply a convenience. In that year "The Secret Sharer," the last first-rate Conrad, appeared in book form, and *Chance,* the first clearly second-rate work that pretended to be of major importance, began to appear as a serial in the New York *Herald*.[18]

It may be objected, on the basis of Chapter II, that this work does not record the response of one common reader to the Conrad canon but rather expresses the wild fancies of a Freudian enthusiast. To this I can only say that I did not plan it to turn out as it did. Falstaff says of Worcester's treason that it "lay in his way, and he found it." So sexual situations seemed to keep turning up when faulty Conradian prose was under scrutiny. In the middle of the twentieth century it is very difficult and rather foolish to think or talk about sex without using some of Freud's perceptions and terminology.

The reader may also object to what seems an excessive use of "we." I do not mean the word to be read as the "royal we," handing down from the throne the key to Joseph Conrad. Nor do I mean it to be read as an "editorial we," which evades responsibility for its criticism. Rather, "we" means "you and I," two common readers, striving to be better readers by venturing together into the dark world of Joseph Conrad's fiction.

I

The Early Conrad's Anatomy of Moral Failure (1895–1912)

Since the end of World War II, a new and serious interest in the novels of Joseph Conrad has been developing. There is little doubt that we have to thank such critics as M. C. Bradbrook, F. R. Leavis, and M. D. Zabel [1] for the rediscovery. Their fresh examinations of Conrad prior to 1946 stimulated critics, students, publishers, and the public to turn again to the man who had been accepted in the early 1920's as England's greatest living novelist but was pretty well forgotten after his death. Each year since the end of World War II, at least one book or major critical article on Conrad has appeared. His collected works have been reissued as well as a number of new editions of individual works. For better or worse, his works are classics. High school students read his "masterpieces"; undergraduates solemnly discover that a heart of darkness beats within themselves; and graduate students expertly trace the involutions of his complicated chronology.

Conrad has at last been "freed from that infernal tail of ships" [2] which so outraged him during his lifetime. His other bête noire, "exotic," no longer dominates discussions of his early work. Instead, we see him now as a serious and complex novelist who uses for very important purposes subject matter which could be merely picturesque. We see him as a profound psychologist, relentlessly exploring the causes of moral failure and the motives that underlie seemingly praiseworthy actions. We see him as something of a political prophet, foretelling with appalling accuracy the political immorality of the twentieth century. And we see him as one of the most audacious craftsmen in the history of the English novel: Conrad the artist packs every page with added meaning through his complex structures and richly symbolic language. Looming over these three Conrads (psychologist, political observer, artist), including them all, stands Conrad the moralist. Surely it is the author speaking when the narrator of *Under Western Eyes* says that "moral discovery . . . should be the object of every tale."

In attempting to uncover the sources and trace the characteristics of Conrad's decline, we need first to consider what he declined *from*. We need to try to define the quality of his good, early work — to describe its moral, pychological, and artistic "world." We need to discover what has value in Conrad's world. What constitutes good and bad action? What are the patterns of action of his characters? Of whom does. he approve, or disapprove? What kind of character interests him most? From these questions we can move on to examine the relationship between moralist and psychologist, between moralist and political observer. Finally, we can look at a few characteristically Conradian techniques, to see how they contribute to meaning.

On the surface, Conrad's ethic seems very simple indeed. Humanity is important; fidelity is the highest virtue. When we come to consider this ethic in relation to the actions of the characters, we shall see that Conrad's interests are much more subtle and complex than these two simple ideas suggest. But we should be misreading him if we failed to appreciate the strength of his intellectual and emotional allegiance to a stoic humanism.

Conrad's early works contain many references to the human community, to the group. In his first artistic successes, the great sea stories, the group is restricted in scope, consisting only of small crews on the last of the sailing vessels. Of the crew of the *Narcissus,* the narrator asks, at the end of the voyage, "Haven't we, *together* and upon the immortal sea, wrung out a meaning from our sinful lives? Goodbye, brothers! You were a good crowd." (The italics are mine.) On the *Judea,* in "Youth," "they all worked. That crew of Liverpool hard cases had in them the right stuff." The exclusiveness of the group in these stories is the natural result of a circumscribed subject matter rather than of any limitation of Conrad's sympathies. When we come to *Lord Jim* (begun immediately after "Youth"), we find that the concept of the group is considerably broader in its implications. It is no longer simply the crew, but the "ranks." Marlow sees himself as one who keeps his "place in the ranks of an insignificant multitude," while Jim is a "straggler yearning inconsolably for his humble place in the ranks." Conrad here has more in mind than the fraternity of faithful seamen. The "ranks" also include the solid folk of England. Jim is "one of us" because "he came from the right place." Toward the end of the novel the author suggests that the ranks Jim belongs to, or should belong to, are essentially the whole community of Western man. For this reason, it is doubtful whether Jim can redeem himself by leaving that community to seek his fortune in the East, in Patusan. "We must fight in the ranks or our lives don't count." Our actions must be "based on a firm conviction in the truth of ideas racially our own, in whose name are established the order, the morality of an ethical progress."

Conrad's conception of solidarity goes beyond the bond of labor and courage on the sea, however — beyond the tradition of the responsible English people, beyond Western man with his belief in ethical progress. Beyond all these, Conrad feels pity and admiration for suffering humanity in general, for the human community confronted by a godless universe. Such an attitude is clear in all the best Conrad from 1900 to 1912. It is implicit in *Lord Jim* and *Typhoon,* explicit in the political novels, *Nostromo, The Secret Agent,* and *Under Western Eyes.* The *Patna* and the *Nan-Shan* carry human cargo. This is why Jim's failure on the *Patna* is so serious, why Captain MacWhirr's heroism on the *Nan-Shan* is crucial in *Typhoon.* Although Conrad does not labor the point, he makes it perfectly clear by vivid visualization of the two cargoes — eight hundred pilgrims bound on an errand of faith, two hundred coolies returning to their homes after seven years of work. He insists on the numbers of the *Patna* pilgrims, their defencelessness, and especially their humanity:

Below the roof of awnings, surrendered to the wisdom of white men and to their courage, trusting the power of their unbelief and the iron shell of the fire-ship, the pilgrims of an exacting faith slept on mats, on blankets, on bare planks, on every deck, in all the dark corners, wrapped in dyed cloths, muffled in soiled rags, with their heads resting on small bundles, with their faces pressed to bent forearms: the men, the women, the children; the old with the young, the decrepit with the lusty — all equal before sleep, death's brother.

In the political novels, dictators, revolutionists, anarchists, secret agents, and self-deluded "reformers" all act within the same frame of reference — the masses, who will inevitably suffer from the political action. In *Nostromo,* Mrs. Gould, traveling in the interior of Sulaco, discovers the "soul of the land . . . a great land of plain and mountain and people, suffering and mute, waiting for the future in a pathetic immobility of patience." Patience and mere numbers become a positive force making trivial the fiercest efforts of the anarchists in *The Secret Agent.* The Professor, maker of bombs, looks upon the London crowds from the top of an omnibus and despairs:

the thought of a mankind as numerous as the sands of the sea-shore, as indestructible, as difficult to handle, oppressed him. The sound of exploding bombs was lost in their immensity of passive grains without an echo.

Even the Russians of *Under Western Eyes* — that portion of
the human community which Conrad, the Pole, found most
difficult to tolerate — even the Russians have his sympathy.
He writes without irony of Nathalie Haldin's love of "our
poor people."

At the end of what we are calling the early period (although it spans well over half of his career), Conrad, in *A
Personal Record,* looked back to those days when he was
writing his first book. He tried to recall his first feelings of
literary inspiration, tried to account for the fact that certain
people whom he had seen in "real life" now sought him out
as fictional characters. He inevitably saw that inspiration in
terms of human solidarity.

It seems now to have had a moral character, for why should the
memory of these beings, seen in their obscure sun-bathed existence, demand to express itself in the shape of a novel, except on
the ground of that mysterious fellowship which unites in a
community of hopes and fears all the dwellers on this earth?

It follows that Conrad should have seen loyalty and service
as the central virtues of his world: "Those who read me
know my conviction that the world . . . rests on a few very
simple ideas. . . It rests notably . . . on the idea of Fidelity." Faithfulness is the key to Conrad's moral code, which
is, essentially, the code of the British Merchant Marine, or,
as Marlow puts it in *Lord Jim,* "the service of the Red Rag,"
"the craft of the sea." One does one's duty; one works hard.
Marlow wants to see Jim "squirm for the honour of the
craft," and he views himself as a "member of an obscure
body of men held together by a community of inglorious
toil and by fidelity to a certain standard of conduct."

It is Conrad the moralist, with his simple idea of fidelity,
who chooses the central situation of the early stories: the
test. Conrad wishes to explore that most important moment
in an individual's life, the moment which reveals whether or
not he is faithful to the community. Here Conrad is the

traditional moralist; each of his stories is a kind of pilgrim's progress (but without God!). Thus his natural story, the voyage, is perfectly congenial to his moral view. Young Marlow's first trip to the East in "Youth" is one of "those voyages that seem ordered for the illustration of life, that might stand for a symbol of existence." In "The Secret Sharer," the young captain stands alone on the deck of his first command, thinking about himself and his ship: "In this breathless pause at the threshold of a long passage we seemed to be measuring our fitness for a long and arduous enterprise, the appointed task of both our existences." Ideally, the voyager returns home with new knowledge. When Marlow returns from his trip into Africa's dark heart, he feels toward the citizenry as Gulliver did after he returned from his travels:

They were intruders whose knowledge of life was to me an irritating pretence, because I felt so sure they could not possibly know the things I knew . . . I had no particular desire to enlighten them, but I had some difficulty in restraining myself from laughing in their faces . . .

Those who fail the test and learn nothing from their failure unconsciously avoid other tests. After Jim deserts the *Patna*, he is good for no other work than that of a water-clerk: "A water-clerk need not pass an examination in anything under the sun."

Conrad sees experience as a test, and his characters' responses to the test determine their place in his moral hierarchy. It is here that the simple Conradian ideas become more involved. In the best works of the early period, we find three major types of character and one minor type, all of them defined through response to a moral crisis, to a question of right or wrong, to the issue of fidelity or betrayal. The first of these types is *the simple hero*: the unreflective, courageous, loyal seaman. He meets his crisis, often some disaster at sea, with unthinking devotion. His guide is the code we have just been considering. This code unites him with a large group of similarly loyal people, so that he is seldom oppressed by any sense of isolation. He is unimaginative and tends not to sympathize with more complex persons. The second type is the man with the "plague spot"; the man who, confronted in isolation with a crisis, necessarily fails. He is Conrad's most difficult, most complicated character, and he is also the central figure in most of the full-length novels of the early period. He has caused many to misread the novels because he often seems to be a conventional hero. Let us call him (since he *does* fail), *the vulnerable hero.* (When we come to consider this type in detail, we shall see that it comprises two major subdivisions.) The third and last major type of character in the early period partakes of aspects of the other two. He understands, appreciates, and subscribes to the ethical code of the simple, unimaginative man. But he shares the terror and the weakness of the man with the plague spot. Unlike the simple seaman, he is complex and introspective. Unlike the vulnerable hero, he meets his crisis successfully. The measure of his success is not, however, the fact of meeting the crisis; his success lies in his achievement of self-knowledge. Let us call him, for convenience, *the perceptive hero.* Finally, there is one minor type. Like the vulnerable hero, he fails his crisis, but unlike him, he would never be mistaken for a true hero. He has no moral sense and, hence, no shame. Moral crises do not interest him. We shall call him the villain.

Readers of Conrad will readily think of examples of his unreflective, heroic seamen, the men at the top of his moral hierarchy. There is old Singleton, the only member of the crew of the *Narcissus* who successfully meets both crises of the voyage. In the face of a gale which half submerges the ship, he sticks to the helm for over thirty hours, his white beard tucked under the top button of his glistening coat. He stands firm against the demoralizing force of the dying

Negro, James Wait. While the rest of the crew pander to Jimmy and lie to themselves, he simply says: "Well, get on with your dying . . . don't raise a blamed fuss with us over that job." Another old man who belongs in this category is Captain Beard of "Youth." Though he is in his sixties, his eyes are like those of a boy, "with that candid expression some quite common men preserve to the end of their days by a rare internal gift of simplicity of heart and rectitude of soul."

These heroic seamen are simple and straight, and, perhaps unconsciously, they subscribe to an idea of decorum. One of their number, the French lieutenant of *Lord Jim*, remains on the *Patna* for thirty hours, despite the fact that her sagging bulkhead may give way at any time. "It was judged proper . . . that one of the officers should remain. . ." Still another of the simple heroes, Captain MacWhirr, lights upon the same word in his advice to a terrified mate during the typhoon: "There's just so much dirty weather knocking about the world, and the proper thing is to go through it. . ." Although the early Conrad would probably not agree with the early Hemingway on the question of fidelity, both writers see an ethical value in skill, in doing a job well. So the simple seamen are not only loyal but very able. Conrad writes in *The Mirror of the Sea*:

> Now, the moral side of an industry . . . is the attainment and preservation of the highest possible skill on the part of the craftsmen. Such skill, the skill of technique, is more than honesty; it is something wider, embracing honesty and grace and rule . . .

Thus MacWhirr's third engineer, Mr. Beale, mans a valve with as much grace as a Hemingway matador might kill a bull: "He seemed to be poising it above his head, as though it were a correct attitude in some sort of game."

Conrad persuades the reader to admire his simple, faithful, hard-working seamen by suggesting that their heroism is of mythical proportions and by magnifying achievement through understatement. Old Singleton clearly belongs among the epic heroes; he could be one of Beowulf's trusted advisors. He resembles "a learned and savage patriarch, the incarnation of barbarian wisdom." Conrad insists upon his size and his great age: "And alone in the dim emptiness of the sleeping forecastle he appeared bigger, colossal, very old; old as Father Time himself." Singleton is the last of his generation, and the account of that generation recalls the regret for the passing of the *comitatus* expressed in the great Anglo-Saxon elegiac poems, "The Wanderer" and "The Seafarer."

The men who could understand his silence were gone — those men who knew how to exist beyond the pale of life and within sight of eternity. They had been strong, as those are strong who know neither doubts nor hopes. They had been impatient and enduring, turbulent and devoted, unruly and faithful . . . they had been men who knew toil, privation, violence, debauchery — but knew not fear, and had no desire of spite in their hearts . . . They are gone now — and it does not matter.

It is perfectly fitting that when Singleton does fall, it is an Homeric collapse, "crashing down, stiff and headlong like an uprooted tree."

At the same time that Conrad suggests that his seamen have quasi-supernatural qualities (MacWhirr is godlike on the bridge: "an enlightened comprehension dwelling alone up there with a storm"), he emphasizes certain unattractive physical details. He draws attention to MacWhirr's ear, "big, fleshy, very wet," Singleton's bleared eyes and black-rimmed spectacles, Captain Beard's bandy legs, and the French lieutenant's tarnished bars, his three stiff fingers, his general appearance of a "snuffy, quiet village priest." These details act as effective understatement. By diminishing his heroes physically, Conrad makes their spirit seem even more intrepid. These men, moreover, are supposed to be ordinary, very much of the human community. They are average men, not particularly bright, getting a trifle old; but sticking it out. Understatement of this kind can come very close to the undercutting of irony. We have to admit that Conrad often pokes gentle fun at his simple heroes, at Beard and MacWhirr especially. This occasional irony suggests that in certain ways Conrad feels uneasy about this type; as an artist, he is, perhaps, not deeply interested in these good men. Certainly Singleton and the French lieutenant play subordinate roles in *The Nigger of the "Narcissus"* and *Lord Jim*. Even in *Typhoon* the focus keeps shifting from the brave MacWhirr to Jukes, his frightened first mate. Perhaps, too, Conrad the psychologist does not quite believe in his moral heroes; his tendency to assign to them more-than-human virtue suggests that they do not exist, are a myth, an ideal.

Conrad's uneasiness can be seen in the characterization of Captain Mitchell, of *Nostromo*, a variation on the simple seaman. He has all the necessary attributes: courage, simplicity, fidelity, lack of imagination. Yet he is the unwitting dupe of the "material interests" that are destroying Costaguana. In the complex political situation he misinterprets every sign and becomes a spokesman for values which the reader learns are false. In short, when confronted by a complex problem, the simple seaman fails.

If fidelity is the highest virtue of Conrad's moral code, its opposite — betrayal — is the central theme of the early period. The second type of character, the man who fails, interests Conrad more deeply than the man who succeeds in the ranks. Even in the apprentice work of *An Outcast of the Islands* and *Tales of Unrest* (especially "Karain" and "The Lagoon"), betrayal of friendship is the subject: Willems betraying Lingard, his only friend, by showing the Arabs the way into Sambir, and Karain shooting his only friend, Pata Matara, on behalf of a woman who does not even know him. Of course, the classic examples of betrayal are found in the major novels of the early period. Jim's sin is the most serious, for he betrays his seaman's trust and jumps impulsively from the stricken *Patna*. Even his "redemption," his self-sacrifice in Patusan, has the look of betrayal, and his faithful wife calls him "false." All the main characters of *Nostromo* betray their friends or their responsibility at some point. The "incorruptible" Nostromo steals the silver of the mine; Charles Gould virtually deserts his wife; Decoud speedily forgets his love for Antonia and his responsibility to the revolution and commits suicide; and Dr. Monygham lives haunted by the confession forced from him years before, which meant the betrayal of his friends. In *Under Western Eyes,* Razumov turns over to the police Haldin, his fellow student who had assassinated the Russian Minister of State, and sets out to inform upon Haldin's family and associates.

The extent to which the early Conrad is concerned with the idea of betrayal is suggested by the fact that his two nonfictional works of the period deal with the same subject. In the most dramatic scene in *The Mirror of the Sea,* Conrad describes his feelings when he learned that the nephew of his closest friend, Dominic Cervoni, had informed the Spanish coast guard of their gun-running activities. And much of *A Personal Record* circles around the fact of Conrad's own abrupt departure from Poland. He does not say that this constituted betrayal, but he admits that he still catches himself answering accusations made against him at the time. It is interesting to note that he uses the same word to describe his departure from Poland that he used to describe Jim's from the *Patna* — the italics are mine: "Mine was the only case of a boy of my nationality and antecedents taking a, so to speak, standing *jump* out of his racial surroundings and associations."

The central characters of the early Conrad belong, then, to the second type, that of the vulnerable hero, the failure, the betrayer. Our brief account of betrayals indicates clearly that the characters involved are not all alike. Some, like

Nostromo, are very simple, unreflective men; others, like Decoud, are complex, ironic, and given to analysis of others and of themselves. The differences between the two are great enough to require their separate consideration. Probably the most interesting of the simple betrayers is Jim. He ought to have been a true hero, a young MacWhirr. Marlow admits that he would have chosen Jim as his first mate: "I would have trusted the deck to that youngster on the strength of a single glance, and gone to sleep with both eyes — and, by Jove! it wouldn't have been safe." It would not have been safe because Jim, unlike the simple heroes, is cursed by an excess of imagination. When the *Patna* strikes an underwater derelict, Jim knows as well what to do as would MacWhirr. But he looks ahead. He imagines the rusty bulkhead giving way, the eight hundred pilgrims in panic. His imagination renders him powerless, and he deserts the ship. Imagination and simplicity prove to be a fatal combination in Nostromo's case, too. When his mission to save the silver partially fails, he assumes that he has been betrayed and so, for the first time in his life, becomes secretive.

The confused and intimate impressions of universal dissolution which beset a subjective nature at any strong check to its ruling passion had a bitterness approaching that of death itself. He was simple. He was as ready to become the prey of any belief, superstition, or desire as a child.

The simple betrayer such as Jim or Nostromo cannot really understand what he has done, let alone express it. For this reason, he requires an interpreter, someone more subtle to explain the failure to the reader. Jim has Marlow. Nostromo has the complex betrayer, Decoud, to express him.

Although Decoud is certainly the prime example of the complex, vulnerable hero, he has some noteworthy colleagues in the same category. We think especially of Monygham and Gould in *Nostromo*, of Razumov in *Under Western Eyes*. These men differ from Jim in several important respects:

they are very intelligent; they recognize their moral weakness (but do nothing about it); they are intellectual and can verbalize their own and other people's dilemmas; they tend to be skeptical and ironic. Of course none of the characters fits the pattern perfectly. Monygham, for example, redeems himself through his devotion to Mrs. Gould and his effective action during the Sulaco revolution, although he remains to the end damned in his own eyes. Razumov's case is less clear. Conrad asserts that he finds peace and self-awareness during his confession of his betrayal to Nathalie; but the description of this redemption is unconvincing. The reader is much more likely to recall Razumov after his confession, when, deafened by a blow from one of the Revolutionists, he wanders through Geneva, "a lost mortal in a phantom world."

The responses of Decoud and Gould to their respective failures represent an interesting contrast within the type of the complex, vulnerable hero. When the evil of the material interests which Gould represents becomes perfectly obvious, Gould suffers much more than Decoud, suffers under the

conviction of irremediable folly. He was too severely practical and too idealistic to look upon its humours with amusement, as Martin Decoud, the imaginative materialist, was able to do in the dry light of his scepticism.

Suffering does not, however, divert Gould from his course; he isolates himself more and more from his wife, and his silver mine becomes an increasingly heavy burden upon the people. Decoud's skepticism may protect him from political despair, but it is helpless against the terrible force of ten days of physical isolation on the Great Isabel island. As he sits alone in the silence,

the vague consciousness of a misdirected life given up to impulses whose memory left a bitter taste in his mouth was the first moral sentiment of his manhood. But at the same time he felt no remorse. What should he regret? He had recognized no other virtue than intelligence, and had erected passions into duties.

Both his intelligence and his passion were swallowed up easily in this great unbroken solitude of waiting without faith . . . His sadness was the sadness of a sceptical mind. He beheld the universe as a succession of incomprehensible images . . . And all exertion seemed senseless.

Yet this condemnation of Decoud's skepticism (reinforced by his suicide) does not give us a complete understanding of the early Conrad's attitude toward skepticism. There are a number of explicit references to its saving grace in this period. Much of mankind's suffering, Conrad says in *Nostromo*, results from the lack of Decoud's point of view: "The popular mind is incapable of scepticism; and that incapacity delivers their helpless strength to the wiles of swindlers and to the pitiless enthusiasms of leaders inspired by visions of a high destiny." Decoud, moreover, is not the only skeptic of the early period. Marlow, who has never been a betrayer, is tinged with more than a little of Decoud's curse. One of his chief reasons for following Jim's case is the desire to conquer his skepticism concerning the moral code by which he lives:

I see well enough now that I hoped for the impossible — for the laying of what is the most obstinate ghost of man's creation . . . — the doubt of the sovereign power enthroned in a fixed standard of conduct.

It is Marlow's doubting, questioning, ironic mind that sheds light on Jim's dilemma and undercuts the importance of Jim's final, apparently heroic, act: "Is he satisfied — quite, now, I wonder?"

Marlow is the chief figure in our third major category of early Conradian heroes: the perceptive hero. This is the kind of man who follows the simple seaman's code, yet has the imagination, skepticism, and self-doubts of the betrayers. He meets his crisis with success; Marlow keeps his place in the ranks, and the young captain in "The Secret Sharer" achieves "the perfect communion of a seaman with his first command."

But the point of their achievement lies not in the successful action but in the inner meaning which they discover through their ordeal. They learn two important truths about themselves, that they are mortal and that they are imperfect and fallible. As Marlow tells Jim's beloved Jewel, "Nobody, nobody is good enough."

"Heart of Darkness," "The Secret Sharer," and *Lord Jim* are all principally concerned with the theme of self-knowledge: we must recognize our potential weaknesses, our plague spots, in order to achieve a perceptive, moral life. Of all the hollow white men in the heart of darkest Africa, only Kurtz, in Marlow's eyes, achieves self-recognition. Kurtz had preached morality, but he had become a god, or devil, for the cannibals and participated in human sacrifice because, Marlow tells us, "there was something wanting in him — some small matter." Yet this man, who has betrayed every human value, at the last moment wins a place for himself among Conrad's perceptive heroes. On his deathbed he looks into his soul, sees the truth about himself, and pronounces judgment: "The horror! The horror!" Through Kurtz, Marlow too gains self-knowledge, comes to realize that Kurtz's "deficiencies" are potentially his own. The young captain in "The Secret Sharer" achieves self-recognition, just as Marlow does, through identifying himself with another who has actually committed a criminal act.

The theme of self-knowledge in *Lord Jim* and Marlow's role as perceptive hero demonstrate how subtle the early Conrad's thinking is, how much more complex the book than the simple "sin and redemption" interpretation it first received. Jim fails on two counts: first, his leap from the *Patna* clearly violates the seaman's code; second, in his inconclusive interviews with Marlow during the Inquiry he avoids the self-knowledge that is Marlow's chief interest. Marlow says of Jim's evasiveness:

I didn't know what he was playing up to — if he was playing

up to anything at all — and I suspect he did not know either; for it is my belief no man ever understands quite his own artful dodges to escape from the grim shadow of self-knowledge.

After Marlow gets to know Jim better, he comments that Jim "made so much of his disgrace while it is the guilt alone that matters." Jim never, as far as Marlow knows, faces up to his guilt. On their last day together, in Patusan, Jim tries to tell Marlow the "real truth" about himself. Marlow is not impressed: "I did not let a murmur escape me: I felt he was going to say more, and come no nearer to the root of the matter."

Marlow does not pronounce judgment on Jim, but he knows where he himself stands on the question of self-knowledge. Moreover, his obsession with Jim's problem has its source in his own continuing self-exploration. Jim serves something of the same function for Marlow that Kurtz does. "Was it for my own sake that I wished to find some shadow of an excuse for that young fellow . . . ?" Marlow's attitude toward self-knowledge in *Lord Jim* differs markedly from that expressed in "The Secret Sharer." In the later story, Conrad seems to be saying that the captain has achieved lasting self-knowledge. Marlow, however, sees the quest as endless, hence the inconclusiveness of his tales. He says that he has

enough confidential information about myself to harrow my own soul till the end of my appointed time . . . we are only on suffrance here and got to pick our way in cross lights, watching every precious minute and every irremediable step, trusting we shall manage yet to go out decently in the end — but not so sure of it after all — and with dashed little help to expect from those we touch elbows with right or left.

With our discussion of Marlow, picking his way through cross lights, we have completed our survey of the major types of character in Conrad's moral world: the simple seaman, the simple or complex, vulnerable hero, and the perceptive hero. These types will be convenient points of reference when we come to consider the characters that interest the later Conrad. For the same reason, let us turn now to a minor type in the early Conrad — the villain. His relative unimportance in the early period is of special interest because in the later novels the villain becomes a major type.

The villain of the early Conrad is the absolute antithesis of the faithful English seaman. He is almost never an Englishman: an obscure central European like any of the anarchists in *The Secret Agent,* a half-caste like Cornelius in *Lord Jim,* a Latin like Montero or Sotillo in *Nostromo.* If the villain is an Englishman, he is often the product of the London slums, like Donkin in *The Nigger of the "Narcissus."* Far from being devoted to some craft, the villain actively dislikes work and can do nothing well. Donkin is

the man that cannot steer, that cannot splice, that dodges the work on dark nights; that, aloft, holds on frantically with both arms and legs, and swears at the wind, the sleet, the darkness; the man who curses the sea while others work.

The Secret Agent is practically a sermon against sloth. Most of its characters are villains. They are revolutionists because they are too lazy to hold a steady job, and they have all gotten fat in their profession. The little work that a villain does is motivated strictly by self-interest. He has no conception of fidelity. Practically none of the whites does any work in "Heart of Darkness," but they are all obsessed with finding ivory. Marlow comments: "To tear treasure out of the bowels of the land was their desire, with no more moral purpose at the back of it than there is in burglars breaking into a safe." The villain's disloyalty extends to the political sphere. He tends to hold what Conrad would consider radical views. Donkin is a rabble-rousing labor agitator. The depth of Nostromo's fall can be measured by the fact that at the time of his death his only friend is a "hater of capitalists."

Although the villain differs markedly from the heroic seaman of our first category, he resembles him in one respect — simplicity. The crew of the *Narcissus* are the children of the sea, and Sotillo and the other revolutionists of *Nostromo* are children too. Perhaps this is why Conrad in some ways displays the same lack of concern with these very dissimilar types. In none of the early novels does a villain play a major role. Conrad the psychologist does not find him sufficiently interesting or sufficiently "real" to merit extensive exploration. If Conrad the artist pokes gentle fun at the simple heroes, he treats the villains with fierce irony. This is especially evident, of course, in the heavily ironic *The Secret Agent*. In *Lord Jim*, Conrad dehumanizes, mechanizes the evil German captain of the *Patna*, with a comic image reminiscent of Swift's *A Tale of a Tub*: "His shoulders reappeared, jammed in the small opening; his head hung out, distended and tossing like a captive balloon, perspiring, furious, spluttering." Some of the scenes between Mitchell and the comic-opera army officers of Costaguana, in *Nostromo,* come very close to pure farce.

Before we leave the villains in the early Conrad, we should note another type of character who lives outside the moral sphere. He is not at all clearly etched, as are the villains we have been talking about. He is the complacent bourgeois. If the early Conrad is conservative and hates revolt, he also scorns complacency. We find, therefore, in the background of the early novels a vaguely defined group of people who appear to be secure only because they have never been tested. These are the stupid citizens of the sepulchral city of "Heart of Darkness," the bovine Swiss of *Under Western Eyes*, MacWhirr's and Jim's families, safe and sound back in England. Conrad's attitude toward Jim's people gives us an interesting key to his early complexity. On the one hand, he idealizes them as the solid folk of England. On the other hand, by contrasting their safe existence to Jim's disreputable failure, he raises serious doubts as to their superiority to Jim. Marlow speaks very ironically of the father's platitudinous letter to Jim about resisting temptation, of his "little thoughts about faith and virtue." Marlow comments on the family: "Nothing ever came to them; they would never be taken unawares, and never be called upon to grapple with fate. Here they all are . . . gazing with clear unconscious eyes. . ." The imperceptive, untested character is really as reprehensible to the early Conrad as his corrupt and comic villains.

Conrad's moral world seems, then, to display considerable complexity. We have noted four types of character and certain variations, each type responding to a moral crisis in a different way. Even more suggestive of the early complexity is Conrad's ability to hold all these types in solution, so to speak, and to juxtapose them in order to convey more subtle meanings. MacWhirr, the faithful seaman of *Typhoon,* is contrasted to the cowardly second mate, who is like Donkin of the *Narcissus,* and to the imaginative and demoralized first mate, Jukes, who would have failed like Jim, if MacWhirr had not been there. In *Lord Jim* the moral hierarchy is implicit on every page. The three major types are all at the Inquiry to try Jim. Two are Jim's formal judges, merchant marine officers conducting the Inquiry. One of them has rugged hands and thoughtful eyes; he asks Jim technical questions and clearly belongs in the category of faithful seamen. But the second, Big Brierly, is nervous, dreamy, looks at his blotter rather than at Jim. Several weeks later he commits suicide to avoid the knowledge of his own guilt. Clearly he belongs among the vulnerable heroes. In the audience at the Inquiry sits a white man directing a glance at Jim which is "not the fascinated stare of the others. It was an act of intelligent volition." This is Marlow, the type of the self-doubting, perceptive hero. Rivaling, perhaps surpassing, *Lord Jim* in its complex handling of moral responses is *Nostromo,* the novel that Robert Penn Warren aptly calls "a chromatic scale of attitudes." [3]

We began our examination of Conrad's ethic by saying that the human community is of primary value. Yet in our survey of the moral hierarchy of characters we saw that the early Conrad devotes his energies chiefly to creating vulnerable heroes who fail to support the human community. Marlow says that the interest that drew spectators to Jim's trial was "purely psychological — the expectation of some essential disclosure as to the strength, the power, the horror, of human emotions." Certainly this is what interests Conrad: not the superficial how of his characters' actions but the fundamental why, and particularly the why of moral failure. Conrad's psychology has been a major cause of his critical revaluation in recent years, and this brief account will be for the most part a summary of the work of others, particularly that of Albert J. Guerard.[4] Here we shall consider the early Conrad's exploration of three ideas: the effect of physical and moral isolation on man's actions, the part that egoism plays in motivating action, and, finally, man's quest for peace and his urge to self-destruction.

Throughout Conrad's early period, his writing is haunted by the recurring nightmare image of a lone man, menaced and terrified by hostile surroundings. This image has such vividness and clarity that it must have been deeply felt. It appears in its most extended form in "Amy Foster," where we see Yanko Goorall, wet and muddy, hiding in a pigpound, frightening children, being lashed by a milk-driver's whip, dodging stones thrown by three boys, running from a barking dog. Jim's dash from the stockade in Patusan contains the same elements: "he arose muddy from head to foot . . . with no pity to expect from any one, like a hunted animal . . . He . . . noticed the little children trying to run for life . . ." Señor Hirsch dashes through Sulaco pursued by dogs and men with guns, and Peter Ivanovitch, in *Under*

Western Eyes, walks across Siberia with a chain about his waist, using a wild beast's cunning to elude his pursuers. Often the lone man has the added handicap of being unable to communicate with his fellows. Goorall and Hirsch sometimes speak in their native tongue without realizing it, and thus appear even more suspicious and incomprehensible to their enemies. After so many weeks cut off from human voices, Peter Ivanovitch cannot speak when help is offered to him.

Isolation in Conrad is, however, more than a striking image. It is the condition of the test which each of his major characters must undergo; it is a chief cause of their failure; and it tempts them to seek unlawful successes. Certainly Jim fails his test on the *Patna* because of moral isolation. He is not physically alone; he has his captain and the other white officers. But they are outside his moral sphere. The "odious and fleshly figure" of the German captain appears to Jim as the "incarnation of everything vile and base that lurks in the world we love." Since "we trust for our salvation in the men that surround us," it is inevitable that the vulnerable Jim should jump when the others do. While Nostromo and Decoud have each other for company on the sinking lighter, they are still isolated; they have "no bond of conviction, of common idea." Finally, the opening pages of *Under Western Eyes* prepare us for Razumov's betrayal of Haldin by filling in a picture of complete loneliness and moral isolation: "He was as lonely in the world as a man swimming in the deep sea. The word Razumov was the mere label of a solitary individuality."

If man's isolation constantly deprives him of the support he needs to avoid moral failure, it also gives him the freedom to act in dubious ways. Kurtz can behave as he does only because he is in the wilderness, in "utter solitude without a policeman," in "utter silence, where no warning voice of a kind neighbor can be heard whispering of public opinion."

Jim's questionable triumph in Patusan takes place under conditions of "total and utter isolation." He is "in every sense alone of his kind there." Nostromo, isolated from his fellows by being sole possessor of the secret of Decoud's and the silver's fate, sees that he can safely steal the silver, and does. So, too, Razumov, because of his secret and lonely existence, can compound his betrayal of the revolutionist Haldin by becoming a spy for the Russian secret police.

Conrad insists that none of these isolated characters is unique; none has any unusual obsession, any really distorted trait of personality. Although Jim is excessively romantic, he is still "one of us." The egoistic Nostromo remains faithful to his name, "our man." The normality of these stragglers from the ranks, these men who fall because of physical solitude or moral isolation, serves to underscore Conrad's belief in universal isolation. This is the lesson Marlow learns through Jim:

> It is when we try to grapple with another man's intimate need that we perceive how incomprehensible, wavering, and misty are the beings that share with us the sight of the stars and the warmth of the sun. It is as if loneliness were a hard and absolute condition of existence . . .

If loneliness is the condition of most of Conrad's characters, it is a condition largely self-imposed. Whether simple or complex, his vulnerable heroes are all egoists. Their deepest impulses and longings are directed not toward a dutiful place in the ranks but toward self-aggrandizement. They are alone chiefly because they have thoughts for no one but themselves. This is one of the central convictions of Conrad the psychologist, that egoism is the motive force of most men's actions. It is probably no accident that Conrad first began to write because, as he tells us in *A Personal Record*, he was haunted by recollections of a man who "governed his conduct by . . . incredible assumptions, which rendered his logic impenetrable to any reasonable person." This is Kaspar Almayer, the first of a series of romantic egoists and vulnerable heroes who were to occupy Conrad's attention through virtually all of his early career.

In *A Personal Record*, Conrad addresses Almayer, the prototype of Willems, Kurtz, young Marlow, Jukes, Jim, Nostromo, Gould, Razumov: "You were always an unlucky man, Almayer. Nothing was ever quite worthy of you. What made you so real to me was that you held this lofty theory with some force of conviction and with an admirable consistency." Consistency is a rather mild word for Almayer and his descendants. Each is obsessed by the fixed idea of his own greatness. Each is a dreamer, and "dream" becomes in the early Conrad a key word — and a pejorative word. Our first view of Almayer reveals him forgetting the bitter reality of the present "in the vision of a great and splendid reward." Willems, in *An Outcast of the Islands*, though completely destroyed, can on the least provocation lose himself in dreams of glory. Kurtz, on the point of death in the Congo, expects to return to Europe and be met at railway stations by kings. While Marlow is trying to lead Jim to an awareness of guilt, he must constantly whisk him back to reality, because Jim keeps forgetting his loss in a "fierce yearning after that missed distinction . . . With every instant he was penetrating deeper into the impossible world of romantic achievements." Jim's "redemption" in Patusan follows the same pattern. Although his duty is to Jewel, he is "torn out of her arms by the strength of a dream."

Conrad tells us explicitly of the tremendous selfishness of his characters. Willems is "ferociously conceited"; Kurtz's "elevated sentiments" consist of "my Intended, my ivory, my station, my river, my—"; Jim looks down on Patusan with "an owner's eye"; Nostromo seems to Decoud "astonishingly simple in the jealous greatness of his conceit."

Conrad, as a psychologist, shows us that one of the major causes of the moral failure of the romantic egoist is his tendency to self-delusion, his capacity for clothing his passionate desires with what Decoud calls the "fair robes of an idea." Jim rises to power in Patusan under the illusion of doing the people good. Kurtz once belonged to the "gang of virtue." In *Nostromo*, the self-deception of the idealist is the main theme, and Decoud's analysis of Gould is probably Conrad's clearest statement of that theme. Decoud tells Mrs. Gould that her husband simply

cannot act or exist without idealizing every simple feeling, desire, or achievement. He could not believe his own motives if he did not make them first a part of some fairy tale. The earth is not quite good enough for him, I fear.

Dr. Monygham analyzes Gould in much the same terms but does not realize that he himself suffers from the same ailment. His ideal conception of his own disgrace tends to make him a dangerous man. Razumov, too, finds in an ideal his excuse for an immoral act. He betrays Haldin in order to defend his ideal autocratic state against misguided revolutionists.

The early Conrad shows that egoism lurks behind even those acts which seem most praiseworthy. The crew of the *Narcissus*, for instance, are very proud of their charity toward the dying James Wait. The truth is, however, that their sympathies are really for themselves. They see in Jimmy's impending death their own mortality, and they cannot bear the sight of it. As Conrad states explicitly: "the latent egoism of tenderness to suffering appeared in the developing anxiety not to see him die." The corruptness behind their sympathy for Jimmy is emphasized by the fact that it leads them to mutiny. Jim's sympathy for Gentleman Brown, the starving renegade who comes to Patusan, is clearly of the same ignominious, self-protective sort. When Brown hints that Jim has as guilty a past as his own, Jim decides to let Brown go free, as he himself would want to go free. This gives Brown the opportunity to murder Jim's best friend.

The egoism of Conrad's vulnerable heroes so distorts reality for them that not only do they fail to understand their own motives, but they always blame someone or something else for their dilemma. The betrayer sees himself as betrayed. Jim feels that the dark powers took unfair advantage of him on the *Patna*, that "on the square . . . there was nothing he couldn't meet." As soon as Nostromo realizes that he is in a dangerous position, his imagination seizes "upon the clear and simple notion of betrayal" to account for his dazed feeling of being in trouble.

Finally, in his anatomy of moral failure, Conrad dramatizes the idea that man, with his egoistic longing to escape reality, desires — more profoundly than power and glory — irresponsibility, peace, even death itself. As the narrator of *Under Western Eyes* says, "Being myself a quiet individual I take it that what all men are really after is some form or perhaps only some formula of peace." We readily recall how many of Conrad's characters find their peace either by committing suicide (Whalley, Brierly, Decoud, Winnie Verloc) or by deliberately bringing about their own destruction (Willems, Kurtz, Jim, Nostromo, Razumov). Jim's retreat to the East after his disgrace is a quest for peace. Although we generally think of Patusan as headquarters for Jim's heroic action, the first words we hear him say there are, "Peaceful here, eh?" The night before Marlow's departure from Patusan he thinks about Jim's success:

> He was going to try ever so many experiments; I had admired his energy, his enterprise, and his shrewdness. Nothing on earth seemed less real now than his plans, his energy, and his enthusiasm . . . It was a great peace, as if the earth had been one grave . . .

Later, Marlow comments upon Jim's decision to atone with his life for Dain Waris' murder: "The dark powers should not rob him twice of his peace." That this is the peace of irresponsibility is made clear enough by Jewel's entreaties, Stein's disappointment, and Marlow's ironic comments on Jim's death.

Although Jim's longing for peace is inherent in his temperament (he is quite happy in his easy berth on the *Patna*), there is little doubt that the quest for death after his failure rises also from a desire to punish himself. The desire is by no means conscious; Jim thinks he is looking for his lost opportunity. But the systematic way in which he loses every job Marlow finds for him, his unarmed entrance into Patusan, his fanatic recklessness as Tuan Jim — all these suggest an unconscious desire for self-destruction. Monygham's will to destroy himself gives him the energy and vigor to outwit Sotillo, though he is saved just as Sotillo is about to hang him. Conrad tells us explicitly that Gould's guilt concerning the way he has treated his wife lies behind his scheme to blow up the mine:

He was prepared, if need be, to blow up the whole San Tomé mountain sky high out of the territory of the Republic. This resolution expressed the tenacity of his character, the remorse of that subtle conjugal infidelity through which his wife was no longer the sole mistress of his thoughts, something of his father's imaginative weakness, and something, too, of the spirit of a buccaneer throwing a lighted match into the magazine rather than surrender his ship.

Most obviously of all, it is guilt over betrayal that drives Razumov to seek out his enemies in Geneva and that keeps him always on the brink of the confession which will destroy him. Though Conrad of course sees self-destructiveness as a fault in his vulnerable heroes, he nevertheless has to admire the vigor with which they go about it. After all, it is Jim's "intensity" that makes Marlow admit that Jim is "none the less true." Most readers respond in the same way. Surely the glamor, the energy, the intensity of the hero of *The Great Gatsby* owes something to the self-destructive Jim.

Conrad is skeptical about the individual's motives not only in relation to himself but in relation to society as well, and here the psychologist becomes a political observer. Because this aspect of Conrad disappears in the later period, we shall note here only two ideas: Conrad is suspicious of all political action; he distrusts especially the language of politics. Conrad's attitude toward political action is probably not far from Razumov's attitude toward the Utopian plans of the Russian revolutionists in Geneva: "As if anything could be changed! In this world of men nothing can be changed — neither happiness nor misery. They can only be displaced at the cost of corrupted consciences and broken lives . . ." *The Secret Agent* shows that revolutions arise from "personal impulses disguised into creeds." It is characteristic of Conrad that he should concentrate upon the psychological rather than the economic or sociological causes of revolution: "the most ardent of revolutionaries are perhaps doing no more but seeking for peace in common with the rest of mankind."

If *Under Western Eyes* and *The Secret Agent* reveal Conrad as anti-revolutionary, the earlier, non-European novels show him to be anti-imperialistic. Imperialism is a major theme in "Heart of Darkness" and *Nostromo*, an implied one in *An Outcast of the Islands* and *Lord Jim*. For Lingard prides himself on the benefits that he has brought to Sambir, and Jim feels the same way about Patusan; yet each leaves his country the worse for his having been there. What imperialism means in the Congo could hardly be more obvious: a French gunboat firing into the wilderness, an inferno of dying Negro slaves, rapacious pilgrims shooting down Kurtz's native woman for sport. Although the situation in Costaguana is somewhat more complex, a striking image of Western "progress" does much to enlighten the reader about imperialism there:

the sparse row of telegraph poles . . . bearing a single, almost invisible wire far into the great campo — like a slender, vibrating feeler of that progress waiting outside for a moment of peace to enter and twine itself about the weary heart of the land.

As a part of his interest in politics, Conrad foreshadows contemporary psychological warfare with his dramatization of the way men's misuse of language enables them to gain power over others. Just as men delude themselves in pursuit of a dubious "ideal," so they delude others by the words they use. Although the simple heroes are usually inarticulate, the villains are quite eloquent. We think of Donkin, a "consummate artist," gifted with a "filthy loquacity" which effectively demoralizes the crew of the *Narcissus*. Deep-voiced men dominate *The Secret Agent* and *Under Western Eyes*. Costaguana has been harried by "pronunciamentos" since the beginning of time, and even the level-headed English engineer becomes infected with the disease and begins to "talk like an expert revolutionist." Charles Gould comes to the conclusion that "the words one knows so well have a nightmarish meaning in this country. Liberty, democracy, patriotism, government — all of them have a flavour of folly and murder." This reminds us of the rebellion of more recent writers against the good old words. Ernest Hemingway, a quarter of a century later, has the hero of *A Farewell to Arms* rage against the words "glory, honor, courage," which sound "obscene" to him.

No one in the early Conrad is so endowed with the gift of persuasion as Kurtz. Before he and Marlow even meet, the latter discovers that he has never imagined Kurtz as "doing, you know, but as discoursing." Kurtz's eloquent seventeen-page report to the International Society for the Suppression of Savage Customs, as ironically rendered by Marlow, gives a frightening insight into Conrad's attitude toward propaganda, politics, and human nature:

The peroration was magnificent, though difficult to remember, you know. It gave me the notion of an exotic Immensity ruled by an august Benevolence . . . There were no practical hints to interrupt the magic current of phrases, except a kind of a note at the foot of the last page . . . "Exterminate all the brutes!"

"Heart of Darkness" — with Kurtz summing up the truth

in "The horror!" — may be an extreme statement of Conrad's pessimism. Yet surely a rather dark view is implied throughout the early period. Most of Conrad's important characters stand on the brink, ready to be betrayed and undone, as Marlow says in *Lord Jim,* by the "Irrational that lurks at the bottom of every thought, sentiment, sensation, emotion." There are, it is true, the MacWhirrs and the Singletons, but they remain fairly inconspicuous. They exist, perhaps, to remind us of what ought to be, the standard by which Conrad vigilantly judges and condemns what *is.*

We have been discussing at some length Conrad the moralist and Conrad the psychologist, with a glance at Conrad the commentator on politics. There remains still another Conrad, in some respects the most important and most complex of all, the Conrad who reveals the morality, the psychology, the politics — Conrad the artist. As before, we shall be able to look only at a few highlights, considering them under the two general headings of structure and language.

Taken in its broadest sense, the term structure means not only the relationship of the parts to each other but also the selection of the parts and the emphasis given to them. Thus, in Conrad's novels, structure includes his use of the personal narrator and the illustrative episode, as well as his violation of conventional chronology. Virtually all of the important early works employ two of these features of structure, and a good number employ all three. We shall draw most of our examples from one novel, *Lord Jim,* because it is the most familiar to the common reader and because, despite certain obvious flaws, it is probably the best written of the full-length novels.

The devices of the narrator, the illustrative episode, and chronological involution resemble each other in that all three are indirect methods. The narrator acts as a barrier or screen between the reader and the action. Although the illustrative episode can be employed fairly obviously, Conrad usually presents it as if it were purely irrelevant, and leaves the reader to see the connections. Conradian violation of chronology takes the reader not into the middle of things but to a point after the fact, then before the fact, then around and around the fact, an artistic evasiveness that brings added perception to his work.

Marlow, as the narrator of *Lord Jim*, contributes meaning in several ways. In the first place, he gives the reader a sense of actuality. After all, he knew Jim better than any one else did. He was there. More important, however, Marlow acts as Jim's interpreter because, as we have seen, he has a more subtle mind than Jim and can see implications that Jim cannot. Marlow is important in his own right, too. He adds a new moral dimension because Jim's dilemma becomes his own. Finally, Marlow acts as an interviewer who brings together and comments upon the testimony of more than a dozen secondary observers of Jim.

All the narrators of *Lord Jim* convey not only information about Jim but also a moral attitude. Conrad's art lies in the way he carefully qualifies each narrator's analysis of Jim and shows clearly that the truth about Jim must be the sum of many perceptions. Let us take the case of Stein, probably the most famous of the secondary narrators in *Lord Jim*. Marlow tells him Jim's story because he is so wise and because he is likely to be sympathetic. Stein confidently diagnoses Jim's case: "I understand very well. He is romantic." He gives the cure: "The way is to the destructive element submit yourself." For some critics these words have been practically the key to Conrad,[5] but to accept them without qualification is to miss all the complexity of Conrad's method. Stein's words are very much qualified by their context, are kept from becoming *the* solution to that subtle knot, Lord Jim, who must remain "not quite clear." Stein's attempt to clarify his very cryptic solution serves to undercut it: "There were things, he said mournfully, that perhaps could never be told, only he had lived so much alone that sometimes he forgot — he forgot. The light had destroyed the assurance which had inspired him." So Stein's uncertainty weakens his position. Moreover, we should not forget that it is Stein, not Conrad, who is speaking. The German words interspersed throughout his conversation remind us of this, remind us that Stein himself is an incurable romantic and not an unbiased commentator. The German words also underline the contrast between this scene and the one with Marlow and the French lieutenant. If the Frenchman could not give the whole answer to Jim, why should the German be able to?

Stein's pronouncement upon Jim is most convincingly qualified by the consciousness of the primary narrator, Marlow. Marlow is not at all sure about Stein's advice, sees it in fact as a dangerous cloak over the truth:

> The whisper of his conviction seemed to open before me a vast and uncertain expanse, as of a crepuscular horizon on a plain at dawn — or was it, perchance, at the coming of the night? One had not the courage to decide; but it was a charming and deceptive light, throwing the impalpable poesy of its dimness over pitfalls — over graves.

And so Stein's way remains *a* way of looking at Jim, but not *the* way. The way must be the sum of all the attitudes with each attitude qualifying the others and each qualified by the personality of the speaker, and all the attitudes transmitted and transmuted by the screening consciousness of Marlow.

Besides providing us with a good example of the secondary narrator, Stein will also serve to demonstrate Conrad's use of the illustrative episode. Before Marlow tells us what Stein has to say about Jim, he digresses for two pages to talk about Stein's past. At that point in the novel, the digression seems only for the purpose of showing that Stein has had an adventurous and noble youth. But the attentive reader will remember those two pages when he comes to Jim's "redemption" in Patusan. Marlow tells us that as a young man Stein had assisted a Celebes prince in establishing control over his country and had married the prince's sister. Unfortunately, with peace almost achieved, the prince was assassinated. Although this made Stein's position extremely insecure, he stayed on until his wife suddenly died, and then he left the country. The reader cannot fully grasp the importance of this seemingly irrelevant episode until he knows the rest of Jim's life. Clearly Stein's adventure with the prince and his marriage to the princess foreshadow Jim's relations with Dain and Jewel. But what is important is the difference: Stein is a romantic, but a selfless one; Jim thinks only of himself. Conrad says of the writing of *Lord Jim* that he "formed the resolve to cram as much character and episode into it as it could hold." [6] The Stein episode suggests that Conrad's purpose was a high one, to make episode illuminate character.

Joseph Warren Beach [7] and others have discussed some of the advantages Conrad gains by violating chronology: that a striking first impression is more effective than the gradual building of a character, that it is more "natural" to acquire information about a character's history unchronologically. Perhaps more important than these advantages, Conrad's jumbled chronology enables him to juxtapose events and characters in a way that would be impossible in an orderly telling of the story. The case of Brierly, one of Jim's judges at the Inquiry, is a useful example of how the rearrangement of events in time can add meaning. Marlow tells virtually the whole story of the Inquiry and of Brierly's end *before* he tells the reader that Jim had jumped and the *Patna* had not sunk, although the Inquiry had taken place a month to six weeks later. Brierly, an extremely successful young captain, had been much disturbed by Jim's disgrace, yet had asked Marlow to help Jim run away before sentence was passed. Barely a week after the Inquiry he leapt from his own ship to his death. Marlow equates Brierly with Jim when he says that while Brierly talked about Jim, he "must have been

thinking of himself." More important, through careful selection of details, Conrad equates Brierly's suicide leap with
Jim's jump from the *Patna*. The reader does not know at the
time that Jim jumped, but he does know that shortly before
the *Patna* disaster, Jim looked at the chart. Conrad draws
attention to this by a close description of the sheet of paper,
the dividers, parallel rulers, the black cross of the ship's position, the straight line of the ship's course. The account of
Brierly's last moments includes a detailed description of him
laying out the course in the chart room. The alert reader
should sense the relationship between Brierly and Jim when
he reads this. When he learns later that Jim jumped too, he
will understand that Jim's jump to save his skin is as reprehensible as Brierly's, is moral suicide. Recalling Marlow's
question about Brierly, "Who can tell what flattering view
he had induced himself to take of his own suicide?" the reader
will realize that Jim is unlikely ever to acknowledge his guilt.
Yet none of these meanings would have been possible if
Brierly's story had followed Jim's in normal chronological
order.

It is difficult to discuss Conrad's technique without referring to its effect upon the reader, for Conrad's masterly
control of the reader's responses is one of the most significant
results of his unorthodox methods and especially of these
time shifts. Rearranged chronology means, of course, that the
writer can withhold a crucial fact to create a feeling of suspense in his reader. But Conrad does more than simply create
suspense. By holding back information and moving forward
and backward in time, Conrad catches up and involves the
reader in the moral situation, makes the reader's emotions
follow a course analogous to that of the characters. In *Lord
Jim*, the reader circles and circles the fact of Jim's jump, for
111 pages, evading that fact just as Jim tries to evade it, even
when he at last blurts out to Marlow, "I had jumped . . ."
and then adds, "It seems."

Structure acts even more powerfully upon the reader's emotions in *Nostromo* than in *Lord Jim*. Perhaps no novel of Conrad's is so demanding of the reader, so calculated to confuse, outrage, and exhaust him. The reader must absorb piecemeal and without apparent order a staggering collection of facts about the history, geography, and the inhabitants of Costaguana. He must endure Nostromo's absence from one hundred pages of the middle of the book. He must wade through nearly two hundred pages and decades of time before he discovers that on the eleventh day of Decoud's solitude he committed suicide. By the end of the novel the reader's state of mind is likely to resemble that of a victim of Captain Mitchell's tour of modern Sulaco who, "stunned and as it were annihilated mentally by a sudden surfeit of sights, sounds, names, facts, and complicated information imperfectly apprehended, would listen like a tired child to a fairy tale." Yet surely this is one of Conrad's chief purposes, so to assault the reader that he will experience some of the emotional chaos of the characters. Conrad's early work, as much by virtue of its technique as by its moral view, seems to fit perfectly Lionel Trilling's statement that the greatness of the novel as a form lies in its "unremitting work of involving the reader himself in the moral life." [8]

In turning to a consideration of Conrad's use of language, let us take "Youth" for an example. Since it is short, its language may be considered, as language should, in relation to the total meaning of the work. A brief explication of "Youth" may be helpful, too, as a conclusion to our survey of the early Conrad, because it contains many of the elements that we have already discussed. All three major types of the moral hierarchy appear here — simple seaman, vulnerable hero, and perceptive hero. Structurally, the story is interesting in its very sophisticated use of the personal narrator. Although "Youth" lacks the explicit seriousness of some of the early works, much serious meaning does come through implicitly. The prose reveals the important qualities of the early style: vigor, irony, symbolic imagination, emotional richness. Finally, "Youth" may be of some interest because it has been generally neglected by Conrad's rediscoverers. Mr. Leavis castigates its "cheap insistence on the glamour," [9] and Mr. Zabel says that it "shows the strain of a cloying lyric verbalism." [10] Yet for the common reader "Youth" seems a most Conradian story.

"Youth" is just what the title implies, a tribute to the strength and, apparently, to the romance of youth. Marlow tells the story, in this his first appearance in Conrad, about a voyage he made to the East as second mate of the barque *Judea*, twenty-two years before, when he was only twenty. During that voyage fraught with many disasters, he discovers that he has the courage and the endurance to be a good seaman. When the *Judea* is leaking badly on one of her attempts to reach the East, young Marlow mans the pumps with his watch for a week and thinks, "By Jove! . . . here I am lasting it out as well as any of these men." Later, the *Judea* burns and sinks in the Indian Ocean, and Marlow brings his fourteen-foot boat safely into port: "I did not know how good a man I was until then."

The accounts of the crew's efforts to save the ship during her various disasters contain some of Conrad's most vigorous, most effective prose, the prose of action which so energizes *The Nigger of the "Narcissus," Lord Jim, Typhoon,* and, to some extent, *Nostromo.*

We forgot the day of the week, the name of the month, what year it was, and whether we had ever been ashore. The sails blew away, she lay broadside on under a weather-cloth, the ocean poured over her, and we did not care. We turned those handles, and had the eyes of idiots. As soon as we had crawled on deck I used to take a round turn with the rope about the men, the pumps, and the mainmast, and we turned, we turned incessantly, with the water to our waists, to our necks, over our heads. It was all one. We had forgotten how it felt to be dry.

Here, short words, abrupt phrasing, and brief clauses create a sense of desperate activity. Pounding parallelisms and frequent repetitions suggest both the monotony of the sailors' battle and the power of their anatagonist. Few adjectives or dependent clauses rise to impede the steady movement of the prose, and the reader knows how it feels to pump a foundering ship.

Although the narrator, old Marlow, admires the strength of his youth, he does not altogether approve of the character of his younger self. In fact, he treats his youthful counterpart with consistent irony. He draws attention to the fact that though young Marlow feels contempt for his sixty-year-old captain and first mate, they are usually right and he is usually wrong. The language frequently underscores Marlow's ironic attitude toward his younger self. When young Marlow leaps into the smoking hold to "show how easily" he can dig down to the fire's source, he faints dead away. Conrad's metaphor for the ensuing rescue succinctly cuts the youthful hero down to size: they "contented themselves by fishing for me with a chainhook tied to a broom-handle, I believe." Often the old and the young Marlow's contrasting attitudes are deliberately juxtaposed: "I sat steering my cockle-shell — my first command." Old Marlow's experience and superior wisdom constantly undercut young Marlow's surprise at each new disaster by such remarks as "of course" or "you see it was to be expected." The same kind of irony diminishes an apparently heroic figure in the first paragraph of *Lord Jim*: "He was *spotlessly* neat, apparelled in *immaculate white* from shoes to hat, and in the various Eastern ports where he *got his living* as a ship-chandler's water-clerk he was very *popular*." (The italics are mine.) This is Jim, after his fall from grace on the *Patna*. On reading this sentence after having finished the book, we are struck by the irony of Jim's immaculate covering. "Immaculate" also gives us Jim's attitude toward himself, toward Lord Jim, the man who wishes to be perfect in an imperfect world. And Conrad's skepticism about Jim is in this sentence too, in the vulgarity of "got his living," in the degrading fact that the only homage that Jim commands is "popularity."

In "Youth," the narrator has misgivings not only about young Marlow's ignorance but also about the nature of his motives. Pretty clearly, some of his most praiseworthy actions arise not out of a devotion to the craft of seamanship, but out of pure egoism. This egoism results in an extreme lack of perception. Young Marlow tries to alter the world according to his own feelings. More seriously, he does not understand his own longings, does not perceive that within his youthful, romantic desire for glamour lies a longing for irresponsibility, repose, and death. Conrad implies this imperception chiefly through language — through his use of certain images of the sea and of the East.

"There was all the East before me, and all life," thinks young Marlow at the beginning of the voyage. Yet the most striking pictures of the Eastern sea and of Marlow's first Eastern port reveal not life, but the coldness and fixity of death.

The sea was a miracle of purity, a miracle of azure. The sea was polished, was blue, was pellucid, was sparkling like a precious stone, extending on all sides, all round to the horizon — as if the whole terrestrial globe had been one jewel, one colossal sapphire, a single gem fashioned into a planet.

Here is beauty, indeed — but the terrifying beauty of an absolute, inhuman perfection. It is significant that in this tribute to youth's eagerness for adventure, the language describing youth's goal, the East, should actually suggest stasis. The bay that Marlow first comes into is "smooth as glass and polished like ice." The morning after his landing he first sees the men of the East; he describes them and their land in language more suggestive of an oil painting than of real life:

these beings stared without a murmur, without a sigh, without a movement. They stared down at the boats, at the sleeping men who at night had come to them from the sea. Nothing moved. The fronds of palms stood still against the sky. Not a branch stirred along the shore, and the brown roofs of hidden houses peeped through the green foliage, through the big leaves that hung shining and still like leaves forged of heavy metal.

Lest there be any doubt about the symbolic meaning of these images of Eastern seas, and lands, and men, Conrad defines them for us: "The mysterious East faced me, perfumed like a flower, silent like death, dark like a grave." Old, experienced Marlow (and Conrad) still respond to the amazing beauty of the East. Yet the fact that they describe this beauty in terms of death indicates that life has taught them something that young Marlow has not yet learned: his youthful desire for heroic adventure masks a yearning to escape life altogether.

The early Conrad states his artistic purpose in his celebrated preface to *The Nigger of the "Narcissus"* of 1897: "My task which I am trying to achieve is, by the power of the written word to make you hear, to make you feel — it is, before all, to make you *see*." By this Conrad means literally what he says, that he wants us to see pictures, images. But he also means "see" as "understand," that is perceive meaning in these images. In short, the imagination of the early Conrad constantly tends toward symbolism. Conrad's use of the East as symbolic of death in "Youth" prefigures the image pattern of *Lord Jim*. There, images of the East, of whiteness, of moonlight are all equated with peace and death. In *The Nigger of the "Narcissus"* images of light are related to the good life at sea, images of dark to the weakness of man and to the ignoble life on the land. In "Heart of Darkness," the pattern is reversed and darkness means truth, whiteness means falsehood.

Images of the East and death in "Youth" gain added meaning through contrast with the death of the *Judea*. Throughout the story the old ship is personified, made symbolic of age and experience. Her death is like the death of a human being and has none of the coldness or fixity of peace in the East. She goes down in a blaze of glory to her reward for faithful duty on the seas:

> She burned furiously; mournful and imposing like a funeral pile kindled in the night, surrounded by the sea, watched over by the stars. A magnificent death had come like a grace, like a gift, like a reward to that old ship at the end of her laborious days.

Just as Beowulf's twelve faithful retainers circle his burial mound in tribute to him, the three boats of the *Judea* move "round her remains as if in procession." In the two paragraphs describing the ship's death, young Marlow becomes an anonymous member of the crew and the speaker shifts from "I" to "we." Thus, through language, Conrad reveals what the older Marlow has learned to value above his former youthful romanticism. The only life which merits a hero's death is the unpretentious life of loyal service in the ranks.

Yet it would be falsifying "Youth" to insist that old Marlow and Conrad separate themselves completely from the romantic egoism of the youthful hero. Though Conrad perceives the weakness inherent in the romanticism of youth, he nevertheless sympathizes with, even loves, a youthful straggler like Lord Jim. In "Youth," the pathos of the passing of these feelings receives its fullest expression in one of those overlong sentences that are virtually the hallmark of the early style:

> I remember the drawn faces, the dejected figures of my two men, and I remember my youth and the feeling that will never come back any more — the feeling that I could last for ever, outlast the sea, the earth, and all men; the deceitful feeling that lures us on to joys, to perils, to love, to vain effort — to death; the triumphant conviction of strength, the heat of life in the handful of dust, the glow in the heart that with every year grows dim, grows cold, grows small, and expires — and expires, too soon, too soon — before life itself.

The reader keeps expecting this sentence to end — after "for ever," after either of the semicolons, or after "expires." Conrad, however, continually adds new words in apposition to "feeling" and new dependent clauses to explain and qualify those appositives. He cannot resist multiplying words and phrases: "the sea, the earth, and all men," "to joys, to perils, to love, to vain effort," "conviction . . . heat . . . glow," "grows dim, grows cold, grows small." There is always more emotion to be expressed, another idea to be stated, a further qualification to make. Such a sentence may overwhelm all but the most incorrigible Conradian. In some of the early Malay stories, sentences like this often seem mere affectation, a mannerism. At its best, however, the overlong sentence of the early Conrad has a particular precision. It can succeed, as it does here, in dramatizing the overflow of human feelings.

Clearly the early Conrad's use of language is but one more aspect of his complexity. Through irony, symbolic imagery, and even sentence structure, he is able constantly to suggest that there are other sides to the question, that things are not quite what they seem. Though his morality is apparently simple enough, his characters' responses to their moral tests, his analysis of their responses, and the organization and the expression of his art — all these are very complicated.

Few novelists using the English language can match Conrad in any single aspect of his art. None, it may be asserted, has ever been able to combine so successfully such moral and psychological awareness with so complicated and rich a technique. We shall be better able to appreciate the height of Conrad's achievement when we examine the complex of conflicting impulses out of which it developed. Though Conrad's period of apprenticeship was brief, it was arduous. Arduous, too, were his efforts to maintain his own "exalted mark." It is not surprising, therefore, that the Conrad whom we have been considering in this chapter disappeared before the historical Conrad stopped writing.

II

The Uncongenial Subject: Love's Tangled Garden
(1895–1924)

Although the early period (1895–1912) saw the production of all of Conrad's important works (half a dozen short novels and four full-length novels), this was not a time of unbroken success. It includes the apprentice work of *Almayer's Folly* (1895), *An Outcast of the Islands* (1896), and *Tales of Unrest* (1898). While these books foreshadow the best of Conrad in theme, characterization, structure, and style, they are what most critics have recognized them to be — minor works. During his apprenticeship, Conrad suffered two disasters, two novels which he could not finish, *The Sisters* and "The Rescuer." Even while Conrad was producing his best work, he was also writing some very inferior fiction. There are, for example, three stories as long but not as substantial as his great short novels: "Falk," "The End of the Tether," and "Freya of the Seven Isles." Conrad may have intended these to be serious; at least they were published in volumes that contain serious work. But all are so marred by sentimentality as to be relative failures. Finally, Conrad wrote during the early period a number of short stories that are frankly potboilers. As he told his publisher in 1908 about *A Set of Six*, "They are just stories in which I've tried my best to be *simply entertaining*." [1]

The early Conrad's apprentice work and his failures strikingly resemble each other in subject matter and in symbolic imagery. Almost all deal in a major way with love. Moreover, even when the love story is apparently romantic and pure (the usual case in these works), powerful but ambiguous sexual feelings clearly lurk beneath the surface of the prose. The poor early works frequently contain patches of adjectival prose, heavy with images of writhing plant life, and straining mightily to express the "unspeakable" and the "impalpable." Conrad was well aware that he indulged in this kind of bad writing. "The Lagoon," he wrote Garnett, is a "tricky thing with the usual forests river — stars — wind sunrise, and so on — and lots of second hand Conradese in it." [2] Conradese contributed to his dubious reputation as an "exotic" writer, and Max Beerbohm's 1912 parody of Conradian excesses remains perhaps its best criticism.[3]

Love, we recall, had no place in our attempt to define the important early Conrad in the first chapter of this study. Yet of the seven novels he wrote after 1912, all but one are centered in love affairs. The fact that the early Conrad's unsuccessful work has the same subject as almost all the later novels suggests that, in our quest for sources of his declining powers, we would do well to scrutinize these early works more closely than Conrad's readers have tended to. We found in the previous chapter that recurrent patterns of action and character relationships gave us valuable keys to the working of Conrad's creative imagination. Might not an awareness of recurrent implausible and ill-conceived love affairs and of recurrent images inappropriate to the intended meaning of the work, help us to understand certain fundamental weaknesses in Conrad's imagination? When we have studied the love affairs and the imagery of the early unsatisfactory work, we should be better able to comprehend the later Conrad's handling of love.

Conrad began to write, as we have seen, because he was haunted by the memory of a man named Almayer whom he met in Borneo. Conrad does not tell us, however, why he felt compelled to include in his first novel the love story of Almayer's daughter, Nina, and the handsome Malay, Dain Maroola. It does not really matter; perhaps his purpose was no more mysterious than a vague feeling that since most novels he knew (particularly English ones) included a romantic love story, his should also.

Whatever the conscious reason for their creation, the two lovers are, artistically speaking, the weakest part of *Almayer's Folly*. They lack the moral and psychological interest of Almayer, the vitality of Babalatchi. Their conventional good looks and their wooden dialogue, consisting primarily of high-flown sentiments, mark them as stereotyped noble savages. Yet their failure is more complex than one simply of dullness. The inconsistency of the lovers' attitudes toward each other, the curious relationship between Nina and her father, the inappropriate imagery used in connection with the lovers — all these suggest that their creator is so seriously confused that he cannot carry out his artistic intentions.

Clearly, Dain is supposed to be stalwart, courageous, and masculine, and Nina is supposed to be his adoring beloved. But at certain crucial points in the love story, the dashing Malay becomes a timorous milquetoast, his submissive Nina *la femme fatale*. One of their most passionate scenes together portrays their first kiss. Dain tries to prevent the kiss by saying, "We must part now." Instead of going, Nina kisses him; his response must disappoint her: "He closed his eyes, surprised and frightened." When Conrad, toward the end of the novel, tries to describe the look of Nina's final, complete "surrender" to Dain, he instead describes her total victory:

> She drew back her head and fastened her eyes on his in one of those long looks that are women's most terrible weapon; a look that is more stirring than the closest touch, and more dangerous than the thrust of a dagger . . .[4]

Although only one critic has noticed it,[5] there is another love story in *Almayer's Folly*, one that tends to obscure the meaning of the novel. This is Almayer's unrequited, incestuous love for Nina. Miserable in his henpecked existence, Almayer gives all the love he possesses to his daughter. Therefore, when Nina finally leaves him for Dain, he rages like a betrayed lover rather than a disappointed father: "When you were *caressing* my cheek you were counting the minutes to the sunset that was the signal for your meeting with that man — there." (The italics are mine.) The reason Nina gives for leaving is on the same basis; she longs for a more vigorous sex-life, a life of "power and love." Almayer's response to this goes beyond normal paternal feeling: "I would have rather strangled you with my own hands." He longs to tell her that his love *is* more powerful than Dain's, but instead shouts that he will never forgive her:

This was the last time in his life that he was heard to raise his voice. Henceforth he spoke always in a monotonous whisper like an instrument of which all the strings but one are broken in a last ringing clamour under a heavy blow.

Nina, on the other hand, rather enjoys this scene in which she rejects her father; her farewell to him has all the characteristics of a coquette being sweet to one of her faithful but unacceptable suitors. The scene thus becomes a sympathetic defense of Almayer, the betrayed lover. But this is to sentimentalize him and negate the central meaning of the book which is that the foolish Almayer has destroyed himself through egoistic longings for wealth and power.

Feelings at variance with intention are also evident in Conrad's use of images in the love scenes between Dain and Nina. Although theirs is meant to be an idyllic romance, the description of the scene of their first kiss is anything but idyllic. It begins glamorously enough with an account of the lovers paddling into a miniature bay "under a low green archway of thickly matted creepers" where immense red blossoms send "down on their heads a shower of great dew-sparkling petals . . . in a continuous and perfumed stream." Then suddenly the tone shifts from enjoyment of this beauty to horror at its sources — death and decay:

all around them in a ring of luxuriant vegetation bathed in the
warm air charged with strong and harsh perfumes, the intense
work of tropical nature went on: plants shooting upward, en-
twined, interlaced in inextricable confusion, climbing madly and
brutally over each other in the terrible silence of a desperate
struggle toward the lifegiving sunshine above — as if struck with
sudden horror at the seething mass of corruption below, at the
death and decay from which they sprang.

The idea of fertility as death recurs in a series of purple
passages toward the end of the novel describing the hideout
where Dain awaits Nina and where their love is finally con-
summated. His clearing is surrounded by the big trees of the
forest which look

down at the growing young life at their feet with the sombre
resignation of giants that had lost faith in their strength. And in
the midst of them the merciless creepers clung to the big trunks
in cable-like coils, leaped from tree to tree, hung in thorny festoons from the lower boughs, and, sending slender tendrils on
high to seek out the smallest branches, carried death to their victims in an exulting riot of silent destruction.

The fate of these trees intrigues Dain, and he looks from time
to time into their dark shade where lie "entombed and
rotting, countless generations of trees," and where their suc-
cessors stand "as if in mourning, in dark green foliage, immense and helpless awaiting their turn." In a sense, this last
phrase applies to Dain's own situation as a stalwart hero,
never before in love, awaiting Nina. Although Conrad intends
marital bliss for Dain, the imagery of a less conscious and more
persuasive Conrad speaks only of death. Moreover, through
frequent references to flowers as well as creepers, Conrad
underlines the femininity of the destructive jungle life. There
in the "forests that were like death," where parasites with
pink and blue flowers strangle gigantic trees, Nina soon comes
to Dain "with quick, resolute steps," and throws her arms
around his neck "with a sudden gesture."

In *An Outcast of the Islands*, Conrad's next novel, love

plays a more obvious part than in *Almayer's Folly* or, really, any other of the early novels. Tyrannizing over his half-caste wife, Joanna, is Willems' chief joy in life until he is caught embezzling funds and has to leave the island. Willems' affair with Aïssa, later in Sambir, leads him to betray his only friend, Lingard, and ultimately brings about his own death at Aïssa's hands. Unlike *Almayer's Folly, An Outcast of the Islands* does not reveal an artist at war with his intentions. The intensity of his contempt for his hero deters Conrad from sentimentalizing him. The novel does resemble its predecessor in certain important ways, however. Like Almayer, Willems must endure having his masculinity held in contempt by the women in his life. Like Dain, Willems at times betrays fear of the woman who seemingly worships him. Finally, the imagery used in connection with his love affair with Aïssa reveals some of the same meanings we saw in the images of *Almayer's Folly*.

After Willems is fired for stealing funds from his employer, he goes home expecting to find, as usual, a suppliant wife, weeping to be consoled, ready to do his wishes. Instead, he finds Joanna changed into a ferocious Mrs. Almayer. Her upper lip is "drawn up to one side, giving to her melancholy face a vicious expression altogether new to his experience." She informs him that he is "less than dirt," and that she is through with him. When he pleads with her, she makes the rejection explicitly in sexual terms: "I do not want you; do not come near me· . . . Ah! Keep off me! Keep off me! Keep off!" Willems thus must go into exile alone and departs for Sambir.

Although Willems easily wins Aïssa, he later suffers a painful, though temporary, rejection at her hands, when she keeps him from her bed until he agrees to betray Lingard for the sake of her Arab friends. The rejection scene takes place just after Aïssa prevents her father from murdering Willems by wresting the kriss from his hands. (Almayer, we recall, in the earlier novel, tries to shoot Dain but Nina stops him.) Shaken by the experience, Willems begs Aïssa to flee with him to the land of the whites. She refuses, tells him to sleep elsewhere that night, and throws her father's kriss at his feet. Willems "instinctively" looks at it and identifies himself with the object. He stoops to pick it up with a "sad and humble movement," and asks himself, "Was this the answer to his pleading, to the hot and living words that had come from his heart? Was this the answer thrown at him like an insult? . . ." He stares at the kriss, drops it, and looks into the "sea of darkness" in which Aïssa has disappeared.

Conrad seems aware of Willems' lack of masculinity as he was not of Dain's; Lingard comments explicitly that Willems "is not a man at all." Certainly Willems presently loses interest in Aïssa's sexuality. When she clasps him round the neck in a burst of passion, he stiffens "in repulsion, in horror." Toward the end of the novel, Willems decides that he must resign himself to perpetual exile in Sambir and let the woman help him to forget. He takes Aïssa suddenly in his arms and waits "for the transport, for the madness," but all he feels is "cold, sick, tired, exasperated with his failure." The next morning he gets up with a "disgusted horror of himself."

As in *Almayer's Folly*, setting becomes symbolic when used in scenes between man and woman. Since *An Outcast of the Islands* deals with some of the same characters in the same East Indies setting, it is not surprising that the symbolic images are of the same sort — creepers, flowers, trees, and, more important than in *Almayer's Folly*, grass. These images occur, however, even in the urban setting of Macassar at the opening of the novel, when Willems is headed toward his "flower-bowered house" where he is accustomed to feed his egoism. This time he must tell his wife of his dismissal; he has no suspicion that she will reject him in his hour of need until he reaches the house. Then suddenly he feels a nameless fear:

The house was a pretty little structure all doors and windows, surrounded on all sides by the deep verandah supported on slender columns clothed in the green foliage of creepers, which also fringed the overhanging eaves of the high-pitched roof . . . He paused at every step. He must tell his wife. He was frightened at the prospect, and his alarm dismayed him. Frightened to face her!

With its supports clothed in creepers as were the doomed trees in *Almayer's Folly*, with a frightening female inside, the house has become a man-trap for Willems.

Whereas Dain's courtship of Nina is especially associated with flowers, Willems' "conquest" of Aïssa is especially associated with grass, though flowers are mentioned, too. Willems first meets Aïssa in a clearing in the forest rich with "long and feathery grass," and before he even sees her, he knows someone has just passed by because the grass on the bank is trembling. He hurries toward the spot, catches sight of Aïssa, but does not reach her until they are underneath the trees. Willems looks into her eyes, then at the forest:

He had been baffled, repelled, almost frightened by the intensity of that tropical life which wants the sunshine but works in gloom; which seems to be all grace of colour and form, all brilliance, all smiles, but is only the blossoming of the dead; whose mystery holds the promise of joy and beauty, yet contains nothing but poison and decay. He had been frightened by the vague perception of danger before, but now, as he looked at that life again, his eyes seemed able to pierce the fantastic veil of creepers and leaves . . . and the mystery was disclosed . . . He looked at the woman . . . the very spirit of that land of mysterious forests . . .

This is much like what we saw in *Almayer's Folly*: the life of the forest producing death and equated with woman. These images recur throughout the courtship, though frequently without sinister overtones. Aïssa seems habitually wrapped in the heavy odors of blossoms, her black hair mingled with pale green orchids.

From the moment that Willems wins Aïssa, however, his doom is evident, and it is expressed in these very images.

When the longed-for day came at last, when she sank on the grass by his side and with a quick gesture took his hand in hers, he sat up suddenly with the movement and look of a man awakened by the crash of his own falling house.

The image of the falling house recalls, of course, Willems' coming home to his wife the day of his disaster and seeing the slender columns of his pretty house menaced by strangling creepers.[6] Aïssa's "quick gesture" echoes Nina's "surrender" to Dain. Willems at last recognizes that this love will inevitably destroy him, and he sees "the sure death — everywhere" in creepers, in huge indented leaves that look to him like enormous hands waiting "to enlace him, to strangle him, to hold him till he died." Then, he thinks, the insects will consume his body until nothing will remain "but the white gleam of bleaching bones . . . in the long grass" that will "shoot its feathery heads between the bare and polished ribs." Willems knows, in short, that the life of the wilderness will finally destroy him, that the grass which was the first signal of Aïssa's presence will at last stab him through the ribs. Willems' literal death is accomplished with a last bit of garden-variety irony: Aïssa approaches singing, flowers in her hands, crimson blossoms in her hair, sees that Willems is about to desert her, flings down the flowers and shoots him dead.

Conrad finished *An Outcast of the Islands* in September, 1895; he did not finish another full-length novel until July, 1900.[7] That period was undoubtedly the most critical in his writing life. As he tells in his "Author's Note" to *An Outcast of the Islands*, he had begun his second novel rather casually in response to Edward Garnett's casual, "Why not write another?" But writing the third novel meant commitment to the profession. Five years of heartbreaking effort followed, including the shelving of two novel-fragments, *The Sisters* (only ten thousand words) and "The Rescuer" (over four hundred manuscript pages). Yet this was far from an unproductive period; for relief from "The Rescuer," Conrad wrote a book of short stories, *Tales of Unrest,* and three great short novels, *The Nigger of the "Narcissus,"* "Youth," and "Heart of Darkness." The period is of particular interest in our examination of Conrad's handling of love since all these works either deal directly with love or else rigorously exclude it. Conrad seems unable to find a middle ground. Moreover, his failure to finish two projected novels at this time may shed some light on his failing powers in the later years.

During the fall and winter of 1895–96, Conrad began and abandoned *The Sisters,* which was published posthumously in its unfinished form. Conrad himself has left no hint of his conscious intentions in *The Sisters,* and, of his friends, only Ford Madox Ford has discussed it in any detail. Ford's speculations, while most intriguing, suffer seriously from being based on a notoriously faulty memory looking back over thirty years.[8] However, the text itself, brief as it is, provides us with enough evidence to make some useful and informed guesses about what kind of story Conrad was trying to write. It consists of seven short chapters, the first four about a young man, the last three about a young woman. Stephen, the wealthy son of *nouveau riche* Russian peasants, has wandered restlessly all over Europe in search of a "creed." His parents die, his brother wants him to come home to help with the business, but instead he settles in a pavilion in a court on the outskirts of Passy, presumably to continue his quest for truth. The scene then shifts across the street to the house of Rita, also an orphan. She is Spanish, and her family are all revolutionists, seeking to restore the Bourbons to the Spanish throne. She lives with her uncle, J. Ortega, dealer in oranges, olives, and wine, but she longs for the "reality" of the days of her youth in Spain. Here the fragment ends. It seems reasonable to assume that the pensive, lonely Slav and the

fiery, lonely Latin were to meet and fall in love. That the
novel was not to end happily is suggested by this hint of
Stephen's early death: "how short his life, how faint his trace
on the earth, was fated to be."

Besides the love affair between Stephen and Rita, which
the structure of the fragment suggests was to have been the
subject of the book, there are distinct hints of a second love
story, of which Conrad may well have been unaware. This is
between Rita and her uncle, old Ortega, and it recalls Almayer's love for Nina. Like Almayer, Ortega has a shrewish
wife who continually browbeats him and shouts his name at
the top of her lungs. Like Almayer, Ortega is timid and gentle,
with a "thin squeaky voice." Rita has become his whole life;
when she is away he is miserable, when she comes back he is
"childishly happy." "He admired her bravery in holding
out — with more or less success — against Dolores [his wife],
he enjoyed her *caressing* ways — that were for him only. . . ."
(The italics are mine.) Rita responds more sympathetically
to her uncle's love than does Nina to her father's; yet Rita
perceives that Ortega's is not a powerful love. (The italics
below are mine.)

> Its helplessness was touching and it seemed to her to be an
> indissoluble part of it, filling her with regret at the thought that
> so much affection must be bound up together with so much weak-
> ness . . . For her uncle as she grew up, she had a *caressing*, a
> deep gratitude — in which, almost unknown to her, lurked a
> faint flavour of disenchanted pity.

In Conrad's first two novels images of trees, creepers and
grass, flowers and perfume, revealed to us the strength of his
subterranean feelings about the love stories he was trying to
tell. We would not expect to find such images in a novel about
Paris; yet we do. The fact that they occur in a setting where
they are completely gratuitous makes us even more certain
that our symbolic readings of the Malay setting were valid.
In *The Sisters* Conrad describes in detail Stephen's retreat

in Passy. Outside his windows is a garden with three or four trees growing in it "as if in a dungeon." They are fragile and are menaced by fertile grass:

> Their pale foliage waved below the windows of the pavilion in a shimmer of green tints that seemed pale and delicate with the pathetic frailness of town children . . . Below in the damp and uniform gloom the grass sprang up, vigorous and conquering, over that desolate remnant of beauty; covering the ground thickly with a prosperous, flourishing growth in a triumph of undistinguishably similar blades that pressed thick, low, full of life around the foot of soaring trunks of the trees; the grass unconquerable, content with the gloom, disputing sustenance with the roots, vanquishing the slender trees that strove courageously even there to keep their heads in the splendour of sunshine.

As it stands, this passage tells only how fertility, or process, destroys at the same time that it produces. Conrad, however, immediately makes this apply directly to Stephen. The birds in these trees are thinking about Stephen; they are "wondering, perhaps with compassion, at the big stone cage where dwelt an immense and unfortunate creature . . ." Thus Stephen is contrasted to the free birds and equated with the trees in their "dungeon."

Conrad's next step, albeit an unconscious one, is to relate the menaced male, through images, to the unknown female next door. He mentions first the flowers in the courtyard which had once been ornamental and kept under control but which now "run wild" and luxuriate in "incult freedom." Then by means of images he shifts the scene from Stephen's house to Rita's:

> Trailing under the archway, over the court; rising as high as the windows of Stephen's studio, a strong perfume of oranges carried amongst brick walls and over sooty bushes a romantic suggestion of dark foliage and golden fruit, of tepid breezes and clear sunshine, of rustling groves in a southern land . . . Inside, the sweet scented silence was almost undisturbed by the feeble tapping of Ortega's hammer.

So completely fused are the ideas of Rita, perfume, and sex
with the menacing garden outside Stephen's windows that
Rita herself becomes a kind of creeping vine "trailing" over
the court and rising to ensnare Stephen. Moreover, the other
male in *The Sisters,* old uncle Ortega, seems relatively helpless and ineffectual here, his "feeble" hammer juxtaposed
against suggestions of female sexuality in the "strong perfume" and "golden fruit."

We cannot help but wonder why Conrad abandoned *The
Sisters.* He was certainly attempting something quite different from *Almayer's Folly* and *An Outcast of the Islands.* Instead of the exotic East Indies, his setting was Western
Europe. He had apparently decided to make the center of his
novel a love story and, again for the first time, a love story
about two whites. Moreover, the fragment suggests that unlike Almayer and Willems, Stephen was not to have been the
object of ironic judgment. In short, Conrad seems to have
tried to write a sympathetic account of love between two
whites; he discovered very quickly (in less than six months)
that he could not.

Whatever the reason for Conrad's inability to continue
with *The Sisters,* there can be little doubt that his decision
was right. Even as a first draft, this is a most unpromising
fragment. The prose exhibits great uncertainty of tone; it
virtually collapses under the weight of abstract nouns: "The
western life captivated him by the amplitude of its complicated surface, horrified him by the interior jumble of its va-
riegated littleness." Although Conrad throughout his career
almost never completely escapes the cliché, *The Sisters* reaches
a low point in banality. "He thought: It is dark now but tomorrow is another day." *The Sisters,* then, would have been
a step backward when Conrad was really on the threshold of
great things; only a few months later he was to begin one of
his most nearly perfect works, *The Nigger of the "Narcissus."*

Conrad abandoned *The Sisters* in order to begin, in March,

1896, "The Rescuer," [9] his third novel of the East Indies, this one to be about Tom Lingard, a character who is mentioned in *Almayer's Folly* and who figures prominently in *An Outcast of the Islands*. Conrad wrestled with the manuscript until some time in 1899, producing over four hundred pages; he laid it aside completely until 1916 when he added a good deal, most of which he later discarded. In 1918–19, he dictated the final half of the novel and published it in book form as *The Rescue* in 1920. Though Conrad wrote Part I with relative ease between March and June, 1896, he then began to work with probably the greatest difficulty of his entire writing career. His letters to Garnett, written over a period of three years, reveal a continuous, and at times complete, creative paralysis: "The progressive episodes *will* not emerge from the chaos of my sensations. I feel nothing clearly. And I am frightened when I remember that I have to drag it all out of myself." [10]

"The Rescuer," then, raises the same question as *The Sisters*: why did Conrad fail to finish it? As he invested more and more time, he had increasing reason to complete it, especially when, in 1898, he sold the magazine rights to McClure. Moreover, on the surface at least, "The Rescuer" would seem to be more congenial to his temperament than *The Sisters*, since it much more closely resembles his first two novels. It tells of an egoistic white man who meddles in native politics for the sake of a young Celebes prince and his sister. Lingard is an honest and courageous adventurer, thus much more sympathetic than Almayer or Willems, but the action he pursues certainly resembles theirs, up to a point. At the delicate moment of coordinating all his forces for a big attack to retake the prince's kingdom, Lingard is confounded by an unexpected complication. The complication is a woman, not a savage like the heroines of the first two novels, but a sophisticated Englishwoman. She, her husband, and a Spanish gentleman [11] run aground in their yacht precisely where Lingard is organizing his expeditionary force. A letter to his publisher indicates that Conrad had introduced these yacht people to please the public: "The theme of it shall be the rescue of a yacht from some Malay vagabonds and there will be a gentleman and a lady cut out according to the regulation pattern." [12]

Both the external evidence of Conrad's progress in writing the novel, as told in his letters to Garnett, and the evidence provided by the manuscript itself indicate that the yacht people were the rock upon which "The Rescuer" foundered. Having finished in June, 1896, Part I, "The Man and the Brig," which describes Lingard approaching his hideout, he wrote Garnett in July that setting the yacht people on their feet was proving to be a "hell of a job." [13] A month later he wrote:

> Your commendation of part I plunges me simply into despair — because part II *must* be very different in theme if not in treatment and I am afraid this will make the book a strange and repulsive hybrid, fit only to be stoned, jumped upon, defiled and then held up to ridicule as a proof of my ineptitude. You see, I must justify — give a motive — to my yacht people.[14]

Ten days later Conrad dropped "The Rescuer" and did not get back to it for over a year. When he did succeed in writing Part II in the winter of 1897–98, it is significant that he evaded the yacht people and made Part II a retrospective account of Lingard's first meeting with the prince, Pata Hassim, Hassim's loss of his kingdom, and Lingard's preparations for its recapture. Finally, in the spring of 1898, Conrad at last tried to create the yacht people; he finished Part III in December. His psychological state is clearly revealed in a letter to Garnett in August, 1898: "I am writing hopelessly — but still I am writing . . . Pages accumulate and the story stands still. I feel suicidal . . . I am utterly out of touch with my work — and I can't get in touch." [15] Sometime in 1899 Conrad completely abandoned "The Rescuer." He appears to have quit at a point in the story between the time when the woman, Edith Travers, moved to Lingard's brig, and the time when she and Lingard sailed together to the mainland. In other words, Conrad gave up when the heroine was completely in the hero's hands. Yet it matters little precisely where Conrad stopped. All the evidence indicates that, after an initial burst of enthusiasm, when the time came for Conrad to create the gentleman and lady, he became acutely uncomfortable.

We are moving, then, toward the same tentative solution we reached with *The Sisters*. The sympathetic treatment of love between a white man and woman is not congenial to the early Conrad's creativity. An examination of a few scenes between Lingard and Edith Travers in "The Rescuer" makes this quite clear. Whether Conrad was conscious of it or not, he felt the relationship between hero and heroine to be a powerfully sexual one. This is made especially obvious in a description of Lingard's actions after he misinterprets a signal from the yacht and believes that Edith is carrying out the plan he had proposed to her. He believes, that is, that he has made a telling impression on her. This rather amusing passage is quoted at length since the later Conrad censored most of it from *The Rescue*.

He bit the cartridges, hammered at the waddings with fierce joyousness, with something impatient in his movements. The ramrods rang and jumped. The table was covered with loaded muskets . . . She has done it — he repeated mentally. She has done it. And why? She does not understand anything of danger. It looks as if she had done it for me. He imagined her in that cabin and with his teeth fastened in a cartridge he stood looking across the table at the settee as though she had been sitting there before his eyes. "I could talk to her just as if I had known her from a child." He muttered flinging a ramrod down the barrel violently . . . The intimacy of his thought with that woman seemed to affect his body like strong drink, so that while cocking a musket he swayed a little. His hand trembled when he picked up a little coppercap that shone like a tiny red spark between his big fingers. He pressed it steadily on the nipple, and his face was very still.[16]

This passage reveals, first of all, that Conrad feels Lingard's response to Edith to be largely sexual. Incongruously juxtaposed against Lingard's innocent thoughts of speaking to Edith as a childhood friend are a welter of obvious sexual references. It is important to remember that this passage, which more stridently than any other in "The Rescuer" describes Lingard's sexual feelings for Edith, takes place while he is away from her and, moreover, arises from a misinterpreted signal.

While Conrad does not deal with Edith's sexual feelings for Lingard, he does depict her as a person longing for a violent and truthful emotional experience. In this respect she reminds us of Rita in *The Sisters*. "As a young girl — often reproved for her romantic ideas" — Edith "had dreams where the sincerity of a great passion appeared like the ideal fulfillment and the only truth of life." Instead she marries a man who appears to be an idealist but proves to be merely selfishly respectable. Edith envies the lot of the native princess, Immada, because nothing stands between her and the "truth of her sensations." Edith feels that she herself "also could be equal to such an existence; and her heart was dilated by a momentary longing to know the naked truth of things." Then Lingard seeks out Edith alone and tells her all his plans: "what I have told nobody." Apparently this is the naked truth of things that Edith has been waiting for: "She felt intensely alive. She felt alive in a flush of strength, with an impression of novelty as though life had been the gift of this very moment."

As in *The Sisters*, we find in "The Rescuer" uncertain characterization and unpromising prose. Conrad had every justification for fearing that "The Rescuer" would destroy his reputation. Still, Conrad handles Lingard better than he had handled Stephen in *The Sisters*. We would expect this, since Conrad had already written about Lingard in two other novels. Moreover, in "The Rescuer" he had two subjects, one the power and beauty of love, the other a meddlesome romantic adventurer creating a kingdom for the sake of an ideal friendship — and his own egoism. The most obvious weaknesses rise out of the love subject: the conversations between Lingard and Edith and the description of their inner lives.

Wooden dialogue destroys the most crucial scene in the manuscript. This is the one in which Lingard convinces Edith Travers of his good intentions toward the yacht people and of the tremendous stakes for which he is gambling. In this passage, Lingard is persuading Edith to try to make her husband move the yacht people over to his brig where they will be safe and will not spoil his plans. She begins:

"You are like other men in this — that you get angry when you can not have your way at once."

"I angry!" he exclaimed in a deadened voice. "You do not understand . . . I am . . . thinking of you also . . . it is hard on me . . ."

"I mistrust not you but my own power. You have produced such an unfortunate impression on Mr. Travers."

"Unfortunate impression! He treated me as if [I] had been a long-shore loafer . . . Never mind that. He is your husband. Fear in those you care for is hard to bear for any man. And so, he . . ."

"What Machiavellism!"

"Eh? What did you say?"

"I only wondered where you had observed that. On the sea?"

"Observed — what?" he said absently.

We note that three times in this short passage the dialogue shifts person through the simple expedient of having one character repeat a word or phrase of the other. Two shifts are accomplished by one asking a question of the other. (Cross-examination is Conrad's chief device throughout this scene.) Edith's "What Machiavellism!" is obviously meant only for the reader, to tell him that the unlettered Lingard has made a brilliant stroke of diplomacy.

Since Conrad is dramatizing the moment when two strong characters fall in love, he must indicate their admiration, their awe for each other. He does so in this fashion. " 'You dared!' She whispered down in an intense tone. . ." And Lingard's words to her: "I told you because I — because I trust you."

Conrad appears to have as much difficulty with passages of explicit analysis of feelings as he has with straight dialogue. It is almost as if he were showing his own discomfort in this account of Edith's reflections:

> And at first it was only an oppressive notion of there being some significance that really mattered in this man's story. That mattered to her. For the first time the shadow of danger and death crossed her mind. Was that the meaning? Suddenly in a flash of acute discernment she saw herself involved in that story, helplessly like [sic] one is involved in a natural catastrophe.

Here, in this central passage foretelling the inevitable tragedy that must come from Edith's involvement with Lingard, Conrad remains on the surface of things. His attempt to elucidate Lingard's inner being fares no better:

> Lingard's soul was exalted by his talk with Edith, by the strain of incertitude and by extreme fatigue . . . He went into his cabin and throwing himself on the couch closed his eyes thinking: I must sleep or I shall go mad.

We see that once again Conrad has abandoned a bad piece of writing. This time there can be no excuse that he had not yet mastered the tools of the trade, for the period of struggle with "The Rescuer" was anything but one of apprenticeship. During this time Conrad wrote three of his finest works, *The Nigger of the "Narcissus,"* "Youth," and "Heart of Darkness," as well as the first pages of *Lord Jim.* This indicates that he abandoned "The Rescuer" because the subject was uncongenial, because he could not write the love story of Lingard and Edith, just as he could not even begin the love affair between Stephen and Rita in *The Sisters.* There is something about the theme of love that elicits only bad writing from Conrad, something that frustrates his most strenuous efforts to create. In order better to understand the nature of Conrad's difficulties with love in "The Rescuer," let us examine those stories which he wrote as relief from his vain struggle. As in our study of the first four works, we shall look specifically at the function of love and, where relevant, at the imagery.

While Conrad was still at work on the first part of "The Rescuer" in May, 1896, he took time out to write a short story, called "The Idiots," about a Breton farmer and his wife. Though hardly a "love story," it effectively dramatizes the disastrous results of one marriage. A naturalistic story in the de Maupassant manner, it tells of a farmer who marries in order to found a family, improve his farm, and pass it on to the next generation. But his wife frustrates his plans by bearing him four idiots. He takes to drink; she murders him and commits suicide.

Finding it impossible to make headway with Part II of "The Rescuer" in June, Conrad began *The Nigger of the "Narcissus,"* perhaps the most aggressively masculine of all his works. The ship Narcissus is a little world which Conrad lovingly memorializes, a self-sufficient, domestic, womanless world. Men happily perform all the housewifely chores and stroll about the decks in "couples." This ideal world contains one woman, it is true, the beautiful *Narcissus*: "She was beautiful and had a weakness. We loved her no less for that." The female of the human species, however, belongs to the dark and corrupt land. The first words spoken to the ship as she moves up the Thames come from a bareheaded woman who screams, "Hallo, Jack!" to the silent ship. When the captain joins his wife, the crew does not even recognize him. And young Charley seeks to disengage himself from his "untidy," "blubbering" mother.

While still at work on *The Nigger of the "Narcissus"* and,

ostensibly, on "The Rescuer," Conrad determined to write a volume of short stories with "The Idiots" as a beginning. The second was "An Outpost of Progress," written in July, 1896. In Conrad's own words to his publisher: "It is a story of the Congo. There is no love interest in it and no woman — only incidentally." [17]

The third, in order of composition, of the short stories for the volume, *Tales of Unrest,* was "The Lagoon," finished in August, 1896. It tells about Arsat, a Malay who falls in love with the servant of his ruler and carries her off with the aid of his beloved brother. They are pursued, and Arsat, because he is in love, becomes cowardly. His brother chides him: "There is half a man in you now — the other half is in that woman." When the three are about to be captured, Arsat, desiring only safety and peace, leaves his brother to die alone and sails away with the girl. For a time they do find peace in their secluded lagoon, but she eventually dies, and the story ends with Arsat, covered with shame, determined to return to his country and die avenging his brother's death. The vegetation imagery of "The Lagoon" represents an interesting variation on the pattern we saw in the first two novels and *The Sisters.* Here the emphasis is not upon the jungle as living, writhing, strangling, destroying, but the jungle as fixed in death. Every creeper and every blossom seems "bewitched into an immobility perfect and final"; lotus blossoms are "silvery," the lagoon "polished and black." This difference may arise from the fact that Arsat's moral destruction is already complete when he reaches the lagoon, whereas Dain's, Willems', and Stephen's are just about to take place. When the woman dies, freeing Arsat to die honorably, the setting changes dramatically to suggest the possibility of redemption:

The breeze freshened; a great brilliance burst upon the lagoon, sparkled in the rippling water. The forests came out of the clear shadows of the morning, became distinct, as if they had rushed nearer — to stop short in a great stir of leaves, of nodding boughs, of swaying branches.

Conrad devoted the time from September, 1896, to February, 1897, to finishing *The Nigger of the "Narcissus,"* and then wrote "Karain," the fourth of the short stories for *Tales of Unrest,* completing it in April. It, too, is a Malay story of betrayal. Karain and his closest friend, Pata Matara, pursue Matara's sister, who has run off with a Dutchman, thus disgracing her brother. Karain and Matara intend to kill them both, but during the years of pursuit Karain dreams constantly of the girl and falls in love with the dream. When they finally catch the couple, Karain, instead of shooting the Dutchman while Matara stabs his sister, shoots Matara. The girl does not, of course, even recognize Karain. He begins wandering, no longer seeing the vision of the girl but only the accusing specter of his friend. For the rest of his life, Karain is a "slave of the dead."

As soon as Conrad completed "Karain," he began the fifth, and last, of the stories for the *Tales of Unrest* volume, still unable to face the crisis of "The Rescuer." Ironically, Conrad had tremendous difficulties with "The Return" almost from the start. A letter to his friend Sanderson recalls his letters to Garnett about "The Rescuer": "What I've written seems to me too contemptible for words." [18] He finally finished it in September and soon hated it heartily. Yet we must examine it rather carefully because its subject, the relationship between a white man and woman, proved to be insuperable in *The Sisters* and "The Rescuer."

On the surface, "The Return" is an indictment of the triviality, the conventionality, the pomposity of a bourgeois London couple, particularly of the husband, Alvan Hervey. We see him first getting off the commuter train in his suburb, then going up the "sordid staircase" with the other commuters, whose backs all look alike, "as if they had been wearing a uniform." Conrad reviews Hervey's marriage five years before and sums up the Herveys' relationship this way:

They skimmed over the surface of life hand in hand, in a pure and frosty atmosphere — like two skilful skaters cutting figures on thick ice for the admiration of the beholders, and disdainfully ignoring the hidden stream, the stream restless and dark; the stream of life, profound and unfrozen.

Conrad further reinforces the idea of Hervey's conventionality by describing him mirrored in his wife's pier glass which multiplies his image into a "crowd of gentlemanly and slavish imitators."

A note from his wife telling him that she has left him jolts Hervey out of his complacency and into the world of "real feelings," and "for less than a second he looked upon the mysterious universe of moral suffering." Hervey is somewhat chagrined when his wife returns and he discovers that he is once again perfectly safe. The world will know nothing of what happened. "It was morally impossible to go wrong. He was not elated by that certitude; he was dimly uneasy about its price; there was a chill as of death in this triumph of sound principles." Hervey reverts briefly to his conventional self and demands an explanation of his wife. She does not respond as he expects; she tells him the truth, that neither of them has ever loved the other, that she returned to him only because she lacked courage. At his words, "I forgive you," she bursts into hysterical laughter. As the evening wears on, Hervey discovers himself longing for "the certitude immaterial and precious — the certitude of love and faith . . . It was the subtle despotism of an idea that suffers no rivals, that is lonely, inconsolable, and dangerous." Twice he approaches his wife to get from her the gift of "love and faith," and twice she spurns him. From his suffering Hervey learns that his middle-class morality is false:

> It came to him in a flash that morality is not a method of happiness. The revelation was terrible. He saw at once that nothing of what he knew mattered in the least. The acts of men and women, success, humiliation, dignity, failure — nothing mattered.

Hervey's statement of nihilism and despair is most unusual in the early Conrad because it is not qualified by either irony or explicit judgment. While Decoud, for instance, thinks such hopeless thoughts in *Nostromo*, Conrad condemns him for it. Moreover, people and their acts certainly *do* matter to the early Conrad. How then can we explain Hervey's despair? It appears from Conrad's letters to Garnett [19] and from the patches of rather crude irony which occur in the story that Conrad *thought* that he was satirizing Hervey, thought that he was rendering him ironically. Yet somehow Conrad became so confused about Hervey that try as he might he could not judge and condemn Hervey's despair.

Conrad's confusion seems to arise from the fact that "The Return" is more about Hervey's sexual difficulties than about his bourgeois ideas. An examination of his reactions to his wife's desertion and return may illuminate the central meaning of the story. When Hervey finds that his wife has left, he does not care so much about losing her as about the personal insult that she has found another man sexually preferable to himself. Conrad accents the quality of Hervey's feelings by describing them in physical terms. Hervey drops his wife's note "as though it had been something hot, or-venomous, or filthy." "He felt very sick — physically sick — as though he had bitten through something nauseous." He cannot accept the fact that he has been involved in

passion . . . the unpardonable and secret infamy of our hearts, a thing to curse, to hide and to deny . . . And it had come to him! It had laid its unclean hand upon the spotless draperies of his existence . . .

As he thinks over the past, his meditations reveal that his married life has not been very active sexually: "Five years of life in common had appeased his longing. Yes, long-time ago. The first five months did that . . ."

Hervey's first reaction to his wife's return comes as something of a surprise. Not at all elated, he stumbles in his anxiety when he hears her footsteps nearing their bedroom.

She had come back! And he very nearly said aloud "Of course!"
— such was his sudden and masterful perception of the indestructible character of her being. Nothing could destroy her —
and nothing but his own destruction could keep her away.

The ensuing scenes between husband and wife certainly bear
out Hervey's conviction of his wife's supremacy over him, of
her determination to destroy him. "He felt himself helpless
before the hidden meaning of [her] look; he resented it with
pained and futile violence . . ." He tries to make her admit
that she has been having a love affair all along, but he gets
no satisfaction from her answers. When, instead, she bursts
into laughter, he bounds toward the door, horrified.

The crucial scene between the two takes place after dinner in a highly atmospheric setting, elaborately prepared.
Throughout the story, images of heat, light, and marmoreal
indestructibility have been associated with Mrs. Hervey.
When she returns and appears before him in the glare of the
menacing gaslight (a "flaming butterfly poised between the
jaws of the bronze dragon"), Hervey can scarcely make her
out for the glare. "He was amazed to see her preserve so well
the composure of her upright attitude in that scorching brilliance which, to his eyes, enveloped her like a hot and con-
suming mist." During their first argument, she sits "with a
lost, unswerving gaze of her eyes which stared . . . at the
crude gas flame." When she bursts into hysterical screams,
Hervey stands still, distracted, "unable to touch her as though
she had been on fire." At the dinner table, Hervey sits in awe
at her "marmoreal impassiveness" and ponders the "impenetrable duplicity" of women.

We are therefore quite prepared to find Mrs. Hervey in the
following setting for their climactic scene:

The coals glowed without a flame; and upon the red glow the
vertical bars of the grate stood out at her feet, black and curved,
like the charred ribs of a consumed sacrifice. Far off, a lamp
perched on a slim brass rod, burned under a wide shade of
crimson silk: the centre, within the shadows of the large room, of

a fiery twilight that had in the warm quality of its tint something delicate, refined and infernal.

This is as we would expect it: the woman set against fire, indestructible and deadly, a sacrifice at her feet. A few pages later, Hervey thinks of their home as a "house of ill-fame." While Hervey's wife sits there with her back to him, he paces back and forth, wondering what she is thinking: "he felt himself insignificant and powerless before her, like a prisoner in chains. The fury of his *impotence* called out sinister images . . ." (The italics are mine.) Hervey again tries to offer her forgiveness. She stands up, "tall and indistinct, like a black phantom in the red twilight." Her movement forces him into the role of a supplicant, and he makes this significant remark — the italics are mine:

"But if my love is strong enough . . ." and hesitated.
He heard something snap loudly in the fiery stillness. She had broken her fan. Two thin pieces of ivory fell, one after another, without a sound, on the thick carpet, and *instinctively he stooped* to pick them up.

Here we find the same language describing the same gesture which Willems made when Aïssa threw the kriss at his feet and told him to go sleep somewhere else, alone. In the present scene, Hervey has said that, if his love is strong enough, they can still have a successful marriage. Still, his love had not been strong enough before to keep her from leaving him for "passion." Her answer to his question, breaking the fan, tells him that his love is *not* strong enough, that she has greater force than he.

Although she has rejected him, Hervey seizes upon the idea that she holds the "very secret of existence." He stands for a moment in a kind of trance and then approaches her:

He made a step forward, putting his arms out, as if to take her to his breast, and, lifting his head, was met by such a look of blank consternation that his arms fell as though they had been struck down by a blow. She started away from him, stumbled over the threshold, and once on the landing turned, swift and crouching. The train of her gown swished as it flew around her feet. It was an undisguised panic. She panted, showing her teeth, and the hate of strength, the disdain of weakness, the eternal pre-occupation of sex came out like a toy demon out of a box. "This is odious," she screamed. He did not stir . . . and looking at that face triumphant and scornful, at that white face, stealthy and unexpected, as if discovered staring from an ambush, he was coming back slowly to the world of senses.

This prose has been quoted at such length not merely to show the repugnance Mrs. Hervey feels towards her husband's sexual inadequacy but chiefly to indicate how completely Conrad loses control when he tries to deal with a sexual subject. The scene purports to show Mrs. Hervey's panic at her husband's approach, but it actually shows how dangerous she is to *him*. With a look as powerful as a blow, moving along like a beast of prey, she seems ready to ambush her husband. We recall that this action takes place as she heads for her lair — their bedroom upstairs.

The last scene takes place in the bedroom. It adds little that is new, but it does help confirm what we already suspect. Contempt for himself finally forces Hervey to follow his wife upstairs. Yet when he reaches the door of their bedroom and advances his hand to open it, he does a very strange thing which Conrad does not explain. Instead of opening the door, he falters, steps back, and hides in the perpendicular folds of the portière, in the manner of an inadequate voyeur lurking outside a strange woman's bedroom, rather than of a man married five years. While Hervey pauses, there occurs the only moving passage in the story, the only sympathetic picture of a human being. Up the stairs, "as if ascending from a well," walks one of the maids; she, too, is associated with light and flame:

At every step the feeble flame of the candle swayed before her tired, young face, and the darkness of the hall seemed to cling to her black skirt . . . as though the great night of the world had broken through the discreet reserve of walls, of closed doors, of curtained windows.

Hervey looks past her at the familiar lighting fixture, the "woman of marble composed and blind on the high pedestal" warding off the "devouring night with a cluster of lights." The girl continues up the stairs, extinguishes the marble woman's lights, and leaves Hervey alone in the darkness to make his discovery that nothing matters. The darkness and the discovery are both intolerable, and he goes, as always, to his wife for help. For a moment he can see nothing but the "dazzling brilliance of the light" in the bedroom; finally he makes her out, her hair streaming on her shoulders like "burnished gold." He finds no help there, of course, and runs out of the house, into the night.

So ends the only serious direct treatment of a sexual subject that Conrad finished during his early period. One may well ask why we have dwelt so long on such a bad piece of writing. For one thing, the situation and the image pattern do have artistic possibilities, as T. S. Eliot clearly demonstrates in his handling of almost identical materials in the first half of "A Game of Chess," in *The Waste Land*.[20] "The Return," moreover, provides us with a kind of *locus classicus* for the near paralysis of Conrad's creativity when dealing with a sexual subject. Finally, it is significant that Conrad's one extended study of a sexual subject should center in an inadequate male who sees female sexuality as an inescapable menace. For Alvan Hervey does not consider his situation unique. He sees in his wife every woman and so becomes suspicious even of the female domestics: "Women — nothing but women round him . . . The sight of a man's face — he felt — of any man's face, would have been a profound relief . . . He would engage a butler as soon as possible." He loathes his wife's "*feminine* penetration" (my italics) and feels drawn to other men, including his rival: "He felt fellowship with every

man — even with that man — especially with that man." Alvan
Hervey sees his unhappiness as simply part of a world in
which women destroy men, a world in which nothing matters.
After finishing "The Return" in September, 1897, Conrad
devoted full time to "The Rescuer," completing Part II in
March, 1898, but then grinding to a halt again in May. For
relief, during late May and early June, Conrad wrote "Youth"
and a few pages of what he intended to be a long short story,
"Tuan Jim: A Sketch." Both must have provided a complete
change from his toils with Lingard and Edith. Woman appears in only one short scene in "Youth": Captain Beard
heroically rescues his motherly wife from a purely imaginary
danger. "Tuan Jim," Conrad's tentative beginning of *Lord
Jim*, was to have been concerned solely with the pilgrim ship
episode and Jim's disgrace; it would therefore have been womanless.

Finishing Part III of "The Rescuer" in December, 1898,
Conrad soon abandoned Part IV to write "Heart of Darkness," which was published in *Youth and Two Other Stories*,
1902. As in "Youth," all the principal characters are male.
But Marlow, the narrator, makes some interesting comments
on women; the last scene, between Marlow and Kurtz's Intended has considerable significance; and the jungle imagery
raises some interesting problems. Marlow's most extended
comment on women comes out apropos of his aunt's expostu-
lations on the great missionary work of the Congo trading
company. Marlow ventures to remind her that the company
is run for profit, and then says in an aside to his male audience on board the yawl in the Thames estuary:

> It's queer how out of touch with truth women are. They live
> in a world of their own, and there has never been anything like
> it, and never can be. It is too beautiful altogether, and if they were
> to set it up it would go to pieces before the first sunset. Some con-
> founded fact we men have been living contentedly with ever
> since the day of creation would start up and knock the whole
> thing over.

In the context of "Heart of Darkness," with its theme of self-discovery, Marlow's assertion that women can take no part in the quest for truth is severe criticism indeed. Marlow says the same thing of Kurtz's Intended: "Oh, she is out of it — completely. They — the women I mean — are out of it — should be out of it. We must help them to stay in that beautiful world of their own."

Though "Heart of Darkness" does not hint that Marlow has any sexual interest in the Intended, their scene together at the end certainly recalls in some respects scenes between the Herveys in "The Return." For instance, though Marlow has been eager to meet her, he is filled with horror when he reaches her door. The fireplace in her drawing room has a "cold and monumental whiteness." Marlow looks at the woman and wonders what he is doing there, "with a sensation of panic in my heart as though I had blundered into a place of cruel and absurd mysteries not fit for a human being to behold." Their ensuing dialogue is halting and wooden, a "bad patch" of prose, F. R. Leavis calls it.[21] Marlow has come there hoping to surrender to her the memory of Kurtz. She instead maneuvers him into telling her a lie: that Kurtz's last words were, not "The horror," but her name: "I heard a light sigh and then my heart stood still, stopped dead short by an exulting and terrible cry, by the cry of inconceivable triumph and of unspeakable pain." Marlow's lie certainly weakens the scene; he has made truth seem too important throughout the novel to persuade the reader now to accept falsehood as salvation.

The extended descriptions of the jungle remind us, not unnaturally, of the vegetation imagery of *Almayer's Folly* and *An Outcast of the Islands*. Here, too, the "vegetation rioted on the earth and the big trees were kings"; the reader finds himself in a "strange world of plants, water, and silence." Yet "Heart of Darkness" does not stress so heavily as the earlier works the strangling effects of tendrils and creepers.

At one point, Marlow does mention the "living trees, lashed together by the creepers," and at another he equates vegetation with woman just as he does not only in the Malay stories but also in *The Sisters*. The jungle woman is, of course, Kurtz's native mistress, "savage and superb, wild-eyed and magnificent." Marlow comments:

> And in the hush that had fallen suddenly upon the whole sorrowful land, the immense wilderness, the colossal body of the fecund and mysterious life seemed to look at her, pensive, as though it had been looking at the image of its own tenebrous and passionate soul.

Any reader of "Heart of Darkness" must recognize that our analysis of it in terms of sexual love hardly scratches the surface. It means far more than this, and herein lies its significance. For the first time Conrad has been able to use material potentially related to sex in such a way as not to ruin his story and, in fact, in some respects to strengthen it. Our account of the imagery of the Congo jungle far from exhausts its meanings; rather, this imagery has the richness and tonality of the true symbol. The jungle stands for "truth," for an "amazing reality." Conrad equates it with the African natives who alone are full of vitality; the whites are but hollow men. Yet the jungle also means the "lurking death," "profound darkness," and "evil," which belong to the prehistoric life of man, our heritage. We cannot escape this heritage; going into the jungle seems to Marlow like traveling into one's own past, into the world of one's dreams, into the subconscious. Thus the vegetation imagery means much more than female menace; it means the truth, the darkness, the evil, the death which lie within us, which we must recognize in order to be truly alive. In the same way, while the scene between Marlow and Kurtz's Intended is imperfect, and while it does show the "inconceivable triumph" of woman over man, it has other, more important functions in the story. The scene can be read, for example, as an indictment of this

woman, safe and ignorant in her complacent, Belgian bourgeois existence; she does not *deserve* to hear the truth. The
scene can also be read as Marlow's reaffirmation of fellowship
with Kurtz. To accept Kurtz's pronouncement, "The horror,"
means accepting damnation; Marlow's sin, the lie, serves to
confirm this.

With the completion of "Heart of Darkness" in January,
1899, and the total abandonment of "The Rescuer" shortly
thereafter, Conrad entered a new phase, which includes his
four best full-length novels, *Lord Jim, Nostromo, The Secret
Agent,* and *Under Western Eyes.* Before we examine his
handling of love in those works, we might pause to observe
the faint outlines of a recurrent pattern of character relationships and the recurrence of a particular type of scene. The
hero seems always to be pursuing the heroine against the
wishes of someone else, usually related to, and often older
than, the heroine, someone who loves her very much even
though he exhibits symptoms of sexual inadequacy. This conflict is sometimes resolved in a crucial scene in which the
relative tries to kill the hero, the heroine saves him, and the
episode still does not redound to the hero's credit. Almayer
tries to shoot Dain, but Nina intervenes. Joanna's effeminate
brother, Leonard da Souza, threatens Willems with a rusty
iron bar; in this case, though, Willems protects himself.
Aïssa's blind and aged father tries to stab Willems, but she
disarms him and throws the kriss contemptuously at her lover's feet. While Ortega has not yet met Stephen in *The Sisters,*
he does worship his niece and sits across the street from
Stephen's house, hammer in hand. In "The Lagoon" the
pattern changes a little; Arsat, the hero, lets the brother of
his beloved die in order to secure her, but this dishonorable
act destroys him. Karain kills Matara in order to prevent him
from killing his own sister, whom Karain loves madly. "The
Return" has only two characters, the Herveys, but Alvan
Hervey broods constantly about his rival. Hervey has am-

biguous feelings about this man, hating him for his dishonor, disdaining him as an effeminate artist, and sympathizing with him as another rejected male. No one threatens Hervey with a weapon, but his wife metaphorically destroys him by breaking her fan and throwing it at his feet. "The Rescuer" alone shows no trace of the pattern, though either Linares or Mr. Travers could have played the role of the ineffectual rival.

After two false starts and three-and-a-half years of struggle, Conrad took up an idea he had had the year before for a short story, worked well over a year on it, and produced his best-loved novel, *Lord Jim*. We cannot help but wonder how he overcame the jinx he had fought so long. And why did he deliberately decide to convert "Tuan Jim: A Sketch" into *Lord Jim,* a "free and wandering tale"? The answer is not far to be sought. He was able to complete a full-length novel, finally, by taming the very materials that had so baffled him. The Patusan portion of *Lord Jim,* the portion that Conrad added to the pilgrim-ship episode to convert the latter from a short story to a novel of sin and "redemption," represents, essentially, a reworking of "The Rescuer." [22] "King Tom" Lingard of "The Rescuer" certainly foreshadows "Tuan Jim" of Patusan. Both are expert seamen but have an unseamanlike attitude toward their trade; both are romantic egoists longing to found a kingdom in which they will be all-powerful. Just as Lingard becomes involved in an adventure into native politics through his friendship for two native leaders, the ironic Hassim and his resolute sister, Immada, so Jim liberates Patusan from cruel oppressors out of friendship for his quietly ironic native friend, the princely Dain Waris, and out of love for Jewel. She, of course, is not a native, but she very much belongs to Patusan and has no use for the white world. Jim's faithful native servant, Tamb 'Itam, who takes Dain Waris' ring to Jim during Gentleman Brown's attack, derives from Jaffir, who swims out to Lingard's brig with Hassim's ring the night of the attack on Wajo. At the height of Lingard's and Jim's success, a boatload of whites arrives and destroys their kingdom as if it had been no more than a dream. While their native friends stand loyally by, the two white leaders vacillate. Wasub begs in vain for Lingard to fight; Tamb 'Itam tries without success to make Jim defend himself. "The Rescuer," though incomplete, hints strongly that Lingard's decision to help the whites and his refusal to fight his disgruntled native allies can result only in disaster. *Lord Jim* can and does end in an even more complete disaster since Conrad is free to kill off the hero as he is not in Lingard's case.[23]

The nature of Conrad's solution to his problem becomes clearer when we note what he eliminated from "The Rescuer" material and what he kept. Briefly, he cut out Edith Travers and substituted Gentleman Brown. That is, he got rid of a powerful yet supposedly sympathetic female, and put into her place one of his most congenial types, the isolated, egoistic, cynical yet romantic figure with a criminal past. Conrad transferred from "The Rescuer" to Jim not only many of Lingard's personal characteristics but also his political involvement. This subject had interested Conrad from the first; politics play a subordinate yet significant role in *Almayer's Folly, An Outcast of the Islands,* and "Karain." There are hints of Conrad's interest in the psychology of revolution in his characterization of Ortega in *The Sisters.* Although Conrad does not assimilate the political material into *Lord Jim* with complete success, it nevertheless heralds what will be his overriding interest for the next decade.

It would be idealizing *Lord Jim* to say that adding "The Rescuer" material to the pilgrim ship episode produced a flawless book. Not only are the political complications presented rather tediously but also the handling of Jim's and Jewel's love affair has serious weaknesses. In fact, whenever Marlow talks about them, he loses his ironic manner, which is one of the great strengths of the novel: "they came together under the shadow of a life's disaster, like knight and maiden meeting to exchange vows amongst haunted ruins." As in "The Rescuer," dialogue between the lovers is wooden, and there is the same insistence upon emotions which Conrad seems unable to dramatize: when Jim discovers that Jewel has been on watch every night to protect him, "it was as if he had received a blow on the chest. He gasped."

The ineffective characterization of Jewel's stepfather, Cornelius, especially points up Conrad's lack of creative involvement in the love story, for Cornelius represents a reversion to the Almayer-Ortega type and a prefiguration of the stereotyped villain of the later Conrad. Timorous, squeaky-voiced, teeth-gnashing, he rages outside his dying wife's bedroom door, demanding to be let in. But his wife rejects him as Joanna rejects Willems; instead, she desires only the company of Jewel, offspring of that romance which still makes Cornelius jealous. Though Cornelius says that he hates Jewel, his actions hint that the hatred arises from jealousy of Jim's love for her. When Marlow says that he is convinced Jim will never leave Patusan and give Jewel back to him, Cornelius bursts into an hysterical attack on his rival. Marlow comments: "One would have thought he had cherished the girl with surpassing love, that his spirit had been crushed and his heart broken by the most cruel of spoliations." Through a detailed description of Cornelius' pose while cursing Jim, Marlow hints at what he means when he calls Cornelius "grotesque":

> He leaned his forehead against the fence, and in that position uttered threats and horrible blasphemies in Portuguese in very weak ejaculations . . . It was an inexpressibly grotesque and vile performance, and I hastened away.

Cornelius, of course, carries out his threats. He plots against Jim with Gentleman Brown, and although Cornelius himself is destroyed, the plot succeeds and Jim dies.

Conrad, nevertheless, "gets by" with this love affair. Though imperfect, it is certainly better than the Lingard–

Edith or Alvan–Mrs. Hervey relationships, perhaps because Jewel, so long as Jim lives, remains safely submissive and dependent, like Aïssa in relation to Willems. Moreover, after Jim's death, Jewel changes dramatically from the stereotyped ingénue of romantic fiction into an extremely effective, utterly pitiless judge of Jim's moral conduct. Jewel gives Marlow an important attitude toward Jim's final, equivocal act: " 'He has left me,' she said, quietly; 'you always leave us — for your own ends.' " Not only does Jewel's characterization have its compensations but the love affair itself serves an important function in the novel. Jim must be possessed as completely as possible by Patusan, the country on which he looks with an "owner's eye." As Marlow says: "but it was they that possessed him and made him their own to the innermost thought, to the slightest stir of blood, to his last breath."

Like "Heart of Darkness," *Lord Jim* contains images which can be interpreted in terms of menacing female sexuality. These occur when Marlow muses about Jim's plans and then looks at the grave of Jewel's mother. (Marlow has previously told us how Jim built the fence of slender saplings around the grave and how Jewel regularly weaves a "garland of leaves and flowers . . . about the heads of the slender posts.") The italics are mine.

Nothing on earth seemed less real now than his plans, his energy, and his enthusiasm; and raising my eyes, I saw part of the moon glittering through the bushes at the bottom of the chasm . . . It threw its level rays afar as if from a cavern, and in this mournful eclipse-like light the stumps of felled trees uprose very dark, the heavy shadows fell at my feet on all sides, my own moving shadow, and across my path the shadow of the solitary grave perpetually *garlanded with flowers*. In the darkened moonlight the interlaced blossoms took on shapes foreign to one's memory and colors indefinable to the eye, as though they had been special flowers gathered by no man, grown not in this world, and destined for the use of the dead alone. Their *powerful scent* hung in the warm air, making it thick and heavy like the fumes of incense.

Though this is someone else's grave, Marlow obviously sees it as an omen of Jim's death. Reading the images of Jewel's interlaced blossoms woven about Jim's slender posts in terms of the pattern we noted in the Malay stories and *The Sisters,* we can certainly interpret this passage as implying that Jewel will destroy Jim. Yet like our analysis of imagery in "Heart of Darkness," this reading does not exhaust the symbolism. These death images must be seen as merely part of a larger pattern. From the first page of the novel, the whole force of Conrad's symbolic imagination is directed toward suggesting the inevitability of Jim's death through self-destruction. Peace and irresponsibility, Jim's chief goals, lie to the East, in a grave of his own making, in Patusan.

Between *Lord Jim* and *Nostromo,* Conrad wrote two first-rate, shorter novels, *Typhoon* and "Amy Foster," published together in *Typhoon and Other Stories,* 1903. While the former, like the other great sea-pieces, deals with women only incidentally, "Amy Foster" contains potentially dangerous materials and therefore merits some attention. It has two lovers, Amy and Yanko; her father opposes the marriage; Amy comes to resent Yanko's "strangeness," to feel "repulsion" toward him; she literally brings about her lover's death; her father concludes that it is "for the best." Yet unlike the previous stories where this pattern obtains, "Amy Foster" is an imaginative triumph. We can make a few surmises about why Conrad succeeds. For one thing, Conrad studiously avoids looking at the love affair; he simply says that each loves the other. He concentrates, instead, upon one of his most congenial themes, man's loneliness and moral isolation. Moreover, he makes few demands upon his characters. Amy remains a passive girl, with just a little imagination. Although Yanko has charm and verve, he, unlike most Conrad heroes, has no inclination to idealize his actions, meddle with others, or worry about his honor. Finally, Conrad may have been helped by the fact that the prototype of Amy, the Conrads' maid,[24] was so emphatically flesh and blood, existing before his very eyes. Amy would thus have less tendency to degenerate into the misty, ubiquitous Rita of Conrad's youth, the ghost whose presence does so much damage in the later period. In *Nostromo,* while Conrad created his only truly successful characterization of a woman, Mrs. Gould, he also wrote one of the worst love affairs of the early period, that between Nostromo and Giselle. Their story very nearly wrecks the last few chapters; the prose describing it falls far below the standard of the rest of the novel:

> She was not conceited. She was no more self-conscious than a flower. But she was pleased. And perhaps even a flower loves to hear itself praised. He glanced down, and added, impetuously — "Your little feet!"

In crises, the lovers can utter only stock phrases: "Giovanni, you must have been mad!" " 'Not that! Not that!' he gasped out." Their story ends in the usual way with the older relative trying, in this case successfully, to prevent consummation of the love. The once henpecked, now senile, Viola with the inevitable weapon, "his old gun," destroys Nostromo, the stalwart lover. Really much weaker than any of the Patusan portion of *Lord Jim,* the last pages can perhaps be partially justified by the fact that they contain, sandwiched between the love scenes, some fine, pessimistic comments on modern Sulaco by Dr. Monygham and Mrs. Gould. And though these pages tell us nothing new about Nostromo (his damnation has been completed with his decision to "grow rich very slowly"), his death is justifiable symbolically. It comes at the hands of the true republican, the Garibaldino, on Great Isabel, scene of Decoud's destruction, with the lighthouse shining over the buried silver, blatant symbol of "material interests."

Even granting the slipshod handling of love in the last pages, we must pay homage to Conrad's triumph with Mrs. Gould. Of all of his women, Emilia Gould alone is admitted to the moral hierarchy. Her quiet, unobtrusive life follows a path of moral involvement and disillusionment similar to that of the male characters. Always scrupulously honest, she conceals information from her husband in order to further Decoud's political scheme, and she suffers pangs of guilt for her meddling. At the end of the novel she conceals the fraud of Nostromo from Dr. Monygham and thus demonstrates her fellowship with Nostromo's corruption even as Marlow commits himself to Kurtz's corruption in "Heart of Darkness." Moreover, Mrs. Gould, unlike Kurtz's Intended, does not need to be lied to. The novel's two most perceptive characters, Decoud and Monygham, lead Mrs. Gould to see the awful truth of her husband's egoism and of the evil wrought by the mine, so that Mrs. Gould pronounces the final judgment upon both. Besides this, and more important, Mrs. Gould is a completely believable and charming creation, rendered in a series of memorable scenes: her wooing in Italy; her tour of Costaguana; bidding good-bye, from her landau, to General Barrios; receiving the politicians at Casa Gould; and, as an older, weary, disillusioned woman, lunching with Monygham. On this one occasion, then, Conrad succeeds in doing an extended, and moderately complex, characterization of a woman. Yet we must remember that her courtship is kept safely in the past, that Conrad avoids any close examination of her married life, and that to the rest of the world she remains an unassailable matron.

Conrad's triumph with Mrs. Gould seems all the more remarkable when we observe that he places her in the same pattern of character relationships which usually evokes bad writing. All three characters are there: the hero, tall, handsome, vigorous, idealistic Charles Gould; the heroine, his wife, the beautiful, gentle, orphaned Emilia Gould; the rival (not related to Emilia, it is true), old, dark, limping, irascible, seemingly traitorous Dr. Monygham. Somehow Conrad keeps these characters in control, never letting the relationship disintegrate in a melodramatic scene of violence. He maintains his ironic attitude throughout; he knows that the apparent hero is inwardly corrupt, the apparent villain a man of greater integrity and perception than any of the other characters. The "villain" proves more effective than the "hero": Monygham fools Sotillo while Gould thinks only of blowing up the mine.

Conrad endangers his artistry again in *Nostromo* by creating another love trio: Decoud, Antonia, and her doting, somewhat ineffective father, Don José Avellanos. Again he succeeds, perhaps less brilliantly, for Antonia never achieves the complexity or the "life" of Mrs. Gould. We notice, too, that Conrad disposes of this group in the usual way, the older relative dying, the hero committing suicide with a gun. A captious critic might quarrel a little with Decoud's death scene, might say that the prose could have been tauter, and less loaded with clichés. The Decoud-Antonia story seems to have had an inauspicious first working in *The Sisters* which may partially account for its minor weaknesses. (Both stories are about the revolutions of Spanish peoples. Like Rita, Antonia comes from a patriotic family, including a fanatic, revolutionary priest. Decoud, a dilettante converted to politics by love, seems to derive from Stephen, perhaps via Linares of "The Rescuer.")

How was Conrad able to create such a character as Mrs. Gould, write two successful love stories, and maintain his ironic manner in *Nostromo* when he failed at a much more modest attempt in the second half of *Lord Jim?* Perhaps Conrad's efforts were too modest in Patusan. That part of the novel does give the impression of having been "eked out," in Mr. Leavis' phrase; [25] that is, its material is thin. There is nothing thin about *Nostromo.* So perhaps Conrad, like his best sailors, found value in the love of the work itself, of the gigantic, almost physical, labor of piling in so many characters and so many actions, so much geography and history. This labor may have been what fired his imagination so that he saw the Goulds and Decoud and Antonia not as knights and maidens but as men and women. We cannot blame Conrad for failing in the last few pages of *Nostromo*; the reader is probably so tired himself that he will forgive the false characters and bad prose.

We can readily understand Conrad's great devotion to *Nostromo*, which, according to Richard Curle, he considered his "principal achievement." [26] Conrad had "gotten in" all of Costaguana, and he had also written successfully the only love story he knew, not once, but twice! Until recent years, *Nostromo* has remained a neglected masterpiece. Conrad would be pleased to find it now at the top of most critics' lists, superseding *Lord Jim*, which Conrad seems not to have liked. Mr. Curle warns us, however, against weighing Conrad's opinion too heavily: "If *Lord Jim* had not been a popular book he might have held a better idea of it." [27] Conrad knew, of course, the true weakness of that novel, that the second part does not perfectly match the first.[28] Whether the incorrigible common reader will bow to the critics' and Conrad's judgment is dubious. If *Nostromo* generally surpasses the bad portions of *Lord Jim,* it never soars as high. If the handling of time seems even more complex in *Nostromo* than in *Lord Jim,* that structure still does not add as much meaning as the structure of *Lord Jim.* Only the first chapter of *Nostromo* has prose distinguished for symbolic richness; and nowhere in *Nostromo* does the prose move with the economy and vigor of the *Patna* scenes in *Lord Jim.* We may admire Conrad's achievement in *Nostromo,* but for the Conradian manner at its most meaningful, we shall return stubbornly to *Lord Jim.*

In 1907, *The Secret Agent* appeared, a worthy successor to *Nostromo* in that it continues Conrad's political explorations and contains a memorable female character, Winnie Verloc. Winnie seems to derive from Amy Foster, who has the same dull tenacity, the same capacity for resolute, even violent, action under stress of terror or hatred. Winnie succeeds as a character not by taking an important place in the moral drama (as Mrs. Gould does) but by eliciting Conrad's ever ready sympathy for the lonely, beleaguered outcast. Although Winnie has, for a while, a husband, a home, a loving younger brother, she strikes us as an utter stanger in the jungle of London, completely unaware of her husband's business or of anything else, trapped by her own "philosophy" of "not taking notice of the inside of facts." Only once do we see Winnie outside the shop before the murder, during the furious cab ride with her mother and Stevie. In its length and complexity, the ride seems almost an expedition. After murdering Verloc, Winnie realizes for the first time her complete friendlessness:

It was so true that, in a sudden longing to see some friendly face, she could think of no one else but of Mrs. Neale, the char-woman. She had no acquaintances of her own. Nobody would miss her in a social way.

Winnie rushes out into the street, terrorized by thoughts of the gallows, yearning to escape abroad. But, to her, Spain and California are

mere names. The vast world created for the glory of man was only a vast blank to Mrs. Verloc . . . She was alone in London: and the whole town of marvels and mud, with its maze of streets and its mass of lights, was sunk in a hopeless night . . .

To find her way out of the maze, Winnie must depend on the robust anarchist, Comrade Ossipon, who knows, at least, that to get out of England one must take a train and then a boat. Like a parent dispatching a timid child to summer camp for the first time, Ossipon calls a cab, pays the cabman, buys Winnie her ticket, sends her to the ladies' room, shows her to her compartment, talks to her until the train starts to roll — then jumps out. The last people to see Winnie alive, the steward and stewardess of the Channel boat, later report that she lay alone, on a deck chair, in the dark, too ill to move. Like the terrified young mother of the four idiots, in Conrad's very early story, who stabs her husband to death and runs away, Winnie dies by leaping into the sea. Throughout her pathetic story, Winnie sustains our interest and our sympathy; yet she remains distinctly a minor triumph, lacking the moral and psychological complexity which informs Conrad's greatest creations.

Conrad succeeds with Winnie not only because he finds her loneliness congenial to his imagination but also because he views her story through the heaviest protective screen of irony he ever employed. The extent of the ironic distortion becomes evident when we look at the "love trio" in *The Secret Agent*. The hero, Mr. Verloc, looks like a villain, with black mustaches and a snarling voice, and pretends, at least, to be ferocious. The blowsy, buxom, apparently impassive, heroine resembles only in her youthfulness the romantic ingénues we have seen. The rival, Winnie's younger brother Stevie, is worse than ineffectual; he is half-witted. Yet, unlike any of the other heroines, Winnie loves the rival far more than she loves the hero. In fact, she loves Stevie with a "militant love," and, when they were children, she used to carry her brother "off to bed with her, as into a heaven of consoling peace." She married Mr. Verloc purely for convenience, as insurance for Stevie's future.

Mr. Verloc resembles early lovers like Willems and Mr. Hervey in having soon lost his physical passion for his wife. When he sees her enter the room and "get into bed in a calm businesslike manner," he feels "hopelessly lonely." He confesses to her that he feels unwell, but she persuades him to get into bed and entertains him with her only topic of conversation, Stevie. Mr. Verloc has little taste for the subject, yet he dreads "facing the darkness and silence that would follow the extinguishing of the lamp." When Winnie asks him if she should put out the light, he is at first held "mute and helplessly inert in his fear of darkness," then makes a "great effort": " 'Yes. Put it out.' "

Ironic distortion in *The Secret Agent* is striking, too, in Conrad's handling of two normally ineffective types of scene, the rival's attempt on the hero's life, the heroine's rejection of proffered love. Unlike most rivals, Stevie adores his sister's husband and would do anything for him; Mr. Verloc likes Stevie: he extends "as much recognition to Stevie as a man not particularly fond of animals may give to his wife's beloved cat." Neither intends any harm to the other, but each destroys the other. While carrying the deadly weapon procured by Mr. Verloc, an explosive with its ingenious detonator, "a thin tube of tin," Stevie trips on a root in Greenwich Park and is literally hoist by his own petard. Mr. Verloc has unintentionally caused his rival to destroy himself; the accident directly brings about Mr. Verloc's destruction at Winnie's hands in a sexual rejection scene. Conrad first establishes, by frequent references to his cutting meat, that the weapon, a carving knife, belongs to Mr. Verloc. Moreover, the knife is related to Mr. Verloc's most intense physical passion, eating. As he tries to reconcile Winnie to Stevie's death, he at times partakes "ravenously" of the meat he has cut. When Winnie determines to leave the house forever, he stops her and tries to assert his physical supremacy with a gesture much like Alvan Hervey's in "The Return": "He advanced, and stretching out his hand, dragged the veil off, unmasking a still unreadable face, against which his nervous exasperation was shattered like a glass bubble flung against a rock." Failing in this approach, Mr. Verloc tries to seduce Winnie, calling to her "in a peculiar tone . . . intimately known to Mrs. Verloc as the note of wooing." Instead of taking her place beside him on the sofa, she reaches past him and seizes the object previously identified with him. Unlike Aïssa and Mrs. Hervey, Winnie does not throw it contemptuously at his feet. Rather she plants it in his fat carcass.

Thus ends the love story of *The Secret Agent*. Using a congenial character-type and a thick screen of protective irony, Conrad has written one of his best accounts of relationships between the sexes. Yet Conrad obtains these results only by severely limiting himself in terms of character and situation — the Verlocs are morally so isolated from each other as to be utter strangers — and these limitations make themselves felt in a full-length novel as they do not in "Amy Foster." *The Secret Agent* lacks the tension of the greatest of Conrad's works.

In *Under Western Eyes*, last of the political novels and of the major, full-length novels, Conrad manages his love story only by restricting it to less than ten per cent of the novel's pages. Originally, Conrad intended to make Razumov's love for Nathalie Haldin, sister of the man he betrayed, the center of the novel. He wrote Galsworthy on January 6, 1908, that he had finished the first part.

> 2d in Genève. The student Razumov meeting abroad the mother and sister of Haldin falls in love with that last, marries her and, after a time, confesses to her the part he played in the arrest of her brother.
>
> The psychological developments leading to Razumov's betrayal of Haldin, to his confession of the fact to his wife and to the death of these people (brought about mainly by the resemblance of their child to the late Haldin), form the real subject of the story.[29]

In view of Conrad's usual bad luck in trying to dramatize courtship and marriage, we must admit that he was probably wise to scrap these plans. Instead, Razumov and Nathalie appear in only three scenes together, of seven, four, and nineteen pages respectively, and the narrator quotes four pages from Razumov's diary which refer to his love for Nathalie. In the first two of these scenes, Razumov suffers so from embarrassment and remorse that he scarcely speaks. The third scene, though very important in terms of the meaning of the novel, proves to be an artistic failure.

The characters who enact that last scene play the familiar roles of hero, heroine, and rival. Razumov, an authentic Conradian vulnerable hero, engenders a good deal of interest throughout the novel as the center of a moral and political drama, but as a lover he fails badly. Although Conrad may have hoped that Nathalie Haldin would develop into another Mrs. Gould, she remains little more than a speaker of noble sentiments, with a frank, healthy walk and a virile handclasp. Conrad deliberately plays the "rival," the English professor of languages, in a low key, minimizing his interest in the much younger Nathalie. Conrad's restraint here is certainly a relief from Cornelius (in *Lord Jim*), but the characterization is so restrained that the reader may find the professor interesting only in his technical role as the obtuse narrator. The three enact a very stereotyped, very unconvincing scene together toward the end of the book in which almost every word of the dialogue rings false. The flaw is particularly serious here since it involves Razumov's confession of guilt as well as his love for Nathalie. Conrad insists too much upon the importance of the scene and tries futilely to make of Nathalie's mother a heroic figure.

Miss Haldin stopped, and pointed mournfully at the tragic immobility of her mother, who seemed to watch a beloved head lying in her lap.
That gesture had an unequaled force of expression, so far-reaching in its human distress that one could not believe that it pointed out merely the ruthless working of political institutions.

The hero accepts his dismissal from the heroine, picks up the object she has dropped to the floor, and runs away. " 'That miserable wretch has carried off your veil!' I cried, in the scared, deadened voice of an awful discovery." Nathalie says that her heart feels "like ice." The inferiority of this scene can be readily felt by comparing it with the excellent last two scenes of *Under Western Eyes*, Razumov's confession to the revolutionists and his punishment, and Sophia Antonovna's account, two years later, of the whereabouts of all the characters.

Though the love affair does little for the novel, one of the minor characters, curiously enough, turns the stereotyped gesture of male abasement before the female into one of the most entertaining scenes in the book. Peter Ivanovitch, a political prisoner in chains, becomes a feminist when a pale-faced girl smuggles to him the file she had intended to give her lover before he died. With the file, Peter Ivanovitch manages to free one leg. "He was going to begin on his other leg when he was overtaken by a terrible misfortune. He dropped his file." He gropes for it in the dark, cannot find it, and almost despairs. Then he feels ashamed of his weakness. "To fail would have been a sort of treason against the sacredness of self-sacrifice and womanly love." To prove his devotion to Woman, he trudges across Siberia carrying his chains. Providence rewards him when the next human being to speak to him proves to be the young bride of a blacksmith. Peter Ivanovitch describes the scene of his liberation in his autobiography (translated into seven or more languages) and Conrad's narrator comments:

> "My fetters" — the book says — "were struck off on the banks of the stream, in the starlight of a calm night by an athletic, taciturn young man of the people, kneeling at my feet, while the woman like a liberating genius stood by with clasped hands." Obviously a symbolic couple.

Never did Conrad more effectively satirize his own tendency to sentimentalize women.

After *Under Western Eyes,* Conrad wrote only one more work which we have mentioned as "early" and "major," "The Secret Sharer," a wholly masculine story in the tradition of "Youth" and the other great sea pieces. Yet *'Twixt Land and Sea* (1912), the volume in which it appeared, contains a story, "A Smile of Fortune," which has had insufficient attention. It is worth brief examination here because it deals directly with the subject of love. It tells about a sea captain, a young man but a determined bachelor, who becomes attracted to Alice Jacobus, the illegitimate daughter of a disreputable ship chandler on a beautiful tropic isle. Since Alice seldom speaks to the captain and since she usually has a chaperone in attendance, his desire for her seems, as he says, "unrealizable." In fact, he wants it that way. He comes only to *look* at her in her thin wrapper that reveals a "young supple body."

> I was looking at the girl. It was what I was coming for daily; troubled, ashamed, eager; finding in my nearness to her a unique sensation which I indulged with dread, self-contempt, and deep pleasure, as if it were a secret vice bound to end in my undoing, like the habit of some drug or other which ruins and degrades its slave.

Alice's every movement betokens tremendous animal power. Even sitting down, her body "drawn together tensely in the deep low seat" looks as if it is "crouching for a spring," and recalls the descriptions of Joanna Willems and Mrs. Hervey. (Apparently Conrad did not intend to suggest such strength. He wrote Galsworthy his irritation at reviewers for calling her a " 'sensual animal,' — goodness knows why. I tried to make her pathetic.") [30] When the captain at last gets her alone and tells her that he has no designs on her, she effectively expresses her disdain for him:

> Leisurely and tranquil, behaving right before me with the ease of a person alone in a room, she extended her beautiful arms, with her hands clenched, her body swaying, her head thrown back a little, revelling contemptuously . . .

Like Hervey, the captain cannot bear to have his manhood ignored. He begins to kiss her:

> She let me go on, not as if she were inanimate — I felt her there, close against me, young, full of vigour, of life, a strong desirable creature, but as if she did not care in the least, in the absolute assurance of her safety, what I did or left undone.

In the midst of this, her father (the "rival") appears; she picks up her wrapper which has fallen to the floor and runs away. By agreeing to pay an outrageous price for some cargo, the captain gets rid of Jacobus and starts looking for Alice. She appears, but the captain unaccountably feels that it is "too late." She speaks to him; her words leave him "unmoved except for a sudden and weary conviction of the emptiness of all things." He feels "terror" at his "complete detachment" from her, and when she offers to kiss him, he withdraws slowly. Once outside, he thinks thoughts very similar to those of Alvan Hervey outside his wife's door:

> I felt in my heart that the further one ventures the better one understands how everything in our life is common, short, and empty; that it is in seeking the unknown in our sensations that we discover how mediocre are our attempts and how soon defeated!

Whatever Conrad's intentions, he wrote, in "A Smile of Fortune," a first-rate story of female sexuality and male impotence. Simply looking at Alice sufficiently satisfies the young captain, until she shows her indifference. This is such a blow to his vanity that he desires her, in order to prove his manhood. All this takes place, of course, with the inhibiting awareness of possible interruption by her father. When the girl returns and the way is clear, the captain finds himself "no longer moved." That Conrad felt this to be the meaning is suggested by the return of some familiar images of menacing female sexuality. Alice lives in a house on a very "grass-grown" alley. She always sits in the garden with its "massed foliage" and "maze" of flowers. To the young captain the garden looks deadly, just as the jungle did to Dain: "The garden was one mass of gloom, like a cemetery of flowers buried in the darkness."

"A Smile of Fortune" marks the end of the second phase of Conrad's struggles with the subject of love. He had been able for over a decade to write first-rate, full-length novels and to keep love more or less under control. Two statements in his letters to Garnett suggest that Conrad was sometimes conscious that this subject threatened his artistry. Of "The Return" he wrote: "There are things I *must* leave alone." When he wrote especially well, he knew why: "The Secret Sharer, between you and me, is *it*. Eh? No damned tricks with girls there. Eh? Every word fits and there's not a single uncertain note." [31] We may wonder why Conrad, rather than subordinating women and love in the full-length novels, did not cut them out altogether and produce only perfect works like *The Nigger of the "Narcissus"* and "The Secret Sharer." One can only assume that the subject seemed to him a necessary condition of painting on a canvas broader than that of a short novel. Such a feeling would hardly make Conrad unique among novelists. Except for *Moby-Dick,* it is difficult to name a major novel that completely avoids women and love.

Even during the halcyon years we have been considering, the presence of certain distinctly inferior works about love suggests that Conrad had the subject just barely under control, that at any moment it might break down his defences and destroy him. One need only look at "Tomorrow" (in *Typhoon and Other Stories,* 1903) or "Gaspar Ruiz" (in *A Set of Six,* 1908) to find disasters equal to those of *The Sisters,* "The Rescuer," and "The Return." Almost as bad results obtain in two stories more ambitious in intention than these potboilers, "Falk" (in *Typhoon and Other Stories,* 1903) and "Freya of the Seven Isles" (in *'Twixt Land and Sea,* 1912).[32]

The first tells about Falk, a "man strong and elemental . . . driven . . . by the power of a simple and elemental desire." He desires Hermann's niece, a girl "built on a magnificent scale" who "could have stood for an allegoric statue of the Earth." Uncle Hermann, a sentimental, selfish German, opposes their union because the girl is so useful to his family as a maid and baby-sitter. Falk's troubled conscience also blocks their marriage; during a shipwreck he had had not only to kill a man who had gone berserk with hunger but also to eat him, in order to survive. When Falk finally tells the truth, his story so moves the girl that she marries him, despite her uncle's protests. Conrad tries hard to draw a serious meaning from the story: the terrific force that drives Falk to eat human flesh and to capture the magnificent girl underlies all our feelings, all our most complex conceptions. Yet overly explicit insistence on this theme makes the reader doubt its validity. Uncertainty of tone, particularly in Conrad's attempts to combine comic and serious elements, also makes the story unconvincing as art. Throughout, the narrator can only assert feelings and ideas rather than dramatize them. Nowhere is this more literally true than in the case of Hermann's niece, who speaks not a single word in the story.[33]

Although "Freya of the Seven Isles" ends unhappily, it suffers from the same faults as "Falk." It is much too long for its simple subject: a young girl caught among three men's absurdities, her lover's "impetuosity," "her father's fears," a rival's "infatuation." (The rival destroys the lover's ship upon which his livelihood and the success of the imminent marriage depend, and the lover degenerates into a beachcomber. Freya's father appalled by the lover's condition and afraid of the rival, makes no effort to persuade the lover to return penniless to her. She dies of grief.) Uncertainty of tone reveals what an effort Conrad is making to write an interesting and convincing love story. Yet this very effort guarantees that the story will not succeed. Though Freya's history is a sorrowful one, Conrad in his confusion tries to tell it in a light and chatty manner, and his attempts at humor prove to be most painful. The characterization of the rival, Heemskirk, also serves to point up the fakery of the story. He is but a fantastic parody of evil, a comic villain from stage melodrama, equipped with curses and gnashing teeth. Only Cornelius, in *Lord Jim*, approaches Heemskirk as a stock villain. It would be fine if "Freya of the the Seven Isles" were a parody. But we cannot forget the ending which Conrad expects the reader to take seriously — Freya's father sobbing over her death with a "heart-rending cry."

"Freya of the Seven Isles" marks a turning point in Conrad's handling of love. More blatantly than in any of the early works, it expresses the pattern of timid hero, powerful heroine, and impotent rival, and clearly prefigures the love stories of the later novels. Jasper, though supposedly an impetuous lover, takes his greatest pleasure in just looking at Freya and readily acquiesces to her whim that they not elope until her twentieth birthday. Freya reveals her power and Heemskirk his lack of it on the morning of Jasper's departure on his fatal voyage. Heemskirk stands at her bedroom door watching the thinly clad Freya wave good-by to Jasper's boat.

The wide sleeve of the dressing-gown slipped back, uncovering her white arm as far as the shoulder. Heemskirk gripping the door-handle, as if to crush it, felt like a man just risen to his feet from a drinking bout.

Freya proves to be a deliberate exhibitionist when she discovers Heemskirk's presence. She thinks: "You are looking on — you will — you must! Then you shall see something." And she blows hundreds of kisses toward her lover. "She was excited, she tingled all over, she had tasted blood!" Though no match for Freya, Heemskirk with his tugboat *Neptune* proves more than a match for Jasper and the fragile *Bonito*. Through a ruse, Heemskirk takes the brig in tow and wrecks it on a reef. Jasper immediately gives up the idea of marrying and equates the loss of the brig with the loss of his manhood: he considers himself a "man disarmed for life by the loss of the brig, and, it seemed to him, made unfit for love to which he had no foothold to offer." The powerful Freya, left alone with her senile father, who had never approved of Jasper anyway, implausibly becomes anemic and dies suddenly of pneumonia.

A final instance of Conrad's ambition to write a serious, romantic love story during the early period is the novel he began in 1906, after completing *The Secret Agent.* The history of Conrad's struggles with *Chance* recalls "The Rescuer," the only other novel that he began, laid aside for a number of years, and then took up and finished. He worked on *Chance* for a year, suffering from the same paralysis of expression that haunted him with "The Rescuer." [34] For relief, he turned to *Under Western Eyes.* After finishing it, four years later, he was debating whether to finish *Chance* or "The Rescuer," deciding on the former because it seemed to promise financial success. [35]

Conrad's decision to finish *Chance* determined his decline. In his early major period, he had, as we have seen, either evaded love or subordinated it to other subjects. *Chance* has love for its central subject, as do *Victory, The Arrow of Gold, The Rescue, The Rover,* and the unfinished *Suspense.* Of the later novels, only *The Shadow Line* does not deal with love. Such a radical shift in subject naturally raises the unanswerable question: why? Why did Conrad cease those explorations into moral failure in the masculine world that had enabled him to achieve artistic success? Why did he turn to a subject that had caused him such misery in his fruitless struggles with *The Sisters,* "The Rescuer," and "The Return"?

One obvious, partial answer is that although his artistic successes had elicited critical acclaim, they had failed with the public. From the outset, Conrad had longed for a large audience; yet, as Edward Garnett said, "Nineteen years of arduous work (1895–1913) failed to bring him into real popularity." [36] And he needed money badly. In the years between *Nostromo* and *Chance,* Conrad, his wife, and two children all suffered lengthy and serious illnesses. Doctors' bills and financially unsuccessful novels drove Conrad to borrow repeatedly from his agent, J. B. Pinker, until the debt was so large that even the profits from *Chance,* his first and biggest best-seller, were insufficient to pay it off entirely. [37]

We must, however, admit the possibility of motives other

than money behind Conrad's shift to the subject of love. He may well have felt that he had explored moral failure as far as he could, may simply have grown tired of it. Conrad himself has noted, in his preface to *The Secret Agent*, that a "change in the fundamental mood" had stolen over him after completing *Nostromo*. Moreover, abandoning *Chance* to return, for relief, to the betrayal theme in *Under Western Eyes* had not proved satisfactory. As Morton D. Zabel says, it "fell flat in England and America"; [38] even today it seems considerably less of a triumph than *Lord Jim* and *Nostromo;* it seems too explicit, as if Conrad were viewing his theme externally. Finally, we must remember that Conrad, however unwisely, sincerely wished, from the beginning of his career, to write about women and love. Perhaps all three motives — quest for popularity, need for a change, desire to write of love because most writers do — contributed to Conrad's beginning, and finishing, *Chance*.

In analyzing the later Conrad's six novels about love, we shall not need to deal with the novels singly, since the love patterns are so similar. Moreover, the pattern is familiar, having appeared in indistinct or distorted form in virtually every early, abortive attempt with the subject. In the early period the pattern consisted of hero, heroine, and rival; in the later, this pattern dominates the novels, and the rival has changed into a dyed-in-the-wool villain. The later hero is always an eligible bachelor, not necessarily youthful. Captain Anthony of *Chance*, Heyst of *Victory*, and Lingard of *The Rescue* are in their thirties. George of *The Arrow of Gold*, Lieutenant Réal of *The Rover*, and Cosmo of *Suspense* are, however, young men. Peyrol, who shares with Réal the lover's role in *The Rover*, is sixty-six. Our heroes tend to be of the strong, handsome, taciturn type, lonely, inexperienced with women. Moreover, Conrad asserts that three, Anthony, Heyst, and Lingard, are of a romantic temperament.

Of the heroines there is little to be said, except that they are in distress. All are young and beautiful; all are victims of unhappy pasts. Flora de Barral, of *Chance* — her mother dead, her father in prison for swindling, herself the victim of a cruel governess' outrage — believes that she is unlovable and twice attempts suicide. Lena, of *Victory*, is "almost a child of the streets," abandoned by her mother to a father who is an incurable invalid. When Lena meets Heyst, she is a member of a traveling female orchestra, utterly friendless and pursued by a violent and disgusting hotelkeeper. The orphaned heroine of *The Arrow of Gold*, Rita de Lastaola, appears to be self-sufficient but is in fact terrified in a world where she has found no friends since the death of her protector, Henry Allègre. Arlette of *The Rover* is another orphan; her parents were executed in the reign of terror in Toulon, and she herself was reduced to virtual imbecility by being forced to take part in the blood-bath and then to "marry" Scevola, one of the Jacobins who orphaned her. In *Suspense*, Adèle de Montevesso also has a husband whom she married under duress, to save her destitute *émigré* family. Only Edith Travers of *The Rescue* deviates from the pattern, perhaps because the plot of *The Rescue* had been conceived during the early period. Mrs. Travers has not really suffered. She has simply married a man who she thought was courageous and idealistic only to discover that he is the opposite.

Our third type of character in the later love story, the villain, is usually grotesque in appearance, older than the other two principals, and sometimes a blood relative of the heroine. He exists to menace the future happiness of the hero and the heroine. Flora's father, for example, opposes her marriage to Anthony and tries to murder him. Rita's cousin, José Ortega, tries to murder her and her lover in Rita's boudoir. In *The Rover* and *Suspense*, the villains are the husbands of the heroines. Scevola prowls about the farmyard with a stable fork, trying to kill Réal, who is in love with Arlette. While the exact intentions of the Count de Montevesso remain unclear in the unfinished *Suspense*, his menacing appearance, his intrigues against Adèle's admirer, Cosmo, and Cosmo's distaste for him mark the Count a villain. *Victory* has four grotesque villains — Schomberg, and the infamous trio of Mr. Jones, Ricardo, and Pedro — but none is related by blood or marriage to Lena. *The Rescue*, once again, proves to be the major exception, having no true villain, although Mr. Travers, Edith's husband, and old Jörgenson possess some of the other villains' characteristics. In fairness to Conrad, we should remember that he intends, in two of the novels, at least, that the hero himself should menace his own and the heroine's happiness because of some flaw in his character. We are thinking, of course, of Anthony and Heyst. To some extent Rita, too, is her own and George's worst enemy.

The later love stories, besides having these three basic characters in common, are alike in providing a brief but perfect honeymoon for hero and heroine. Anthony and Flora are finally united in the handsome cabin of a stout ship. Lena and Heyst enjoy at least a few nights together on a tropical isle; Lingard and Mrs. Travers share one night of love in Borneo. Rita and George have several months together in the "Maritime Alps, in a small house built of dry stones and embowered with roses." Arlette and Réal spend a few weeks in a little farmhouse near the western gate of Toulon and then move to Arlette's ancestral home, far out on an almost deserted peninsula in the Mediterranean. Whether the conclusion of *Suspense* would have given Cosmo and Adèle such bliss, we shall never know.

Conrad's later love stories share, finally, an intended moral of a rather dubious nature: love between man and woman is the most important thing in life. This theme is stated with painful explicitness in several of the novels, with such explicitness, in fact, that the passages have become among the most frequently quoted in Conrad. In *Chance*, Marlow, as *raisonneur*, makes this pronouncement:

Of all the forms offered to us by life it is the one demanding a couple to realize it fully, which is the most imperative. Pairing off is the fate of mankind. And if two beings thrown together, mutually attracted, resist the necessity, fail in understanding and voluntarily stop short of the — the embrace, in the noblest meaning of the word, then they are committing a sin against life, the call of which is simple. Perhaps sacred.

In much the same vein are Heyst's words to Davidson, after Lena's death: "Ah, Davidson, woe to the man whose heart has not learned while young to hope, to love — and to put its trust in life!"

In the novels after *Victory*, the moral is not stated as obviously, yet there is no doubt that it is fully intended. When, for example, Lingard and Mrs. Travers, who are "made for each other," have their night together, on the beach of the lagoon, in the "glow of dying embers," he has found "reality," and she understands that these are "moments that would never come to him again on this earth." Again, in *The Rover*, after Réal has overcome his "pedantic conscience," he is "ready to clasp forever to his breast that woman touched by the red hand of the Revolution; for she . . . had brought to him the sense of triumphant life."

Sometimes Conrad's affirmation of the excellence of love carries him so far as to value love *over* life, to see love as something much too good for this world. Mills advances this theory while trying to explain to George why Rita has left him. Mills says, gently, "You know that this world is not a world for lovers . . ."

Our consideration of the basic elements in the later Conrad's love stories, rather than answering any questions, merely poses some new ones. How can a writer as complex and profound as Conrad have written these stories? Their stock characters belong in the romantic melodramas of inferior magazines, as do their conventional love-trysts, and their pernicious, sentimental "message." Can a writer suddenly stop writing serious books and begin to turn out work indistinguishable from popular trash? Or are we, perhaps, doing Conrad an injustice in our résumé by dangerously over-simplifying his work?

Mr. Paul L. Wiley, in the chapter of his book on Conrad called "The Knight: Man in Eden," [39] the only extended study of Conrad's handling of love, offers a much more complex version of the later stories than our own summary and presents this complexity as Conrad's intention. With considerable insight, Mr. Wiley bases his interpretation chiefly upon the relationship between the hero and the villain, as "man" and his evil double, and theorizes that the villain represents, especially, the hero's erotic impulses. The hero must learn to conquer his two unworthy motives, false chivalry and sensuality, in order to win the heroine and make normality triumph over abnormality.

Yet even this complicated interpretation of Conrad's love stories is very different from — in fact diametrically opposed to — the Conrad we have known in this study. No longer is the woman a vigorous character, like Jewel, ready to judge her beloved as "false," or, like Mrs. Gould, capable of making a judgment even against herself. Now the woman is defenceless, existing to be rescued. No longer is man menaced by woman, as were Dain, Stephen, Karain, and Hervey; no longer is man destroyed by woman as were Almayer, Willems, Yanko, and Verloc.

We must conclude, then, either that Conrad's fundamental attitude toward women and love has changed, or else that Conrad hopes that it has changed and Mr. Wiley is describing Conrad's conscious intentions rather than the stories themselves. That is, in 1913 either a new Conrad was born or else the old Conrad began to write love stories, the intended meanings of which ran counter to the deepest impulses of his being. The second alternative seems to be the correct one. Certain serious flaws, particularly in the conclusions of some of the later novels, suggest strongly that Conrad does not have control over these books, that the intended meaning is at variance with the actual meaning.

We recall the implausible ending of *Chance*, a weakness immediately noted by Hugh Walpole.[40] In a melodramatic and unconvincing scene, young Powell, by a series of the most dubious chances, happens to observe de Barral poisoning Anthony's brandy-and-water. Thereupon Anthony's and Flora's misunderstanding is somehow resolved in a few moments; they consummate the marriage; de Barral drinks the poison himself and falls dead at Powell's feet. Yet, as Mr. Guerard writes, "this conflict between Anthony's immaturity and Flora's arrested development could in fact have been prolonged indefinitely . . . there was no reason why the book should end at all." [41] Conrad compounds the implausibility of *Chance's* conclusion by revealing five pages after this scene that some four years later Anthony went down with his ship, by chance, thus leaving the way clear for young Powell to marry Flora.

The conclusion of *Victory* is at least as preposterous as that of *Chance*. The confused relations between Heyst and Lena are resolved in a scene of violence which turns upon three chances: Mr. Jones' strange fear of women, the incredible arrival of Davidson, and Wang's unmotivated interference. Within five pages, Lena, Heyst, Jones, Ricardo, and Pedro are dead, Lena and Jones killed accidentally.

The melodramatic endings of *Chance* and *Victory*, these serious lapses in artistic integrity, have been explained as "commercialism" [42] or as excessive concern with the external shape of the book.[43] Certainly these interpretations have possible validity. Yet if we realize that Conrad's intentions here may run counter to his deeper impulses, then we can partially explain the endings by seeing them as evidence of Conrad's desperation over an insoluble problem. Remembering the menace of female sexuality which we saw in the early love stories, may we not deduce, for instance, that Conrad saves Anthony from de Barral by such a thin thread because unconsciously Conrad feels that he is not saved at all, feels that as soon as Anthony becomes involved with Flora he is doomed? This theory seems more plausible in the light of Anthony's casual extermination, years later by chronological time, but immediately by narrative time, since Conrad neither dramatizes nor summarizes any of Flora's and Anthony's life together. Then there is this fact about their marriage, presented in such a strange manner by young Powell, in answer to Marlow's question:

"Any children?"
Powell gave a start. "No! No! Never had any children," and again subsided, puffing at his short brown brier pipe.

Here at least we detect a resemblance to love in the early Conrad, for almost without exception the marriages which take place during a Conrad story produce no children. The couple in "The Lagoon," Jim and Jewel, the Goulds, the Verlocs — none of these marriages bears fruit. Yanko Goorall and Amy Foster *do* have a child, yet the child, "a bird in a snare" like his father, exists to show man's unceasing isolation, generation after generation. Marriages occurring before the beginning of a story sometimes produce children: the Almayers have Nina, and the Willemses "sickly Louis." The closest approximation to a happy family in the early Conrad is probably the Violas in *Nostromo*. Thus in *Chance*, although the later Conrad asserts the importance of the "embrace, in the noblest meaning of the word," he cannot bring himself to let that embrace be fulfilled through children.

We see desperation in the ending provided for *Victory*, too. The inner Conrad, incorrigibly denying his conscious intention that Heyst is to be saved through his love for Lena, effectively demonstrates his disbelief in the resolution of the theme by making the resolution of the plot utterly incredible. Also, by killing off the lovers so hurriedly, Conrad saves him-

self from the difficulty of trying to write about the couple
after they have come to understand and fully to accept one
another. *The Arrow of Gold* and *The Rover* share with *Chance*
supposedly happy resolutions to the love affairs. But again, as
in *Chance*, the indecent haste with which the sacred "pairing
off" takes place makes us doubt that Conrad really believes
in his happy ending. We recall that in *The Arrow of Gold*
Rita rejects George even after their intimate night together
and would have left him forever had she not met in the doorway her implacable sister. Rita realizes that she does not have
the "courage to deliver [her]self up to Therese" and rushes
back into George's arms. Conrad then passes over their honeymoon in two pages without giving a single particularized detail of their life together. The reader of *The Rover* does see
M. and Mme. Réal once, "many years" after their marriage.
They are talking of the past, of old Peyrol, but nothing about
the scene suggests that the Réals are a married couple, that
they share a life together. As usual, there is no mention of
children.

We do not, of course, require Conrad, simply because he
asserts the importance of love, to detail the consummation of
each marriage for the edification of the reader. (At least one
lady reader did write Conrad of her disappointment at not
seeing Rita and George "embrace." Conrad answered coyly,
"You will easily understand that of this affair not everything
could be set down. The inner truth of the scene in the locked
room is only hinted at.") [44] Yet even if Conrad's new attitude
toward love does not require him to write bedroom scenes,
the reader may nevertheless reasonably expect some dramatization of the give-and-take of human beings who are in love.
That Conrad cannot do this suggests that he does not really
believe that his lovers exist.

Conrad appears to be conscious, in *The Arrow of Gold,*
that his intended theme is demanding more of him than he

can fulfill. At the end of the novel he seems to be apologizing to his readers for his deficiency, or excusing himself.

Love as is well known having nothing to do with reason, being insensible to forebodings and even blind to evidence, the surrender of those two beings to a precarious bliss has nothing very astonishing in itself; and its portrayal as [George] attempts it, lacks dramatic interest. The sentimental interest could only have a fascination for readers themselves actually in love. The response of a reader depends on the mood of the moment, so much so that a book may seem extremely interesting when read late at night, but might appear merely a lot of vapid verbiage in the morning. My conviction is that the mood in which the continuation of his story would appear sympathetic is very rare. This consideration has induced me to suppress it . . .

The ineffective, melodramatic conclusions to some of the later novels suggest misunderstanding of material as well as willingness to pander to a popular audience. We can see from Conrad's failure to dramatize the relationship between lovers that his creative imagination is not cooperating with the intended theme that "pairing off is the fate of mankind." Thus we are faced with the question of whether or not a second meaning lies beneath the surface of the later works. Is there an implicit pattern different from the imposed pattern of Conrad's conscious intention? If so, how does this inner meaning relate to the early Conrad's attitude toward love?

One way to approach the problem is through the character of the villain. Although we cannot, as Mr. Hewitt says, take him seriously as a character,[45] we may find him a useful key to the real meaning of the love stories. The villain is interesting because he represents something new and unusual in Conrad. The early Conrad, we recall, is concerned primarily with normal human beings. But the villain of the later period is a grotesque, both in the literary sense of being a caricature, and in the psychological sense of exhibiting abnormal attitudes toward love.

All the villains show symptoms of marked distaste for

physical love. Mr. Jones of *Victory* loathes women; as his lieutenant says, "He can't stand them at all." Old Jörgenson, although he has a wife back home, seems, in the second half of *The Rescue*, to feel almost as much antipathy for women as Mr. Jones. Although some of the other villains are married and one even has a child, they clearly do not love their wives, tend to mistreat them, and show, in fact, a surprising taste for celibacy. We recall the suffering of Mrs. de Barral, who finally dies "from neglect, absolutely from neglect" by her husband. The cruelty of Schomberg, Scevola, and de Montevesso toward their wives needs no documentation. What is a little less obvious is the evidence that de Montevesso, for example, may never have slept with his wife at all. The reader of *Suspense* will recall that de Montevesso, after a year of marriage, sends Adèle back to her parents because living with her is "too much of a torture for him." Later, friends offer to have the marriage annulled. Finally, de Montevesso and Adèle come to an agreement whereby she lives with him one month out of the year "to save appearances." In *The Rover*, Conrad states explicitly that Scevola and Arlette have never slept together. Critics have tended to take at face value Conrad's explanation to Garnett that he made Scevola so sexually diffident in order to keep Arlette "untouched" [46] for Réal, suggesting that he is pandering to his readers' sentimentality.[47] But, seen in the larger context of Conrad's villains, Scevola's remarkable ability to curb for ten years his "growing impatience" (as Mr. Wiley sympathetically describes it),[48] seems to result from something more than a desire to please the public.

Although the villain shows distaste for woman as a sexual partner, he is nevertheless capable of exhibiting abnormally possessive feelings over some woman to whom he relates, literally or figuratively, as father to daughter. The best example here is, of course, de Barral. When he gets out of prison, he tells Flora of his love for her in terms that go far beyond the usual expressions of parental affection: "I lived only for you . . . There were only you and me . . . I did nothing but think of you! . . . You haunted me, I tell you." When he learns of his daughter's marriage to Anthony, he chokes until he collapses, and then a "jealous rage" affects his brain like "fumes of wine." When father and daughter go aboard the *Ferndale*, de Barral talks to her as if she were a prostitute (recalling Alvan Hervey's tirade); he tells her that she has "sold" herself, watches her go into her cabin "as if into a house of disgrace," and "gnash[es] his teeth at her" when she goes to speak to her husband. Closest to de Barral as the insanely jealous blood relation is José Ortega, the impotent lover of Rita, his cousin. The other villains whom we have mentioned — Mr. Jones, Schomberg, Jörgenson, Scevola, and de Montevesso — would seem not to fit into de Barral's category since they have no daughters, nor even any nieces (except de Montevesso, who shows considerable dismay over his niece's admiration of Cosmo). Without straying too far from reason, however, we can see that Scevola and de Montevesso stand in relation to their wives as fathers rather than husbands. Of course, they show little fatherly regard, but they perform the father's function of affording shelter and protection for their weak, young wives. Arlette obviously could not have returned to her anti-revolutionist parents' home at Escampobar without the protection of the Jacobin, Scevola. Nor could the anti-revolutionist Adèle Armand and her family have survived without the financial aid and political power of de Montevesso. Even Schomberg (a less likely father one could never expect to meet!) bases his hopes of winning Lena chiefly on the fact that she is "worse than friendless" and he is a "man of substance."

Although the married villains show little active interest in sleeping with their wives, they guard their wives' virtue with the devotion of a father protecting his only daughter. Scevola tries to kill Réal. De Montevesso seems to be planning Cosmo's death. Of course, one reason for the extreme jealousy of these villains where their wives are concerned is that fear of ridicule which so besets Alvan Hervey. De Montevesso, especially, worries about what people will say about his qualifications as a husband.

Fear of sexual inadequacy suggests another characteristic of the villain. Just as he disdains sexual relations with his woman, so is he disdained by her. Moreover, although the villain may come close to triumphing over his male rival, he endangers the woman but little, even though Conrad asserts that she is weak. Instead, the woman triumphs over him. We see that this is true even in the case of de Barral. While he ultimately destroys his wife by neglect, his wife dominates him in the most important step of his life, taking a job in a bank. Even little, unhappy Flora does not consider her father a serious obstacle to the consummation of her marriage with Anthony. De Barral's statements of extreme devotion do not move her. She meets his anger with "absolute candour." When he becomes hysterical, Flora proves to be physically stronger, pulling him back into the cab with ease. Flora returns to her father and ceases quarreling with him only after Anthony rejects her.

The chief villains in *Victory* prove to be no match for their women either. Schomberg plays the bully and his wife the terrified automaton, but she shows more courage than he in searching Mr. Jones' room. She twice interferes with his evil designs, first by helping Lena to escape with Heyst, later by telling Davidson about the Schomberg-Jones plot against the lovers. Ricardo, whom we have not yet discussed, seems at first not to fit any of our categories of villains. After all, Mr. Jones calls him a "woman-lover — [a] prevaricating, sly, low-class, amorous cuss!" As "instinctive savagery," Ricardo seems intended to be an almost allegorical figure of lust. Yet his actions do not match the characteristics attributed to him. We recall his much-heralded charge into Lena's bedroom.

("The instinct for the feral spring could no longer be denied. Ravish or kill — it was all one to him . . .") What an anticlimax the battle proves to be! Despite Conrad's long, solemn account of Lena's strong motivation to resist, the reader knows that her victory over Ricardo results simply from her powerful grip on his windpipe.

Ortega and Blunt, Jörgenson, Scevola, de Montevesso, are all helpless against female opposition. Rita twice frustrates Ortega's efforts to conquer her and laughs at him both times. She, moreover, refuses Blunt's proposal of marriage, tells George the whole story, and then laughs "her deep contralto laugh." When Jörgenson tries to use Mrs. Travers as a messenger to Lingard, she pretends to agree in order to be with Lingard but then betrays Jörgenson by not delivering the message, and precipitates the disaster that costs Jörgenson his life. Scevola is simply another Ortega, "the butt of all the girls," chased by a "mob of angry women," easily managed by old Aunt Catherine, and circumvented even by the timid Arlette, who woos Réal right under her husband's nose. De Montevesso has already been rejected by one woman when he meets Adèle, and he marries her chiefly to spite the first one. Although de Montevesso treats Adèle brutally, he often behaves like a supplicant rather than a master.

Detesting the woman with whom he is coupled, desperately desiring a woman whom he must not have, rejected and dominated by both women, the villain remains an outsider, an onlooker at love's feast. He is, in short, a voyeur, and his most characteristic action is to rage obscenely outside the door of a room where a woman he cannot touch lies waiting for his rival to make love to her. In such a scene, the villain often holds in his hand a deadly weapon which he intends to use against his rival. But the woman or her agent (*not* her lover, the villain's rival) usually frustrates the villain, and the weapon proves adequate only for the self-destruction of its holder. This scene, incidentally, almost always evokes from

Conrad his flabbiest prose and his most melodramatic action. The reader will know which scene in *Chance* best fits the pattern: de Barral's attempt to murder his son-in-law. "His fixed idea was to save his girl from the man who had possessed himself of her." Conrad describes the scene in close detail, from the point of view of Powell, and the prose emphasizes the "weird and nauseous" look of de Barral's hand as it appears, "short, puffy, old freckled" from behind the curtain, carrying the poison. Powell warns Anthony; Flora and Anthony clear up their misunderstanding; and the foiled de Barral watches their embrace, "puckering his eyes." Anthony carries Flora into the stern cabin to consummate their marriage while de Barral and Powell carry on a strange conversation immediately outside the door. De Barral asks Powell three times, "Did you see it?" Powell thinks that "it" means the poison, but de Barral is really referring to the awful sight of the couple embracing. De Barral, knowing that he has been defeated, begins to compare himself with his rival; then, after a few remarks on the baseness of his "wicked little fool" of a daughter, swallows his own poison.

Schomberg's earlier appearance in "Falk," in *Typhoon and Other Stories*, 1903, revealed the traits of the voyeur — gossiping, eavesdropping, "embracing every human being within range of the tongue" — which he displays in *Victory*. Schomberg's actions are even more clearly prefigured by Cornelius in *Lord Jim*. Cornelius resembles Schomberg in hating his wife, in desiring a girl young enough to be his daughter, and in wishing revenge on the man the girl loves. Too timid to accomplish the revenge himself, Cornelius enlists the aid of a piratical figure with an anonymous name (Brown–Jones) who does succeed, helped by a villainous crew. The scene of Brown's final capture, with his two parched companions in the longboat, Conrad used again in *Victory* for the arrival of Mr. Jones and his two companions on Samburan. In *Lord Jim*, however, Cornelius dies and Jewel persists, whereas in *Victory* Schomberg survives and Lena dies.

But it is Ricardo, in that novel, to whom we must turn for the fullest development of the voyeur in all Conrad. Although Conrad asserts that for Ricardo, unlike Heyst, "life was not a matter of passive renunciation but of particularly active warfare," Ricardo's actions prove that all he wants to do is watch. As soon as he arrives at the island, he takes on the role of "an observer with his faculties greedy for signs." "For what he was watching for was a sight of the girl — that girl! Just a glimpse across the burnt patch to see what she was like. He had excellent eyes." Upon reaching the curtained doorway of Lena's room, Ricardo, like Hervey outside his wife's bedroom door, pauses to finger the texture of the cloth. Then he peeks in and sees Lena doing up her hair, her bare arms raised, silhouetted "against the unshuttered, uncurtained square window-hole."

At last he plunges through the door, and in the ensuing struggle, Lena quickly defeats him and the two act out a scene with sexual implications of the most childish sort. Lena, sitting on the edge of her bed, readjusts her sarong, "which had come undone during the fight." The supposedly "feral" Ricardo, perhaps out of a sense of fair play, decides to expose himself too, thus making another characteristic voyeur gesture. His exhibition is purely symbolic and without doubt unconscious on Conrad's part, but it is nonetheless obvious.

"All right. I never meant to hurt you — though I am no joker when it comes to it."
He pulled up the leg of his pyjamas to exhibit the strapped knife.

Remembering that Ricardo meant to "ravish or kill," we are surely justified in seeing the knife as a phallic symbol. Certainly Lena reacts to it in this way, for she glances at the knife with scorn and murmurs, "Ah, yes — with that thing stuck in my side. In no other way." After a short but friendly chat, Ricardo leaves, first asserting, symbolically, that he is still potent: " 'I carry a pretty deadly thing about me . . .' He tapped his leg."

Lena and Ricardo complete their symbolic battle for his masculinity in a struggle over the dagger at the climax of the novel. On the realistic level, Lena has two purposes in trying to acquire the dagger: to disarm Ricardo and to rearm Heyst, who has been deprived of his revolver. At the same time, the reader cannot miss the fact that Ricardo himself has virtually no potency left, once he comes into Lena's presence. He tells her that during the day every time he thought about her he thought that his heart would burst one of his ribs. "It has knocked itself dead tired, waiting for this evening, for this very minute. And now it can do no more. Feel how quiet it is!" Ricardo's vigor has been expended upon himself, while he was away from the woman whom he thought he wished to ravish.

Ricardo is clearly doomed. "Dog-tired," he drops to the floor (Lena occupies the only chair). Lena looks down on him thoughtfully: "Woman-like, all her faculties remained concentrated on her heart's desire — on the knife." Ricardo again makes his exhibitionist gesture, tapping his leg; he is "surprised, flattered, by the lighting up of her face." Lena bends over him and asks for the knife; Ricardo obediently hands it to her, claiming now no powers for it, saying only that it is a "good friend." Ricardo has been completely destroyed: "The very sting of death was in her hands; the venom of the viper in her paradise, extracted, safe in her possession — and the viper's head all but lying underneath her heel." We notice here, besides the sexual connotations, Conrad's painful borrowing from Shakespeare: Lena, the Cleopatra of Samburan, conquers her Roman, receives a wound under her "swelling breast" — but when she dies, it is without ever having had a real Antony. Ricardo finds himself defeated by Lena and ambushed by Mr. Jones and Heyst. Like Hervey with the fan and Willems with the kriss, he looks "all over the floor" for the dagger and then runs out into the darkness.

Victory's melodramatic voyeur scene departs from the pattern we have outlined in one striking particular, the death of Lena. Were Conrad following his usual train of events, Ricardo rather than Lena would have died by Mr. Jones' bullet; Heyst would still have died by fire; but Lena would have persisted, eliminating unsatisfactory males until the end of time . . . Although the voyeur scenes as a group are badly written, Lena's death seems, to one critic at least, Conrad's "later writing at its worst." [49] Perhaps Conrad wrote thus because he simply did not believe in Lena's death.

The Arrow of Gold, The Rescue, and *The Rover* all fit the pattern. Rita and Ortega, in *The Arrow of Gold,* perform the ritual twice, the first time in early childhood. Rita tells George about the occasion, remarking that Ortega "wasn't much bigger than myself but he was older." (The villains are rarely much bigger than the heroines. We recall that Flora easily subdues her father and that Lena is actually bigger than Ricardo and even boosts him out of a window when Heyst approaches.) Like Ricardo, Ortega is an exhibitionist. He dresses well to impress Rita, and he lets her "look at him for half an hour." Rita feels that he, in turn, is staring at her: "I remember trying to hide my bare feet under the edge of my skirt as I sat below him on the ground." Later, Ortega approaches with the inevitable weapon, a switch, in hand. Rita obediently lies down, stiff with fright, but Ortega simply bends over and kisses her neck. This seems both to satisfy and to frighten him: " by that time I was gone dead all over and he could have done what he liked with the corpse but he left off suddenly." For the next two months they enact the same scene daily with Ortega sometimes throwing stones at the entrance to a cavelike shelter where Rita hides.

Years later, Rita and Ortega reënact the scene, this time with George as spectator. Once again it is an interior scene, a room where the woman lies in a negligee, ready for bed (we recall Flora in her robe, Lena first in a sarong, then in a fetching black gown), waiting for George, not Ortega. But the voyeur rages outside the door. Like Alvan Hervey, Ortega fears the ridicule of public opinion: "This story will be all over the world . . . Deceived, decoyed, inveigled, in order to be made a laughing-stock before the most debased of all mankind, that woman and her associates." Ortega carries his weapon, although it is antique and inadequate for the intended purpose: "It was an Abyssinian or Nubian production of a bizarre shape; the clumsiest thing imaginable . . . a mere cruel-looking curio of inconceivable clumsiness to European eyes." It serves, however, to save the lovers by wounding Ortega himself when he trips on the stairs.

In *The Rescue*, Jörgenson and Mrs. Travers go through their scene aboard the *Emma* with little emotion. Jörgenson, in fact, shows virtually no interest in Mrs. Travers' charm. He does, however, hold a prolonged colloquy with her at her bedroom door about Lingard's watch, now in Mrs. Travers' possession — and stopped, of course. Jörgenson is surprised that Mrs. Travers opens her door wide, and while he disapproves of her sarong, he nevertheless looks at her. They speak of Lingard, Mrs. Travers casts down her eyes "in intolerable desire," and Jörgenson hastens away. She comes on deck in pursuit and discovers him with a deadly weapon of an unconventional sort. It is a time-fuse which he is making with "several bits of rather thin and dirty-looking rope."

He tried to wave her away with the stump of the pencil. He did not want to be interrupted in his strange occupation. He was playing very gravely indeed with those bits of string.

Jörgenson intends to set off the powder magazine should his and Lingard's plans fail. Because Mrs. Travers does not give Lingard Jörgenson's message, the plans do fail, and one more voyeur dies. Jörgenson, it is true, does not die by his original weapon, the fuse; still, he has a lighted cigar clamped between his teeth when he jumps to his death through the inevitable doorway, the hatch of the powder magazine. In *The Rover*, the voyeur scene is developed only slightly, and in *Suspense* there is just a hint of it. Throughout *The Rover*, Scevola slouches about spying spitefully upon Arlette and Peyrol, Arlette and Réal. When Arlette lies down on Réal's bed, Scevola tries the handle of the locked door. Later that night he seizes his awkward weapon, the stable fork, and sets out after Réal, whom he believes to be hiding in the cabin of Peyrol's boat. Like Ortega, he shouts imprecations outside the door, but then finds himself thrust into the cabin, made a prisoner, and later shot by the British. In *Suspense*, the two voyeur scenes are extremely shadowed and are viewed exclusively from within the heroine's boudoir. Adèle appears first in a dressing gown, then décolleté, each time accompanied by Cosmo. On both occasions there is some evidence that the lovers are being observed: a door moves slightly; footsteps are heard. It is interesting to notice, incidentally, that the watcher in the first scene is not Cosmo's male rival, de Montevesso, but the latter's sixteen-year-old niece, Clelia. This reminds us that there are minor feminine versions of the voyeur in several of the late love stories. These women object to hero and heroine coupling, often on moral grounds (Mrs. Fyne, Therese, Catherine), but there are sometimes strong hints that, like Clelia, they have designs upon the hero. This does not apply perhaps to Mrs. Fyne, but clearly Therese is interested in George, who detests her, and Catherine has longings, if not for Réal, then surely for his old colleague in love, Peyrol.

It is hardly necessary to note, here, that the voyeur scenes which recur with painful regularity in the later novels are clearly prefigured in the early love stories. Dain, Nina, and Almayer; Willems, Aïssa, and her father; Nostromo, Giselle, and Viola, all act in such scenes. But the scenes represent

relatively minor flaws in their works, and the rivals are far
from stock villains. Only in the triangle of Jasper, Freya, and
Heemskirk, at the very end of Conrad's major period, do we
see the full-blown villain appear. The extent to which villains
dominate the later novels provides us with a good indication
of the depth of Conrad's decline.

If we put together all the characteristics of the villain, what
is the composite picture? We see a short, dark man, mous-
tached, unhealthy, violent, cowardly, a foreigner and a
political extremist (of either party, but tending to be a
Leftist or, simply, an "anarchist"). Can we discover the source
of the Conrad villain? Douglas Hewitt suggests the "school-
boy's adventure story"; [50] we might add the stage melodrama
and the ballad. The Conrad villain has further, more omi-
nous, analogues. He is the liberal's image of a fascist, and
the conservative's image of a communist. He is the stereotyped scapegoat of every generation; he is, at times, that
eternal scapegoat, the Jew. We reject the Conrad who makes
Cornelius "The Nazarene." Heemskirk, a Dutchman, does
not look like a Dutchman, being dark, swarthy, with a
"hooked nose." Conrad's intentions about de Barral are
fairly clear:

"Was he a foreigner?" [The narrator asks Marlow.] "It's clearly
a French name. I suppose it *was* his name?"
"Oh, he didn't invent it. He was born to it, in Bethnal Green, as
it came out during the proceedings. He was in the habit of allud-
ing to his Scotch connections. But every great man has done that.
The mother, I believe, was Scotch, right enough. The father, de
Barral, whatever his origins, retired from the Customs Service
(tide-waiter I think), and started lending money in a very, very
small way . . ."

A survey of the villains reveals also that Conrad intends
them to represent something beyond themselves. To virtually
every one of them he attaches the adjective "fatal" at least
once, and the later ones he explicitly calls the Devil or Satan

(Heemskirk, Mr. Jones, Ortega). Critics have tended to defend the overly explicit characterizations of the later villains
as part of Conrad's new, allegorical method.[51] Yet we wonder
how one can defend their appalling lack of vitality. We must
nevertheless admit that Conrad does succeed with these
villains to the extent of making their actions relate to their
function of symbolizing evil. He accomplishes this partly by
an emphasis on their interest in accumulating wealth. A number of the voyeur-villains share a longing for quick and easy
money. We think, in particular, of the Great de Barral, the
gambler Mr. Jones, and Scevola, who gained a prosperous
farm by marrying Arlette. Although interested in money, the
villains care nothing for work, for production, for converting
money into usable goods. Their characteristic place of business is a dingy, dilapidated office, often in or near a warehouse
full of merchandise too old and dusty to be sold. Marlow
refers to de Barral's headquarters as "an old enormous rat-in-
fested brick house." Ironically, although de Barral has chosen
such a place by instinct rather than design, his customers immediately see it as symbolic of de Barral's devotion to his
motto, "Thrift, Thrift, Thrift." In their hunger for money,
Conrad's villains have more important antecedents than the
bad men of the boy's adventure story: Conrad is in the tradition of writers like the Dickens of *Bleak House* who see evil
as *keeping*.

When we turn to examine the role of the heroine in the
later love story, we remember the hallmark of the early
heroine — garden imagery. We saw the male's fear of the
predatory female expressed in those images of rich foliage, of
creepers especially, strangling the masculine trees. In the
later novels, when Conrad's style is in general much barer of
images, the gardens virtually disappear. We do notice traces
in Conrad's explicit and rather clumsy application of the
Garden of Eden myth in *Victory*. The myth is of course quite
convenient — Heyst as Adam, Mr. Jones as Satan, and Lena

as Eve — but it serves only to label and not to give meaning to the characters.

While the heroine of the later novels has been taken from her garden, she is still surrounded by heat and light. In our *locus classicus* for the Conrad love story, "The Return," we saw glowing fire and dazzlingly brilliant light associated with Mrs. Hervey and opposed to Mr. Hervey. In virtually every rejection scene throughout Conrad, one or both of these images appears. Nina rejects her father by the light of a campfire. Aïssa rejects Willems once by firelight, once in extremely bright sunlight. When Jewel throws her arms around Jim, just before his suicide, the sky over Patusan is "blood-red," but when she pronounces her judgment against Jim to Marlow, the imagery is reversed:

> Her figure seemed shaped in snow; the pendent crystals of a great chandelier clicked above her head like glittering icicles . . . I was chilled as if these vast apartments had been the cold abode of despair.

At the end of *Nostromo,* after the hero's death, Linda climbs up to the top of the lighthouse and looks "like a black speck upon the shining panes." Freya waves good-by to Jasper on his last voyage with the rosy glow of the rising sun on her face. When Flora enters the cabin to choose Anthony over her father (thus to destroy both), "the light fell strongly on her." She appears to the watching Powell "whiter than the lilies." The most flamboyant of these scenes is, of course, Lena's conquest of Ricardo. But we also notice the emphasis given to firelight, gaslight, and candlelight in the Rita-Ortega–George scene at the end of *The Arrow of Gold.* In *The Rescue,* Mrs. Travers approaches Lingard, bearing his destruction and a lighted torch. Conquered, he lies with his head on her knee in the glow of dying embers.

We have already seen how Conrad defines some of these images within the contexts of their particular stories. In "The Return," the fire is equated with Mrs. Hervey's evil, female, sexual passion. Whiteness has unpleasant connotations throughout "Heart of Darkness." It is associated with Brussels (the sepulchral city) and the inhuman ivory traders; it is associated with falsehood and death, whereas darkness seems to mean truth and vitality. In *Lord Jim*, whiteness, the East, and Patusan form a group of images which express Jim's romantic dreams, his unconscious longings for peace and death. We must be cautious, however, in generalizing about whiteness. In *The Nigger of the "Narcissus,"* whiteness has only good connotations; so it is possible, too, that the later Conrad's use of whiteness with reference to his heroines has meanings which differ from earlier ones. After all, is not Flora "whiter than the lilies"? Conrad's intentions about whiteness are even clearer in *Victory*: Lena dies with "divine radiance on her lips"; while she is dying, Heyst and Davidson look "mournfully at the little black hole made by Mr. Jones's bullet under the swelling breast of a dazzling and as it were sacred whiteness." Again a religious implication — but the awkwardness of "as it were" makes us a little suspicious, makes us want to scrutinize the imagery of the Lena-Ricardo scene.

The scene takes place in a room brilliantly lighted by that somewhat implausible and quasi-religious prop, the eight-branched candelabra. The color and the meaning of the light change dramatically when Lena seizes Ricardo's weapon:

> At the moment when she bent forward to receive it from him, there was a flash of fire in her mysterious eyes — a red gleam in the white mist which wrapped the promptings and longings of her soul. She had done it!

Although Conrad may assert divine purity for Lena, he has not really departed from his attitude toward Mrs. Hervey in "The Return," where a red gleam meant destructive female passion. In the final crisis between man and woman, Conrad sees woman this way. It is perfectly fitting, symbolically, that Heyst should die in flames in the hut which he shared with Lena.

Conrad rarely accepts this deep-seated terror of the heroines who are always destroying villains and heroes alike. Except in the cases of Amy Foster and Alice Jacobus, he vitiates his female characterizations by sentimentalizing over them. Thus he attributes purity to Flora, sacred divinity to Lena. Even over Aïssa, whom Conrad intends to be purely savage, he must wring more than one false tear. In this respect, Conrad differs from Hemingway, who suffers some of Conrad's difficulty in creating women. Except for the mannish Brett Ashley of *The Sun Also Rises,* the heroines of Hemingway novels tend, it is true, to be sentimentalized, particularly Catherine in *A Farewell to Arms* and Maria in *For Whom the Bell Tolls.* In the short stories, however, Hemingway successfully exploits his misogynous feelings in a way that Conrad could not. The classic example is the bitter account of the woman who murders her husband in "The Short Happy Life of Francis Macomber." [52]

There remains to be considered of our love trio only the hero. A survey of the lover–heroes shows that a triangle does not always obtain, that Willems and Yanko, for example, are destroyed without the presence of a villainous rival. This reminds us of Mr. Wiley's perception that the heroes and villains are doubles.[53] The hero and the villain have the same basic weaknesses which the villain acts out explicitly in socially unacceptable behavior. Like the villain, the hero is, essentially, an impotent voyeur, destined to be destroyed when he becomes involved with a woman. In *Lord Jim* and *Nostromo,* Conrad scrutinizes the motives of the defeated lovers' suicides, but in the later novels he does not. The reader may nevertheless wonder whether it is loss of love which motivates Peyrol's and Heyst's suicides or whether it is hurt pride at having proved inadequate lovers. An astonishing number of the major Conradian heroes who become involved with women die violent, melodramatic deaths: Willems, Jim, Decoud, Nostromo, Anthony, Heyst, and Peyrol. Razumov is deafened and George seriously wounded. It is perhaps symbolic of Conrad's career that we leave the hero of the unfinished last novel headed away from his beloved, out to sea . . . Of the lover–heroes only Charles Gould is spared a violent death. As far as the quality of the style is concerned, Jim's death, alone, is told in first-rate, Conradian prose.

We must guard against being surprised, shocked or horrified at Conrad's negative attitude toward love. How could it be otherwise? Conrad sees man as lonely and morally isolated, harried by egoistic longings for power and peace, stumbling along a perilous path, his only hope benumbing labor or, in rare cases, a little self-knowledge. Conrad could not possibly reconcile so dark a view with a belief in the panacea of love, wife, home, and family. In "Amy Foster," Conrad expresses this clearly. Yanko's true state is symbolized by the wretchedness of his arrival in Colebrook; his marriage to Amy is a futile, uncritical, romantic gesture doomed to destroy him. Conrad makes it clear that Yanko's son will have to follow the same journey.

More unusual than his pessimism is the inhibiting effect of sexual subject matter on Conrad's creative processes. The failure of imagination in the love stories can be seen in the woodenness of the actors and their lack of perception. Let us take Conrad's villains as an example. Insofar as they participate in love stories, they fail as caricatures. Although the short account of de Barral's adventure into finance is one of the most interesting passages in *Chance*, de Barral as a jealous father is an utter fraud. These love villains do not fail because Conrad is an inept caricaturist. Conrad at his best creates many successful caricatures although they are never his major interest. All of Jim's doubles are memorable not only for shedding light on Jim's moral problem but also for their vigor as personalities. We think of the fat skipper of the *Patna* and his friend, the "old stager" with delirium tremens. We think, too, of the French lieutenant and of Stein, who come to life, partly at least, because Conrad insists upon their external, national traits. Only Cornelius fails. He infects Jewel, Jim, and the prose, which becomes pretentious and verbose. But when Gentleman Brown, ironic reminder of Jim's guilt in the white world, supplants Cornelius, the prose tightens, the action is again absorbing. Douglas Hewitt denies that the villains of the love stories are true doubles for the very good reason that they "lead . . . to no further knowledge"[54] of the hero. This is just another way of saying that when Conrad writes about love he does not understand his subject. Conrad is very honest in his preface to *The Arrow of Gold*: "what is lacking in the facts is simply what I did not know, and what is not explained is what I did not understand myself, and what seems inadequate is the fault of my imperfect insight."

Conrad differs radically from other great modern novelists in his lack of understanding, in his almost belligerent lack of genuine, dramatic interest in sexual problems. Although the Conradian villains could be labeled neurotic, exhibitionist, and unconsciously homosexual, they are really just cardboard figures plucked from nowhere and thrown up as obstacles to sexual consummation. Yet such characters would inspire a Dostoevski to his most intense efforts. Ford Madox Ford claims that Conrad was fascinated by the subject of incestuous love, and we have seen some suggestions of incest. But once again, incestuous love exists in Conrad's novels only as a barrier to sexual consummation, not as a deeply felt human emotion. We must turn to William Faulkner to find a writer who has a truly creative interest in the question of incest.

If Conrad, unlike other modern writers, cannot attack the subject of sexual feelings directly, he seems nevertheless able to give meaning to these feelings when his principal subject is a more congenial one. In "Youth," Conrad puts into the older Marlow's account of his first view of the East almost all the images of his stereotyped, lifeless scenes of the rejected voyeur. Conrad calls particular attention to the phallic-shaped object in Marlow's hand, mentions the mist, the red light, the perfume of female passion, and the ice of death. But this is not a love story at all — the woman is safely meta-phorical — and the prose is Conrad at his richest and most meaningful.

And this is how I see the East. I have seen its secret places and have looked into its very soul; but now I see it always from a small boat, a high outline of mountains, blue and afar in the morning; like faint mist at noon; a jagged wall of purple at sun-set. I have the feel of the oar in my hand, the vision of a scorching blue sea in my eyes. And I see a bay, a wide bay, smooth as glass and polished like ice, shimmering in the dark. A red light burns far off upon the gloom of the land, and the night is soft and warm. We drag at the oars with aching arms, and suddenly a puff of wind, a puff faint and tepid and laden with strange odours of blossoms, of aromatic wood, comes out of the still night — the first sigh of the East on my face. That I can never forget. It was impalpable and enslaving, like a charm, like a whispered promise of mysterious delight.

The failure of the lover's masculinity, which we have seen to be the implicit subject of the later novels, resembles, of course, the early Conrad's central concern with the test of a man's moral fitness. How often the various early heroes see their test, like the later lovers and voyeurs, through an open door! Young Marlow looks into the burning hold of the *Judea,* then leaps recklessly through the hatchway; an older Marlow peers at Africa's dark heart through the shutters of his cabin; Jim looks into the *Patna's* hold by lantern-light and sees a bulging bulkhead ready to give way; Jukes flinches at the spectacle of coolies rioting in the *Nan-Shan's* hold; the young captain cannot forget his double, sometimes asleep behind the bed-curtains, sometimes bolt upright behind the bathroom door. "The Secret Sharer" reminds us of the love stories in another way: it has two scenes in which at a critical moment a character drops an object in another's presence.

The untested captain's lighted cigar, symbolic of his ignorant complacency, plops into the sea when he discovers Leggatt, like a headless corpse, at the bottom of the ladder. When they separate forever at the end of the story, Leggatt drops the captain's hat while swimming and thus provides him with a mark by which to save the ship. In none of these fine scenes does sex intervene, and the images become richly symbolic, bringing added life to Conrad's dramatization of the moral test of manhood.

We might seem to have solved the riddle of Conrad's decline: he tried to write about a subject which he did not understand. Fortunately, we are saved from such an oversimplification by the existence of *The Shadow Line,* a later novel that has nothing to do with women and love. Since *The Shadow Line* does, however, share with the rest of the late work certain serious faults, it suggests that Conrad's decline must stem from something more general than his choice of subject matter. Even without *The Shadow Line* we would be wise not to oversimplify. We should scrutinize our statement that Conrad *chose* to write about love. The fact that Conrad could relax his critical judgment enough to choose love for the subject of a major novel suggests a shift in fundamental attitude. While Conrad's critical comments about himself are not very revealing, he was in practice a fairly good judge of his own work. He was right in abandoning *The Sisters,* "The Rescuer," and *Chance.* He abandoned them because the subject was painful, but also because he knew he was writing badly. But by 1910 Conrad could decide to finish *Chance,* a long novel on a subject that he did not understand. He was looking at things in a new way; he was turning his back on moral judgment.

III

The Later Conrad's "Affirmation"
CHANCE, VICTORY, THE SHADOW LINE, and THE RESCUE

Although Albert J. Guerard and Douglas Hewitt raise serious doubts about the Conrad of 1913 to 1917 and dismiss completely the last novels, most critics have insisted upon the fundamental seriousness of some, or all, of the work from *Chance* to *Suspense*. One idea informs these discussions of the later novels: affirmation. Somehow, the argument goes, Conrad rose above his earlier pessimism to arrive at the serenity of acceptance. Frequently quoted in this connection is the epigraph to *The Rover*, from Edmund Spenser's *Faerie Queene*:

> Sleep after toyle, port after stormie seas,
> Ease after warre, death after life, does greatly please.

Miss Bradbrook, one of the critics who discriminate among the later novels, finds affirmation in those she likes. She calls *The Rover* "Conrad's *Tempest*." Although somewhat dubious about *Chance*, she admires *Victory*. There the hero and heroine "stand for humanity at large, betrayed to evil, but uncorrupted, and in pathos and dignity their fate cannot be matched in all Conrad's work." [1] F. R. Leavis rejects everything after *The Shadow Line,* "one of Conrad's masterpieces," has some affection for *Chance*, "certainly a remarkable novel," but his real love in the later period is, like Miss Bradbrook's, *Victory*. He recognizes, on the one hand, that *Victory* is of a "decidedly lesser order than *Nostromo*," yet places it "among those of Conrad's works which deserve to be current as representing his claim to classical standing." In discussing *Victory*, Mr. Leavis sounds the clarion call of affirmation:

complementary to Heyst, we realize, are Morrison and Davidson, upright, sensitive and humane individuals, in whom seems to be present a whole background of routine sanity and decency — "we sailors," the feeling is . . . It is this background . . . which makes the intention of the "victory" unequivocal. The voice that winds up the story in a brief account of the tragic end is Davidson's — Davidson's "placid voice."

Of Lena's death at the end of *Victory*, Mr. Leavis remarks: "It is an ironical victory for life, but unequivocally a victory." [2] Like Mr. Leavis, Morton D. Zabel has some doubts about the novels after *Victory*. He sees, nevertheless, in *The Rover*, more clearly than in any of the last books, "the final release of [Conrad's] spirit into reconciliation." [3]

In the same way, those critics who do not make distinctions about the relative value of the later novels still tend to consider 1913–1924 a clearly defined period informed by an affirmative spirit. Walter F. Wright discusses this spirit in terms of "romance," a quality of which he is particularly aware in the later period, although he finds it throughout Conrad. Mr. Wright's comments on *The Arrow of Gold* indicate the high seriousness of his approach: "It was because of its power to suggest the infinite that romance, to Conrad, was supremely sane." [4] For Paul L. Wiley, it is the Garden of Eden myth which illuminates Conrad's writing from *Chance* to *Suspense*; he believes that the later Conrad reveals "the triumph of the normal over the abnormal." Mr. Wiley concludes that Conrad's "steady vision in these years of the importance of traditional human values in a century of growing unrest and confusion gave added force to his great endowment in artistic power." [5]

All these are rather large claims. This chapter proposes to test the later Conrad to find out of what his affirmation, or reconciliation, consists. It also proposes to search the later Conrad for traces of the early Conrad, to see what has happened to the complex moralist, psychologist, and artist of *Lord Jim, Nostromo,* and the great short novels. By examining certain recurring situations in the early period, we discovered the significance for Conrad of test and betrayal. In the later period, these moral interests yield to an acceptance of chance as the force controlling human action. Our discussion of Conrad's altered view of the world will center in four novels, *Chance* (1913), *Victory* (1915), and *The Shadow Line* (1917), because they are the most respected of the later works, and *The Rescue* (1920), because it attempts to fuse the early interests with the later. We have observed in the previous chapter what an important part accident plays in the resolution of the love affairs. In *Chance*, for example, Powell's lucky peep at de Barral is possible only because of the "precise workmanship of chance, fate, providence, call it what you will!" *Victory*, too, moves by accidents: Heyst just happens to go in to see the orchestra and is actually on the point of leaving when he notices Lena; the evil trio appear utterly unexpectedly at Schomberg's hotel; they almost fail to reach Heyst's island; "their apparition in a boat Heyst could not connect with anything plausible." Love comes by chance to Captain Lingard in *The Rescue.* The nonromantic *Shadow Line* depends also upon chance happenings: the young narrator gains his first command by a series of "miracles"; the crisis arises when he discovers, to his amazement, that the quinine he is counting on to cure the crew is not quinine at all.

To be sure, chance serving the plot, creating the crisis, is hardly a new development in Conrad. In *Lord Jim*, nothing could be less expected that serene night than that the *Patna* should strike a submerged derelict. In *Nostromo*, too, the collision of the lighter with the troopship (the only two ships moving in a huge bay) is utterly unexpected, and this absurd accident destroys Decoud and Nostromo. We have already seen that the early Conrad is interested in these unlooked-for disasters in terms of the human response they evoke as well as the irony of fate that brings them about. Chance in the early Conrad remains subordinate to its result, the test. The crisis tests one's fidelity to the solidarity of mankind, tests one's humanity, essentially. Never to be tested is to be disdained, as Captain MacWhirr is disdained until the typhoon strikes. Even Jim recognizes this and longs for a second chance, that perfect opportunity to prove his superiority to ordinary men.

Not only does the chance crisis in the early Conrad try one's physical courage; it also tries the inner man. In fact, the accidental test usually symbolizes the weaknesses of those to be tested. In *The Nigger of the "Narcissus,"* there are two tests: of the outer man in his response to the fury of a storm; of the inner man through James Wait, who personifies the terror that each member of the crew (except, perhaps, Singleton) feels about his own death. In "The Secret Sharer," chance and inner weakness are equated. Only because the young captain unaccountably violates sea tradition to take the watch himself is the ladder permitted to hang over the side and save Leggatt, the captain's other, darker self. Mr. Zabel effectively defines chance in the early Conrad:

an . . . enemy lies in wait . . . leaping from unknown coverts, sometimes from the hiding places that fate has prepared, but more often and seriously, like James's beast in the jungle, from the unfathomed depths of our secret natures, our ignorance, our unconscious and untested selves.[6]

For the true heroes of the early Conrad, whether simple and unthinking or complex and perceptive, chance is never an excuse for failure. Only those who are morally insensitive try to make excuses and blame fate. This is Jim's case. He feels sure that "on the square" there is nothing that he could not meet. Marlow answers:

"It is always the unexpected that happens," I said in a pro-pitiatory tone. My obtuseness provoked him into a contemptuous "Pshaw!" I suppose he meant that the unexpected couldn't touch him; nothing less than the inconceivable itself could get over his perfect state of preparation. He had been taken unawares . . .

Nostromo responds to the accidental sinking of the lighter with the feeling that, somehow, he has been "betrayed." His further response, like Jim's aboard the *Patna*, is to betray in return. Marlow and the ironic narrator of *Nostromo* know that their heroes are guilty of betrayal. To the obtuse Captain Mitchell, on the other hand, disasters are unrelated to char-acter and can all be explained under the simple heading of "fatality."

If chance remains essentially a *device* for exploring moral failure in the early novels, it has, or seems to have, more im-portant meanings in the later Conrad. Marlow, in *Chance*, his last appearance in Conrad's works, talks a good deal about it. He points out unfailingly how vital a part it plays in the story: the reader can easily find twenty chance happenings which elicit a Marlovian comment. But Marlow does more than simply point; he asserts a serious justification: chance serves to bring about awareness of evil. The first crisis in Flora de Barral's life comes, we recall, wholly as a result of chance. It is none of her own doing. De Barral has hired the evil governess by chance; the disaster occurs through the collapse of de Barral's fortunes, an event unrelated to Flora. Marlow comments that the night before the disaster is Flora's last sleep in

unconsciousness of the world's ways . . . her unconsciousness was to be broken into with profane violence, with desecrating circum-stances like a temple violated by a mad, vengeful impiety. Yes, that very young girl, almost no more than a child — this was what was going to happen to her. And if you ask me how, wherefore, for what reason? I will answer you: Why, by chance! By the merest chance, as things do happen, lucky and unlucky, terrible or tender, important or unimportant.

Conrad thus underlines the importance of the ensuing scene with the governess. After all, it is then that Flora comes to the conclusion that she is absolutely unlovable. Her reaction to the governess' cruelty is as determining to her career as Jim's jump is to his. After Flora collapses in her arms, Mrs. Fyne says to herself something which reminds us of the early Marlow's idea about Jim: "That child is too emotional — much too emotional to be ever really sound." But the later Marlow's comment upon Mrs. Fyne's statement does not sound like the Marlow of *Lord Jim*: "even in the best armour of steel there are joints a treacherous stroke can always find if chance gives the opportunity." The early Conrad believes that the *best* men can withstand any assault of the dark powers.

The first half of *Chance* is, in some ways, a feminine version of *Lord Jim*. Flora and Jim both suffer unexpected disasters which affect their way of looking at life and partially incapacitate them for effective action. Both contemplate suicide as a way out, but both feel contempt for such an escape. Friends (the Fynes in *Chance*, Marlow in *Lord Jim*) try to find jobs for them, but because of their psychic wounds, their hypersensitivity, they prove unsatisfactory. Yet the difference between the two chance disasters gives us a key to the shift in Conrad's attitude. In *Chance*, the evil is *outside* Flora. All that is required of Flora is that she open her eyes to it. She has no responsibility during her crisis. She remains passive until the governess says that de Barral is a swindler, and then she screams. When the governess and her lover leave the house, Flora runs next door to the Fynes, the only people she knows. Jim's response to his disaster does resemble Flora's in certain respects. Like Flora, he remains passive at the beginning, and then he jumps. Yet there are many things Jim could have done, things he ought to have done as a responsible ship's officer; and Jim is aware of these responsibilities at the time, and afterwards, when talking with Marlow. " 'Ah! what a chance missed! My God! what a chance missed!' he blazed out . . ." The *Patna* disaster had been Jim's chance, his test, which he failed because of weakness *within himself.* For Flora, the inner problem is secondary to her discovery of how bad *other people* can be. Throughout the novel, Flora's conduct is impeccable. All her difficulties result from the inhumanity of her father and the timorous and chivalric behavior of Captain Anthony. Flora herself perfectly justifies Marlow's confidence in her: "How far Flora went I can't say. But I will tell you my idea: my idea is that she went as far as she was able — as far as she could bear it — as far as she had to . . ."

The disaster that comes by chance to Lena in *Victory,* Ricardo's attack on her, brings about the same kind of moral awareness as the governess' attack on Flora. As Lena and Ricardo sit facing each other, Lena ponders the meaning of her test: "It seemed to her that the man sitting there before her was an unavoidable presence, which had attended all her life. He was the embodied evil of the world." The key phrase here is "of the world." Ricardo represents for Lena the wickedness of other people. This is very different from "Heart of Darkness." When Kurtz is confronted with an "instinctive savagery" far more powerful than Ricardo's, Kurtz is able to pronounce judgment, not only against the world, but against himself.

These opposite responses to crises might seem simply to reflect Conrad's inability to understand women, his tendency to sentimentalize female characterizations. Let us look, therefore, at the chance disaster in the later Conrad's only masculine story, *The Shadow Line.* On the surface, the young captain's response to his crisis seems to be quite different from Flora's and Lena's. When he finds that the bottles do not contain the quinine that his crew needs so badly, he immediately acknowledges his own responsibility: "The person I could never forgive was myself. Nothing should ever be taken for granted. The seed of everlasting remorse was sown in my breast." Throughout the rest of the novel, the captain periodically accuses himself of failure; he feels oppressed by a "sense of guilt," the "weight of [his] sins," his "sense of unworthiness": "My first command. Now I understand that strange sense of insecurity in my past. I always suspected that I might be no good. And here is proof positive, I am shirking it, I am no good."

Certainly, these are explicit references to inner weakness, rather than to evil embodied in others. Yet we have found the early Conrad most seriously involved with his material and most convincing where he is most ironic, where meanings are implicit rather than explicit. Perhaps, then, we should look a little more carefully at evil in *The Shadow Line* by comparing the novel with its predecessor, "The Secret Sharer." It can be demonstrated that *The Shadow Line* is essentially a reworking of the materials of the earlier, shorter novel. But our present purpose is simply to examine some of the ideas in the two novels to see if they reflect the same or different attitudes toward moral awareness. In "The Secret Sharer," the captain lets evil board the ship in the person of Leggatt; he immediately reveals through his own *actions* that he knows that he is guilty. He calls no one to help; he talks in a whisper to Leggatt; he hides Leggatt in his cabin; and he deals with his crew in such a bizarre manner that he makes himself suspect to everyone.

Although the captain in *The Shadow Line* says that he feels guilty, his actions belie his statement. He makes no effort to conceal his "guilt" about the quinine or to put the blame on anyone else. Instead he rushes out of his cabin, tells his mate, Mr. Burns, and the faithful Ransome of his discovery. Then he makes a speech to the crew, suffering during it more than a "confessed criminal" would have. To his surprise, the men do not reproach him at all; in fact they encourage the captain in a "low assenting murmur." This is very different from the attitude of the crew of "The Secret

Sharer." When they hear it said that Leggatt may be hidden aboard their ship, they immediately pass judgment against such a deception: "As if we would harbour a thing like that." Until the end of the novel, they show no confidence whatsoever in their peculiar and distraught young captain. In *The Shadow Line*, however, the crew behaves as faithfully as could be expected of men almost dead from fever. Through all their suffering, they never blame their captain: "I expected to meet reproachful glances. There were none."

Conrad tries to suggest the presence of evil in *The Shadow Line* in two ways: by references to the former captain, and by emphasis on the physical disability of Ransome, the faithful and heroic cook. By frequently calling the former captain the "old man," and the "old dodging Devil," Conrad indicates that he intends him to be symbolic. Yet he remains a very external evil. He does not make his presence felt aboard the ship; he tempts no man's soul. Rather, he lies buried at the entrance to the Gulf afflicting the ship with calms and unfavorable winds in order to bar her passage. The young captain, his mate, Ransome, and the crew, all, like Flora, act impeccably. In the case of Ransome, however, Conrad tries to symbolize the presence of an internal weakness. He pictures him "going up the companion stairs cautiously, step by step, in mortal fear of starting into sudden anger our common enemy it was his hard fate to carry consciously within his faithful breast." When we recall that the common enemy which Ransome carries is his heart trouble, a purely physical flaw, we realize that, in *The Shadow Line,* the only evil lies at the bottom of the sea.

"The Secret Sharer" contains no satanic figure like the late captain. Rather, evil is represented by a straggler from the ranks, Leggatt, the captain's double, who looks "like a patient, unmoved convict." Leggatt reveals his nature through action; he kills a man. While there are extenuating circumstances, Leggatt is responsible, and his act of violence is the result of a flaw in character. Moreover, the flaw does not exist in Leggatt alone; the captain shares it:

> "Fit of temper," I suggested confidently.
> The shadowy, dark head, like mine, seemed to nod imperceptibly above the ghostly grey of my sleeping-suit. It was, in the night, as though I had been faced by my own reflection in the depths of a sombre and immense mirror.

In short, "The Secret Sharer" belongs to Conrad's early period where the dark powers lurk within us all. The attitude toward evil that *The Shadow Line* dramatizes places it, however, with *Chance* and *Victory*. In these, the crises that come to us by chance reveal that, while we may be surrounded by disease and evil, we are basically sound. When trouble comes to us, we are in no way responsible for it. The fault lies elsewhere, in other people.

Old garrulous Captain Giles sounds the moral at the end of *The Shadow Line* in very interesting language: "a man should stand up to his bad luck, to his mistakes, to his conscience, and all that sort of thing." We note that Conrad's *raisonneur* here equates "bad luck" and "conscience." This reminds us that in the later novels chance serves not only to reveal an evil external to the main characters but also to blur the problem of their moral responsibility, to confuse failure of luck with failure of conscience. We need only think of the quinine. Conrad nowhere establishes that the captain has a clear-cut responsibility for the contents of every bottle in the medicine chest. A "humane doctor," the captain's closest friend during the weeks of delay because of the crew's ill health, anticipates the captain's worry about the medicine chest and carefully inspects the ship's supply of drugs before it departs. "Everything was completed and in order." It is not surprising that the crew do not blame their captain for the absence of quinine. On the other hand, the "chance" of the ladder that saves Leggatt in "The Secret Sharer" is really no chance at all, but the result of the young captain's violation of

sea tradition in taking over a watch himself. His own "strangeness" prompts "that unconventional arrangement," and although his first mate conceals "his astonishment," the second
mate raises his voice "incredulously" at the "unheard-of
caprice." In short, the captain's strange act betrays an inner
weakness which his officers immediately and correctly judge
as unworthy of a ship's captain.

   Chance blurs responsibility in *Chance* and *Victory*, too.
We have already noticed how young Powell's chance peep at
de Barral and the poison saves Captain Anthony's life and
gives him Flora. It also effectively prevents Anthony from
having to face the real problems in his marriage. In *Victory*
there is a series of perfectly plausible misunderstandings between Heyst and Lena rising out of her secret plan to trick
Ricardo. Heyst finally becomes suspicious of Lena. His chance
arrival with Mr. Jones at precisely the wrong moment, when
Lena is bending over Ricardo, results in Heyst's natural mis-
interpretation of the scene. Heyst makes no effort to prevent
Mr. Jones from shooting, and the bullet intended for Ricardo
kills Lena. At the end Heyst blames himself for not putting
his "trust in life," but surely chance, not conscience, is at
fault.

   We have been trying to define the quality of the later
Conrad's "affirmation." We have seen how his use of chance
makes this a very evasive affirmation: the point is not that
man is basically good or even has potentialities for good, but
rather that the world is full of evil, except in certain characters whom Conrad likes. Furthermore, when pain and
suffering come by chance to the untainted, the responsibility
for the evil lies elsewhere. That is, the heroes and heroines
of the later Conrad are sinned against, themselves unsinning.

   We may well wonder if there is any positive value in the
later affirmation. In the early Conrad, we found that the
unquestioned values were integrity and work for its own
sake. Marlow says in *Lord Jim* that the "only reward" of life

at sea is the "perfect love of the work." The value of work is rarely referred to in the later period; instead Conrad asserts that man can achieve goodness and fulfill himself through romantic love. While this affirmation may be defensible, we should scrutinize it carefully to see whether Conradian love is really positive and creative.

The most noteworthy affirmation through love in the later novels is Lena's unequivocal (Mr. Leavis' word) victory for life. Yet an examination of the last pages of *Victory* reveals that the terms of Lena's victory are all *against* life. Mortally wounded, she feels "relieved at once of an intolerable weight"; she is "content to surrender" to Heyst an "infinite weariness." She looks at her own form on the bed and feels "profoundly at peace." Lena's triumphant union with Heyst is a curiously possessive one. "I was thanking God with all my sinful heart for . . . giving you to me in that way — oh, my beloved — all my own at last!" She will look "for his glance in the shades of death."

In *Chance,* however, neither lover dies until long after the reconciliation. Yet even here, where we know so little of the relationship between hero and heroine, Conrad gives us one brief hint of the meaning of Flora's and Anthony's triumphant embrace. Young Powell approaches the door of the captain's cabin where the two are at last consummating their marriage and comments: "It was very still in there; still as death."

Once again, *The Shadow Line* seems to be an exception to our generalizations about the later works. Since it has no love affair, it cannot be guilty of asserting that the love which brings escape into eternal peace is man's greatest good. In fact, *The Shadow Line* appears to stand against peace and to reaffirm the early Conrad's faith in work. The young captain tells old Captain Giles at the end of the novel that he will be off at daybreak, despite the fact that he has spent seventeen days on deck and has had no sleep at all in the last forty hours.

"There's no rest for me till she's out in the Indian Ocean and not much of it even then." Captain Giles approves of the young captain's vigorous attitude toward life and adds, "Precious little rest in life for anybody. Better not think of it." Nevertheless, even in *The Shadow Line,* Conrad cannot quite criticize the longing for death. The novel ends with the reader's attention directed, sympathetically, upon Ransome "in a blue funk" about his heart, moving cautiously, headed for the "quiet" to which he has a "right." We cannot fail to contrast this with our last view of the secret sharer, "a free man, a proud swimmer striking out for a new destiny."

Our analysis of the meaning of chance and love in the later novels has revealed that a new moral attitude now obtains. Conrad no longer sees his characters as part of the world community of suffering and damned humanity; rather he sees them as figures of purity afflicted by an external evil. Their greatest good is to lose themselves in a love that will blot out all awareness of the world and bring the semblance of death.

Conrad's new attitude clearly separates him from his early convictions. Those of his early characters who are in love with death he consistently views ironically and judges adversely, even though, at the same time, he is sympathetically aware that longing for peace is a universal human failing. We think of the terrified Jukes, "corrupted by the storm that breeds a craving for peace." We think, especially, of Jim. Conrad treats ironically his longing to be lord, to be perfect, to be dead, from the very first page, with its account of Jim "appareled in immaculate white," and with "Ability in the abstract," to the end of the novel when Jim embraces death. The true Conradian hero of the early period stands firmly against death, and for life.

Although the early Conrad associates love with death, as *An Outcast of the Islands* makes abundantly clear, he nevertheless views that association with horror. It is difficult to point precisely to the time when his attitude shifts from horror to passive acceptance, but this seems to have taken place shortly after the completion of *Chance*. We have already seen the theme in *Victory*, which Conrad says, in a prefatory note, that he finished May 29, 1914, after, according to M. Jean-Aubry, nineteen months of work.[7] This would put the beginning of *Victory* in the fall of 1912, some six months after the completion of *Chance*.[8] Conrad abandoned *Victory* only once, toward the end of 1913, to write "The Planter of Malata." Though the story has, on occasion, been taken seriously,[9] Conrad's own doubts about it seem well founded.[10] It is interesting, however, as a "break" from *Victory* and important as an aid to dating the beginning of Conrad's willing acceptance of the association between love and death.

"The Planter of Malata" closely resembles its exact contemporary, *Victory*, both in characters and story. The hero, Renouard, is another Heyst, sensitive, romantic, withdrawn from society. Like Heyst, Renouard has retired to an island after gaining a dubious reputation from explorations that cost several of his associates their lives. Renouard, too, falls in love and takes his beloved with him to his private island. When she discovers that he has lied to lure her there, she rejects him and leaves. Renouard's only friend, a newspaper man, visits the island to see what has happened and finds evidence that Renouard has committed suicide by drowning.

By the end of 1913, Conrad's surrender to the association between love and death is fairly complete. Renouard equates his love for Felicia Moorsom with a return to unconsciousness, even before he has lost her and decided to commit suicide. In fact, immediately after Felicia gives the first hint that she may be attracted to Renouard, he slips off his yacht into the water: "He swam away, noiseless like a fish, and then struck boldly for the land, sustained, embraced, by the tepid water. The gentle, voluptuous heave of its breast swung him up and down slightly . . ." As he swims back to the ship, toward his "desire," he feels a "mournful fatigue."

It was as if his love had sapped the invisible supports of his strength. There came a moment when it seemed to him that he must have swum beyond the confines of life. He had a sensation of eternity close at hand, demanding no effort — offering its peace. It was easy to swim like this beyond the confines of life looking at a star . . . He lay in his hammock utterly exhausted and with a confused feeling that he had been beyond the confines of life, somewhere near a star, and that it was very quiet there.

Soon afterwards, Renouard commits suicide by swimming "with a steady stroke — his eyes fixed on a star." That Conrad had accepted this attitude and expected as much of the reader is indicated by the sentimentalism of the last sentence of the story:

A black cloud hung listlessly over the high rock on the middle hill; and under the mysterious silence of that shadow Malata lay mournful, with an air of anguish in the wild sunset, as if remembering the heart that was broken there.

Clearly then, the later Conrad has a new attitude toward the world, though hardly an affirmative one; he now considers evil to be external to his heroes and heroines and sees man's greatest good as complete repose, usually achieved through love. Such an extreme shift in attitude almost necessarily results in a drastic reorientation of Conrad's artistry. Perhaps the best way to see the effect of the later Conrad's attitude upon his early moral hierarchy of characters and upon his complex handling of structure and language is to compare *The Rescue* of 1920 with those portions of its first version, "The Rescuer," which were written in the nineties.[11]

"The Rescuer" displays all of the important, early types of character that we defined in the first chapter, except one; it contains no perceptive hero like Marlow. We have already noted that the Tom Lingard of "The Rescuer" seems to be a first attempt at Lord Jim, the simple vulnerable hero. Linares prefigures Decoud, the complex vulnerable hero. Carter belongs among the ranks of simple, faithful seamen like Singleton and MacWhirr. While Mr. Travers and Jörgenson do not precisely fit any of our categories, they resemble certain characters of the early period. Mr. Travers has much in common with Alvan Hervey of "The Return," and Jörgenson belongs in the gallery of caricatures who serve as doubles for Lord Jim.

The most significant alteration of "The Rescuer" is the simplification and emasculation of Lingard. Through certain crucial cuts from the original manuscript, the later Conrad obscures the most important and interesting facts of Lingard's psychology: the subtle difference between himself and other seamen, his egoistic longings for power, his lack of self-knowledge, his moral isolation. As a result, he has none of the vitality and intensity of Conrad's great self-destructive heroes.

In revising the manuscript, Conrad cut out two passages that tend to cast doubt upon Lingard's qualifications for membership in the fraternity of loyal seamen. As originally described, Lingard does not quite *look* like a seaman, and his motivation is *not* a perfect love of the work itself. "The Rescuer" portrays him as a man who holds "himself very straight in a most unseamanlike manner." He has "also — for a seaman — the disadvantage of being tall above the average of men of that calling." Moreover, although the Lingard of "The Rescuer" is passionately devoted to his ship, as any good sea captain ought to be, his devotion seems to be the expression of something different from a perfect love of his calling. The later Conrad obscures Lingard's questionable attitude toward his craft by cutting out the following description of Lingard bringing his brig to anchor:

A sudden listlessness seemed to come over him. It was one of his peculiarities that whenever he had to call upon his unerring knowledge of his craft upon his skill and readiness in matters of his calling that big body of his lost its alertness, seemed to sink as if some inward prop had been suddenly withdrawn.

"The Rescuer" tells us further that Lingard expects his brig to answer "without hesitation to every perverse demand of his desire."

That the later Conrad is acting to distort his original conception of Lingard as motivated not by love of the craft but rather by love of self becomes more evident in the account of Lingard's motives for interfering in the political affairs of the native state of Wajo. *The Rescue* follows "The Rescuer" here:

> There was something to be done, and he felt he would have to do it. It was expected of him. The sea expected it; the land expected it. Men also. The story of war and of suffering; Jaffir's display of fidelity, the sight of Hassim and his sister, the night, the tempest, the coast under streams of fire — all this made one inspiring manifestation of a life calling to him distinctly for interference.

The Rescue omits, however, the most important of Lingard's motives — his egoism. "The Rescuer" continues the passage thus:

> But above all it was himself it was his longing, his obscure longing to mould his own fate in accordance with the whispers of his imagination awakened by the sights and the sounds, by the loud appeal of that night.

As originally conceived, Lingard's apparently charitable assistance to his native friends was to have been motivated by unlawful desires for personal power and even violence. The later Conrad cannot tolerate the implication that his hero contains any of the old Adam, and so he eliminates this very damning passage about Lingard's response to the opportunity to make war and history:

the islands, the shallow sea, the men of the islands and the sea seemed to press on him from all sides with subtle and irresistible solicitation, they surrounded him with a murmur of mysterious possibilities, with an atmosphere lawless and exciting, with a suggestion of power to be picked up by a strong hand. They enveloped him, they penetrated him, as does the significant silence of the forests and the bitter vastness of the sea. They possessed themselves of his thoughts, of his activity, of his hopes — in an inevitable and obscure way even of his affections.

But if Lingard obeyed the complex motives of an impulse stealthy as a whisper and masterful as an inspiration, without reflecting on its origins, he knew well enough what he wanted even if he did not know exactly why . . .

The absence of this passage from *The Rescue* deprives the reader of several of the early Conrad's most profound perceptions. The passage reminds us that the romantic's seemingly free act of will, his act of interference, immediately costs him his freedom and brings about slavery to the dark powers. (We recall how Kurtz belongs to the jungle and how Jim is possessed by Patusan.) This remnant of "The Rescuer" also reveals Lingard's lack of self-knowledge. He does not reflect upon the origins of his inspiration and does not know "exactly why" he is doing what he does.

A final, important insight into Lingard that the later Conrad finds of no use is the increasing isolation that results from his egoistic involvement in an unlawful adventure. In revising "The Rescuer," Conrad cut out the account of the change that takes place in the once hearty, bluff, and friendly Lingard, the change to a man isolated and guilt-ridden. Some of his friends try to draw him out by chaffing him but he repulses them:

they grew distant and Lingard had a subtle sense of solitude, the inward loneliness of a man who is conscious of having a dark side to his life. It hurt him. He needed the good fellowship of men who understood his work his feelings and his cares . . . Before he had been many months engaged in his secret enterprise he began to feel unreasonably like an outcast . . . he imagined himself, at times, to be the object of universal detestation.

Lingard's sense of isolation parallels Jim's in Patusan and, like Jim's, becomes even more intense when white visitors from the West appear to break into his adventurous Eastern dream.

For the later Conrad, Lingard has little in common with the romantic egoists of the early period. The second half of *The Rescue*, wholly written during 1918–19, carries the emasculation of Lingard further by absolving him of responsibility for the deaths of his best friends and by sanctioning his passive acceptance of repose as his greatest good.

In this later portion of *The Rescue* Conrad raises a clearcut moral issue, presumably to make Lingard decide whether to follow his duty to his native friends or his sudden love for Mrs. Travers. By an unfortunate chance, however, Lingard is unaware that Hassim and Immada have been seized as hostages, and thus he never has a real choice. Moral responsibility for the disastrous outcome of *The Rescue* would seem to lie with Mrs. Travers, who conceals Jörgenson's message to Lingard, and perhaps more seriously with Lingard himself, for loving and trusting such an unworthy person. In fact, critics who admire *The Rescue* tend to interpret it this way.[12] The truth is, however, that although the later Conrad sets up a clear moral problem, no one is really to blame for the evil outcome. Instead, Conrad excuses Mrs. Travers' actions and makes her a victim of chance, unaware of the content of the message, suspicious of Jörgenson's intentions toward Lingard, and convinced by d'Alcacer, the voice of reason, that for Lingard's own good this obscure message must be concealed. Mrs. Travers' dilemma reminds us of similar situations in the later novels, especially in *Victory*. Like Lena, Mrs. Travers deliberately deceives her lover, but with the best intentions in the world. Disaster comes through the agency of an external, implausible, evil figure resembling Mr. Jones: "By the mad scorn of Jörgenson flaming up against the life of men . . ."

If Mrs. Travers is not guilty, then Lingard is utterly blameless. Bad luck, coincidence, the misunderstanding of good intentions, someone else's madness — all these are to blame, not the impeccable hero. Yet like the zealous young captain of *The Shadow Line*, Lingard nobly asserts his guilt. He says that even if Mrs. Travers had given him the message "it would have been to one that was dumb, deaf, and robbed of all courage." Later Mrs. Travers protests: ". . . why don't you throw me into the sea? . . . Am I to live on hating myself? . . . No, no! You are too generous . . ." The reader surely understands the moral of *The Rescue*: responsibility lies not with hero and heroine, but somewhere else.

The later Conrad perverts his original characterization of Lingard in another way, by sapping him of his powerful, if unacknowledged, longings for self-destruction. Although the Lingard of the nineties is a worthy forerunner of the intense, guilt-haunted Jim and Razumov, the Lingard of the second half of *The Rescue* is utterly debilitated. The highest point of his experience seems to be sitting at his beloved's feet, his head upon her knee, telling her, "I care for nothing in the world but you. Let me be. Give me the rest that is in you." He looks upon her as a

waking dream of rest without end, in an infinity of happiness without sound and movement, without thought, without joy; but with an infinite ease of content, like a world-embracing reverie breathing the air of sadness and scented with love.

It must be emphasized that the later Conrad presents all this absolutely without irony. There is not a hint of judgment against Lingard's lapse into passivity.

The later Conrad's handling of the early Lingard shows simply that Conrad either no longer understands his original creation or chooses to ignore it. What had begun as a most promising portrait of a romantic, egoistic, meddlesome figure becomes in the published book the characterization of a conventional hero of popular fiction, a generous, brave, inherently good man brought low by bad luck, human misunderstanding, and the machinations of fate.

Conrad makes fewer interesting revisions in the other important male characters of "The Rescuer." Yet it is clear from the changes he does make and from the essentially new roles these men assume in the last half of *The Rescue* that he views them in a new light. Linares, converted into d'Alcacer, loses his ironic perceptiveness, Carter his stern, unsentimental rectitude; Jörgenson and Travers become less complicated and more villainous.

Because the early Conrad sketched in Linares much less fully than Lingard, the later Conrad could leave him much as he found him although he saw fit to change his name to d'Alcacer. As originally conceived, Linares prefigures Decoud: a cosmopolitan Spaniard, he is an ironic and skeptical observer of the human comedy. He is immediately attracted to the "picturesque" Lingard, just as Decoud responds to the incorruptible Nostromo. But, unhappily, in the second half of the novel, d'Alcacer becomes more of a Heyst than a Decoud, with his "cultivated voice" speaking "playfully." Although he seems to be the *raisonneur,* his analysis of Lingard is actually inept, stuffy, and pretentious:

> More of a European than of a Spaniard he had that truly aristocratic nature which is inclined to credit every honest man with something of its own nobility and in its judgment is altogether independent of class feeling. He believed Lingard to be an honest man and he never troubled his head to classify him, except in the sense that he found him an interesting character. . . He was a specimen to be judged only by its own worth. With his natural gift of insight d'Alcacer told himself that many overseas adventurers of history were probably less worthy because obviously they must have been less simple. He didn't, however, impart those thoughts formally to Mrs. Travers. In fact he avoided discussing Lingard with Mrs. Travers who, he thought, was quite intelligent enough to appreciate the exact shade of his attitude. If that shade was fine, Mrs. Travers was fine, too . . .

D'Alcacer's imperception results naturally from his creator's loss of understanding of Lingard. The early Conrad would never have seen Lingard as "simple" unless, like Jim, he was simple in a complicated way.

Carter suffers even more seriously from Lingard's emasculation. As originally conceived in "The Rescuer," he belongs in the company of Singleton and MacWhirr. He is the calmest person aboard Travers' yacht, but also the one most aware of its dangerous position. He approaches all problems practically and unemotionally. Although he is as young as Jukes and Jim, he differs from them in his readiness to meet unexpected disasters. As "The Rescuer" makes clear, Carter always maintains "the professionally wide-awake state of a man confronted by rapid changes of circumstance." In the later half of *The Rescue,* Conrad does not bother to make Carter's actions plausible; he does not tell us how Carter can accomplish the ten-day job of rehabilitating the yacht in sixty-six hours. More important, the able and experienced ship's officer of "The Rescuer" has regressed and must go through a maturing experience. "His personality was being developed by new experience, and as he was very simple he received the initiation with shyness and self-mistrust." Although Conrad asserts that Carter has not yet matured, he makes him sound like an old retainer in his solicitous conversation with Lingard after the catastrophe: "Why not lie down a bit, sir? I can attend to anything that may turn up. You seem done up, sir."

A long expository passage on Travers in "The Rescuer" (cut completely from *The Rescue*) shows clearly that Conrad intends him to be of the type of Alvan Hervey, in "The Return." Travers is described as a too wealthy, egotistical bourgeois; unimaginative and conventional, he despises other men yet longs for reputation. Conrad's failure with Alvan Hervey makes it unlikely that Travers could ever have become a successful creation. Yet the early Conrad at least makes an effort to understand him and permits him to have a little human inconsistency and to be a somewhat sympathetic figure. For example, in "The Rescuer," Travers seems honestly suspicious of Lingard's motives; he believes that Lingard is lying about the danger from natives in order to trick Travers into letting him seize the yacht for salvage. In revising "The Rescuer," Conrad eliminates any explanation of why Travers is hostile to Lingard. He also makes him completely unsympathetic by deleting passages that show Travers hearing out Lingard and restraining his indignation against Carter, and by removing indications that Carter and Mrs. Travers have some respect for him. Although Travers appears frequently in the later half of the novel, he can hardly be said to exist. He spends almost all of the time in bed, occasionally making some petulant remark from between the sheets.[13]

Jörgenson becomes rather a bore in the second half of *The Rescue*. Yet as originally conceived, he holds much interest. He is, perhaps, the first true double, prefiguring the gallery of caricatures in *Lord Jim*, all of whom, from the "old stager" to Gentleman Brown, serve to illuminate Jim's romantic psychology. As Jörgenson appears in "The Rescuer," he is obviously meant to foreshadow by his past the inevitable destruction of Lingard's hopes: "He demonstrated one way . . . in which prosaic fate deals with men who dream quickly and want to handle their dreams in broad daylight." Even though Jörgenson has been virtually destroyed by his early adventure into native politics, nevertheless, by his act of joining with Lingard in a new adventure, he reveals the power of those illusions that lure the ego into action and self-destruction: "at times the invincible belief in old illusions would come back, insidious and inspiring." In *The Rescue*, "old illusions" become "the reality of existence." To the later Conrad, the adventures in which Jörgenson and Lingard engage are the essence of existence; he finds it difficult to distinguish between illusion and reality.

The early Conrad emphasizes the physical closeness of Jörgenson and Lingard. As soon as Lingard begins to collect supplies for his adventure, Jörgenson starts to shadow him, finally lengthening his stride to come abreast and engage Lingard in conversation. They become partners, and their doubleness

is apparent to the other characters. So Belarab, recalling to
Lingard Jörgenson's help in former days, says abruptly, "He
resembled you." Even Lingard recognizes the equation, in a
conversation with Edith. She asks,

"And this — this — Jörgenson, you said? Who is he?"
"A man," he answered, "a man like myself."
"Like yourself?"
"Just like myself," he said with strange reluctance, as if ad-
mitting a painful truth. "More sense, perhaps, but less luck."

This technique of employing a subordinate character to illuminate the psychology of the main character culminates in "The
Secret Sharer." In the later half of *The Rescue*, however, it
is lost entirely.

The Jörgenson of "The Rescuer" combines with his symbolic function a persuasively human quality. He may be a
skeleton, but he is a "powerful skeleton"; he is a drifter who
cadges drinks from the traders, but he can also pilot a ship
through the Straits of Rhio. Jörgenson is enough of a human
being to have inspired the devotion of a native "girl," with
a "wrinkled brown face, a lot of tangled grey hair, a few black
stumps of teeth." Jörgenson returns her affection, and even
though he cannot resist Lingard's enterprise, he still demands
that the girl be looked after, indicating a greater sense of
responsibility than Lingard has. Jörgenson's past is as if it
had never been, in the second half of *The Rescue*. The later
Conrad easily convinces us of Jörgenson's "other-world aspect," but this is all that Conrad has to say about him, and
he says it many times. The later Jörgenson, with a rather un-
grateful disregard for the years he has spent with his "girl,"
has now become an unassailable misogynist who expresses his
opinions in a childish vocabulary and manner:

"Woman! That's what I say. That's just about the last touch —
that you, Tom Lingard, red-eyed Tom, King Tom, and all those
fine names, that you should . . . come along here with your

mouth full of fight, bare-handed and with a woman in tow. —
Well — well!"

We must agree with Mrs. Travers' analysis of the later Jörgenson: "He was invulnerable, unapproachable. . . He was
dead." Jörgenson and Travers take their places among the
tedious and unbelievable caricature-villains of the later novels. Although they occupy far more space than do the caricatures of the earlier novels, they are greatly inferior to them.
The reader longs nostalgically for Jim's many doubles, or for
the fine gallery of republicans, revolutionists, and counter-
revolutionists in *Nostromo*.

The later Conrad's oversimplification of potentially interesting characters comes as no surprise. A view of the world
which finds men not responsible for their actions will hardly
reveal great complexity. The emasculation of Lingard is rep-
resentative of the fate of other similar heroes. Only Captain
Anthony of *Chance* can be said to partake at all of the qualities of the simple, excessively romantic, exaltedly egoistic
Lord Jim. Yet Anthony has none of the intensity and vigor
of Jim. Moreover, one does not feel that Conrad really senses
any plague spots in him.

Again, Conrad's handling of d'Alcacer in the second half of
The Rescue is of a piece with his treatment of the ironic,
skeptical, vulnerable hero in the later period. Only Heyst
seems even superficially to partake of this type. He is somewhat skeptical, somewhat ironic; he is detached from society,
although he has in the past been twice tempted into action,
first exploring in New Guinea, next managing a coal company in the tropics. The second venture comes about, like
Decoud's intervention in Costaguana politics, through a personal involvement rather than through commitment to an
ideal. Yet Heyst is really much less like Decoud than critics
have suggested.[14] In fact, Heyst partly resembles a character
completely different from Decoud, Charles Gould. Heyst
recalls Gould not only because of his mustache and the ironic

equation with "portraits of Charles XII of adventurous memory," but also because he is called a "utopist." It would be an interesting departure, an exciting development, if the later Conrad were trying to combine the character of the skeptic with that of the man of action, if Conrad were revealing that the utopian and the unbeliever share an "infernal mistrust of all life," that romanticism and skepticism are sometimes two sides of the same coin. Yet the feeling persists that Conrad simply does not know what he wants to make of Heyst. This is amply borne out by the conclusion in which, as we have seen, Heyst emerges as neither a romantic nor a skeptic, but as a good man brought down by chance and "other people."

Conrad's revisions of Carter in *The Rescue* are of interest because they signify not only the end of the type of the simple, faithful seaman, but the emergence of a new type. (For the faithful seaman does disappear; Conrad may have intended Peyrol to be a descendant of Singleton but he is not, as we shall see in the next chapter when we turn to *The Rover*.) Carter's altered role as immature hero has several counterparts in the later period. We have already seen in *The Shadow Line* one example of this type of character — the character for whom Conrad posits a development from naïveté to self-awareness but who, in fact, acts effectively from the beginning and never attains true maturity. There are other examples: young Powell in *Chance*, George in *The Arrow of Gold*, and Cosmo in *Suspense*. We shall see in the next chapter how seriously Conrad fails in his handling of George and Cosmo.

The emergence, in the later period, of the boy-hero, reminds us that there is another type, a new one which we have not yet considered — the heroine. In the best Conrad of the early period there is no special category for women; the most effective heroine, Mrs. Gould, succeeds insofar as she partakes of the qualities of the complex, perceptive hero. Therefore we shall have difficulty in contrasting later with early heroines. Moreover, "The Rescuer" will not help us much here because Edith Travers is ill-conceived from the first. It might appear, too, that we had exhausted the subject in our discussion of women as obstacles to Conrad's creativity, in the second chapter. Nevertheless, the heroine as a character in the later novels is worth a digression because, surprisingly enough, in the cases of Flora and Lena, she is somewhat more successful than other characters. The later women tend to vacillate between two states: homeless waif and assertive heroine. An examination of Flora and Lena will help us to understand how Conrad succeeds with his women only so long as they remain objects of pity. An analysis of Marlow's comments on women and Mrs. Fyne's character in *Chance* may explain why the appealing waifs must always degenerate into aesthetically unconvincing heroines.

The passages in *Chance* which the common reader is likely to find most moving are close in spirit to the sympathetic descriptions of Winnie Verloc in *The Secret Agent*. Unhappily, these successful scenes represent a very small part of a very long book. In the lengthy account of Flora's childhood which Marlow elicits from the Fynes, there is, perhaps, only one touching incident. The Fynes are on watch in their room in the private hotel next to the big Brighton house de Barral rented for his daughter and her governess. First the odious young man strides out the door, then the governess. At last, out flies the deserted Flora,

right out on the pavement, almost without touching the white steps, a little figure swathed in a holland pinafore up to the chin, its hair streaming back from its head, darting past a lamp-post, past the red pillar-box. . .

Fyne bounds down the stairs of the hotel, scattering porters, page boys, white-breasted waiters, to catch Flora:

What might have been their thoughts at the spectacle of a middle-aged man abducting headlong into the upper regions of a respectable hotel a terrified young girl obviously under age, I don't know.

This scene is quite effective. It may have been the inspiration for a fine scene in a novel better than *Chance,* the scene in Elizabeth Bowen's *Death of the Heart* in which young Portia, learning of her sister-in-law's treachery, runs away to the retired Major Brutt's attic in the Karachi Hotel.

Another scene in *Chance* which depends for its effectiveness on the idea of Flora as a homeless waif also takes place outside of domestic security on the pavement. This is at the end of Marlow's conversation with her in London on East India Dock Road, outside a door marked "Hotel Entrance." After Flora has told Marlow the history of her affair with Anthony, Marlow remarks that her lover must be eager to see her, and Flora admits that she has arrived too early. But for once Conrad does not sentimentalize Flora, does *not* have her say that she came early because of her deep and abiding love for this man whom she does not even know. Instead, Flora says, "I had nothing to do. So I came out." And Marlow has an intuition: "I had the sudden vision of a shabby, lonely little room at the other end of town. It had grown intolerable to her restlessness." Here, for a moment, Flora de Barral is not Woman to Conrad, but a lonely and ignorant person, staying in a rented room in the biggest city in the world, willing to stand outside the hotel that contains the only person among the city's millions who would even recognize her face.

Conrad has, on occasion, the same kind of perception into Lena's character in *Victory.* Although Heyst's first meeting with Lena is told in undistinguished and overwritten prose, the reader cannot fail to respond to Lena's brief explanation of her inability to defend herself: "They are too many for me." On the island, Lena often evokes sympathy for her bewildered incomprehension of Heyst's peculiar reasoning and capricious changes in mood. Lena acts like a child entrusted to a parent or guardian whom it suspects of being inadequate protection. When she talks with Heyst, her tone betrays "always a shade of anxiety, as though she were never certain how a conversation with him would end." During their futile quest for shelter on the road to the native village, Lena alternately clasps and drops Heyst's hand as her faith waxes and wanes. Her attitude toward Heyst reminds us a little of Flora's embarrassment at the antics of her father after he is released from prison. Although Conrad's stereotyped rendition of the sexual situations in both books may distress us, we still sympathize with the homeless waif who dwells within the two heroines.

We seem to be involved in a contradiction here, since we have already found that Conrad's characterizations of women usually fail, particularly in the later period. If Flora and Lena arouse our sympathy, how can we say that they fail as characters? The answer seems to be that all the failures we noted in the previous chapter occur in the most important scenes, the scenes that ought fully to express the intended meaning of the novel: Flora capturing Captain Anthony in the last chapter, and Lena defeating the evil of the world. Conrad's failure in these crucial scenes and, as a matter of fact, in virtually the entire presentation of Rita, Mrs. Travers, Arlette, and Adèle, comes about from a combination of two basic conditions of Conrad's art: his moral view and his almost irrepressible misogyny.

While Conrad does sympathize with the homeless female waif, his sympathy is not as complete as Hardy's or Dreiser's. He will not believe with Hardy that man deserves better than he gets or with Dreiser that man is the pawn of heredity and environment. Conrad's temperament is not that of the naturalist. His characters' crises are moral crises; his characters must *act*, and their actions must be judged. Although Conrad relaxes his moral judgment in the later period, the later novels still move in the same pattern as the early ones. Now, however, Conrad asserts (but cannot show) that his characters are morally triumphant.

Conrad's moral sense, demanding that his characters act upon their own volition, conflicts with his misogyny. Woman in action, woman as the competitor of man, is insufferable. Thus, Conrad's sympathy for the homeless waif vanishes as soon as she makes a gesture of self-assertion. Marlow's comments on women and Conrad's characterization of Mrs. Fyne in *Chance* both seem to evolve from unconfessed misogynistic feelings. Conrad tries, early in the novel, to convince the reader of Marlow's impartiality: "A woman is not necessarily either a doll or an angel to me. She is a human being, very much like myself." As so often in the later work, Conrad's assertions do not match the evidence, and Marlow's prejudices about women soon become clear:

As to honour — you know — it's a very fine mediaeval inheritance which women never got hold of. It wasn't theirs. Since it may be laid as a general principle that women always get what they want, we must suppose they didn't want it. In addition they are devoid of decency. I mean masculine decency. Cautiousness too is foreign to them. . .

They were all alike, with their supreme interest aroused only by fighting with each other about some man: a lover, a son, a brother.

Women don't understand the force of a contemplative temperament.

Compunction! Have you ever seen as much as its shadow?

It is the man who can and generally does "see himself" pretty well inside and out. Women's self-possession is an outward thing; inwardly they flutter, perhaps because they are, or they feel themselves to be, encaged. All this speaking generally.

Speaking generally indeed! Marlow apparently expects us to believe that, in general, women are dishonorable, indecent, without caution, without compunction; that only a man can engage a woman's "supreme interest"; that most women lack true self-possession and true self-knowledge, but that most men do have these qualities.

In the early period the narrator's ironic generalizations are of vital interest — Marlow's observations upon Jim reveal the whole inner meaning of "heroism." But the veneer of irony does not disguise the flaws in the later Marlow's commentary. The voice that attacks feminine self-assertion in *Chance* has lost much of its power to persuade.

> As to women, they know that the clamour for opportunities for them to become something which they cannot be is as reasonable as if mankind at large started asking for opportunities of winning immortality in this world. . .

Conrad attempts to dramatize his distrust of feminine self-assertion through the characterization of Mrs. Fyne. Primarily she is a caricature, with her two repeated poses of folded arms and seated immobility, suggesting strength and intransigence. Mrs. Fyne appears first of all as a kind of Carrie Nation, with what Marlow calls a "knock me down" feminist doctrine:

> that no consideration, no delicacy, no tenderness, no scruples should stand in the way of a woman (who by the mere fact of her sex was the predestined victim of conditions created by men's selfish passions, their vices and their abominable tyranny) from taking the shortest cut towards securing for herself the easiest possible existence.

Because of the cruelty of her selfish father, Mrs. Fyne has come to meet the world with a cold detached manner. She is "neutral" toward her children; she makes a slave and a dupe of her husband; and their marriage, of course, produces only daughters. The Fynes are a caricatured middle-class family with the "usual unshaded crudity of average people" and the "semi-conscious egoism of all safe, established existences." Unlike most feminists, caricatured or not, Mrs. Fyne (whom Marlow calls "practical") seems to have no specific program, a lack that casts doubt on her authenticity.

Conrad seems particularly to lose control over Mrs. Fyne when he attempts to show her interactions with Flora. Although her major interest in life is caring for downtrodden women, she does not really like Flora. Moreover, although Mrs. Fyne usually favors the woman over the man, and although she has made herself personally responsible for Flora's future welfare, she violently opposes Flora's conquest of Captain Anthony. This is especially strange since Mrs. Fyne does not love her brother and, in fact, has "nothing in common with that sailor, that stranger." We can only guess that Conrad loses control because he has no feeling for Mrs. Fyne as a character and because his own impulse is to oppose the Flora–Anthony marriage, or any marriage. Thus, Mrs. Fyne, whose single-minded feministic attitude should have made her a convincing object of Conrad's irony, is rendered implausible by the very feelings that created her.

The later Conrad's hostility to feminine self-assertion results in the immediate destruction of his women as soon as they embark upon a plan of action. Virtually all the scenes with women which we noted as unsuccessful in the previous chapter are scenes in which the woman acts for herself. Since Rita, Mrs. Travers, and Adèle assert themselves from their first appearance, they are unsuccessful from the first.

The active woman in Conrad seems to move in one of two directions, toward Society or Sex. Conrad intends Rita and Mrs. Travers to be brilliant and sensitive leaders of salons. Presumably he would like them to approach the complex humanity of a Henry James heroine, but most of Conrad's society women seem rather to derive from books of the quality of Bulwer-Lytton's *Pelham*. (This is the novel that old Singleton reads, and the early Conrad calls its sentences "polished and so curiously insincere," its language "elegant verbiage.") Lena and Arlette are swiftly transformed into symbols of sexual power and the life force; Conrad seems to hope that they will achieve the complex humanity of Shakespeare's

Cleopatra. But only in Amy Foster and Winnie Verloc does Conrad dramatize successfully sexual force, and in neither characterization does he attempt to be explicit. Rita de Lastaola apparently represents Sex as well as Society; Mills calls her "old Enchantress." The reader is not fooled, however, knowing that one reference to Shakespeare does not make a Cleopatra. Nor does it make a Desdemona. Although Captain Anthony is "swarthy as an African" and Flora "whiter than the lilies," Flora in action convinces us no more of her humanity than do the other Conradian heroines of the later period.

We have seen that the later Conrad's denial of individual guilt and his espousal of repose result in the almost total destruction of the early, profound hierarchy of characters. In the place of faithful seaman and vulnerable hero, we find the untried boy and the impeccable hero. The perceptive hero disappears; the popular-magazine heroine and the unremittingly black villain dominate the scene. The only bright spot in the later characterizations, the handling of Flora and Lena in certain scenes, seems rather the reflection of the early Conrad's sympathy for lonely figures than of any new perception into his characters.

How does Conrad's simpler, apparently less pessimistic, view of the world express itself in his technique? Do the later Conrad's structure and style reveal the richness and complexity that we found in the early period? In studying structure we shall use as our touchstone *Chance* because it has been almost universally admired for its complexity. To see how the later Conrad's methods compare with the earlier, we shall consider *Chance* in relation to *Lord Jim*. In studying style, we shall confine ourselves to the revisions of "The Rescuer" to see whether we can discover the later Conrad's attitude toward his early style. In the next chapter we shall study other aspects of the later Conrad's style in relation to the problem of fatigue.

Ever since Henry James first praised the structure of *Chance* at the time of its publication, critics have commented in awe-struck terms about the technique of the novel. Joseph Warren Beach [15] and Edward Crankshaw [16] both analyze the structure in some detail. Mr. Crankshaw calls it "contrapuntal" and invokes Mozart, Schubert, and Beethoven, Berlioz, Sibelius, and William Faulkner. Even critics less wildly enthusiastic about *Chance* find its technique impressive. F. R. Leavis says that Conrad applies his technique "successfully" in *Chance*.[17] Douglas Hewitt's comment on this matter is especially interesting because in general his interpretation of *Chance* is most convincing; he believes that one should not take the question of Conrad's technique too seriously in dealing with any of the novels:

> Certainly Conrad displays extraordinarily fine craftsmanship — and by the word "craftsmanship" I mean his mastery of multiple narration, shifts in time and viewpoint and so forth, which can be too easily discussed in isolation from the total meaning of the work. But he displays them *as much in his worst novels* and stories as in the best.[18]

If Mr. Hewitt is correct, then Conrad's complex techniques are indeed superficial and are not what we saw them to be in the first chapter — the expression of a complex view of the world. The central question in relation to *Chance* seems to be this: does its structure evolve from inherent complexity as in *Lord Jim* and *Nostromo*, or does it merely conceal a fundamental naïveté?

Chance appears to reveal most of the attributes of structure which we admire in *Lord Jim*. It has a personal narrator who comments perceptively and ironically upon the action and who also takes some part in the action. This narrator obtains evidence about the story from witnesses to the action who become subnarrators. As a result of this multiple narration, the reader often sees the action filtered through several intervening planes of consciousness. *Chance* further resembles

Lord Jim in its frequent violations of conventional chronology. Nevertheless, a closer look at these resemblances shows that they are more apparent than real.

Chance has apparently the same narrator as *Lord Jim,* but this namesake is really very different from the earlier Marlow. We have already found ourselves in disagreement with his generalizations about women in *Chance,* though we found his philosophical comments in *Lord Jim* profound. The later Marlow may seem to resemble his predecessor in the ironic tone of his voice. Yet the quality of the irony in *Chance* differs markedly from that of *Lord Jim.* It is forced, capricious, and inhuman. Marlow must constantly remind the reader that what he is saying is ironic. He speaks of "my chaffing humour," tells the reader that his remarks to Mrs. Fyne are banter. At times Marlow's ironic attitude seems most inappropriate. The "desire of laughter" is at his "very lips" when he hears how Fyne raced down the hotel staircase to intercept Flora's terrorized dash from the governess. Marlow sees "something comic" about Flora standing outside the hotel waiting to see if Fyne can dissuade Anthony from marrying her. When Flora tells Marlow how she left the Fynes' house that night in order to commit suicide and was saved by Anthony, Marlow coughs "down the beginning of a most improper fit of laughter. . ." What Marlow's irony shows most conspicuously is his lack of rapport with the story he is hearing and recounting, rather than, as in *Lord Jim,* the conflict of his moral judgment with his inherent sympathy. The Marlow of *Chance* is confused and so most of what he says is inappropriate.

We also notice a difference in the roles that the two narrators take in their respective novels. In *Lord Jim,* Marlow helps Jim actively throughout the novel, comes to love him like a son, and identifies himself with Jim's moral dilemma. Marlow's role in *Chance* is much simpler: he never even sees the hero, Captain Anthony; he talks with the heroine once, briefly; he has one short glimpse of de Barral in a friend's office; he dislikes his chief link with the story, the Fynes, and does not see them again after Flora's elopement. In short, Marlow is neither personally involved nor morally threatened by the subject.

Lord Jim seems more complex than *Chance* in terms of the witnesses which each narrator employs. There are many more witnesses in *Lord Jim,* and they vary greatly in temperament and in ethical attitude. The reader of *Lord Jim* depends for information and attitude upon the following commentators on Jim's character: the author (a character in the novel, since Marlow writes him a letter), Jim himself, Marlow, the chief engineer of the *Patna,* Brierly, the two Malay quartermasters, the French lieutenant, Chester, Jim's first employer (the owner of a rice-mill), his second employer (Egström), Stein, Jewel, Cornelius, Jim's father (in a letter given to Marlow), Gentleman Brown, Tamb 'Itam. In *Chance,* the list of witnesses to the love of Flora and Anthony is short indeed: Marlow, Fyne, Mrs. Fyne, a "fat little financier" (who says three sentences about de Barral), Powell, Mr. Franklin, Mrs. Brown, and Mr. Brown (the last three all presented secondhand by Powell). What strikes the reader about the witnesses in *Lord Jim* is their personal involvement in the case. Each has a stake in the question of Jim's guilt. If Jim is guilty, he is no better than Gentleman Brown. But if Jim can redeem himself, he helps justify Stein's romantic view of existence. Except for Marlow and Stein, Jim's character witnesses are fairly simple people; they are, nevertheless, highly articulate. The French lieutenant, although he is a simple seaman, has a thorough awareness of his philosophical position and can express it succinctly. All the others, except Cornelius, succeed technically as caricatures. Their particularized traits of personality, their "tags," convince the reader of their reality and of the consistency of their attitude.

The witnesses in *Chance* are disappointing both in their

lack of variety and in the uncertainty of their attitudes. Marlow dwells upon the fact that all (except Flora, perhaps) are crude, so that he must do much of the psychological interpretation. None of the witnesses has, for example, Gentleman Brown's instinctive capacity for hitting a man's weak spot. The witnesses on board the *Ferndale* are hopelessly obtuse, with little awareness of detail and no moral sense. Mrs. Fyne to be sure, is a rather well-conceived witness. She is a feminist, and hence, she should be on Flora's side, just as Stein, the romantic, develops an immediate interest in Jim. She has had an unhappy childhood and has suffered from an indifferent father. This, too, reminds us of Stein and his background of adventure which makes him more sympathetic with Jim's longing for glory. But although Conrad posits a plausible set of attributes for Mrs. Fyne, she fails as a witness because Conrad does not understand her as a character. This lack of understanding comes out clearly in some careless contradictions as to the reliability of Mrs. Fyne's evidence. She, like her husband, is "neither subtle nor profound." Yet, for the purposes of the plot, Mrs. Fyne has to be suspicious about the governess and her "nephew"; Marlow comments: "It was very acute of Mrs. Fyne to spot such a deep game," then wonders where her acuteness has now gone. When Flora's cousin comes to pick her up, "Mrs. Fyne, with the fine ear of a woman, seemed to detect a jeering intention in his meanly unctuous tone. . ." What these inconsistencies mean is that Conrad is not really filtering the story through a particular consciousness, but merely saying that he is. He is giving to Mrs. Fyne the attitude and the amount of awareness that will serve the particular moment.

It must be admitted that, in one sense, the narration of *Chance* appears more complex than that of *Lord Jim*. The reader seems often to stand at a much further remove from the action than at any time in *Lord Jim*. Mr. Zabel admires this technique:

It becomes an instrument of consciousness, a mode of sympathy, a means — especially in *Chance*, where the narrator is sometimes five times removed from the event he is detailing — of presenting experience and intelligence in their fullest possible complex of handicaps, prejudices, distortion, and human obstacles.[19]

It is possible, of course, to make a case in these terms for great complexity in *Chance*. For example, one can say that when we read the governess' words, "What are you screaming for, you little fool?" we are reading through four intervening consciousnesses: Flora has quoted the governess' words to Mrs. Fyne "years afterwards"; Mrs. Fyne tells Marlow; Marlow tells the author, some time after the two meet Powell; the author tells us. Yet all that the reader *experiences* is that Flora describes her scene with the governess and Marlow comments upon it. Since Flora is an innocent girl, and since she was utterly ignorant of why the governess was attacking her, the only perceptive attitude toward the subject is Marlow's. In short, the method has been so little exploited as to add no meaning to the story. The method would, in fact, probably pass almost unnoticed if Marlow did not make so many comments on it:

"You may be surprised at my knowledge of these details. Well, I had them ultimately from Mrs. Fyne."

"— — You understand," Marlow interrupted the current of his narrative, "that in order to be consecutive in my relation of this affair I am telling you at once the details which I heard from Mrs. Fyne later in the day, as well as what little Fyne imparted to me with his usual solemnity during that morning call."

These remarks the reader may well consider intrusions, for they contribute nothing to meaning, simply remind us that Marlow talked to Fyne in the morning, Mrs. Fyne in the afternoon. And they make painfully clear that the narrative belongs to Marlow and to Marlow alone.

Although there is little true filtering of the story through various planes of consciousness, some of the early Conradian talent for making every episode illuminate the central problem does appear. We notice, for instance, that Flora's suffering during her scene with the governess has come about through the governess' long repression of her own natural desire to be loved. This foreshadows, of course, Flora's suffering from Anthony's repression. In the same manner, Flora's childhood misery is prolonged because the Fynes do not interfere: "With that fatal diffidence in well doing inherent in the present condition of humanity, the Fynes continued to watch at their window." Even after Flora's rescue by the Fynes, she is not permitted to enjoy the full sympathy of another woman because of Mrs. Fyne's detachment, the neutral attitude she early acquired to protect herself fom her father. Once again, Flora believes that she has found a sympathetic person in the head of the German family she works for, but the truth is simply that he wants to sleep with her and has so "masked" his desires in respectability that the girl misunderstands him. When his furious wife erupts, his "cowardice of respectability" makes him unable to do anything but stand by and nod, instead of defending Flora's complete innocence. Yet these instances in which isolated episodes serve to illuminate the central theme of repression and diffidence are fairly rare. *Chance* has little of the density of *Nostromo* or *Lord Jim.*

Chance resembles superficially the two early Conrad masterpieces in its violation of chronology, its use of the celebrated time shift. Here again the resemblance is especially close to *Lord Jim.* Both novels devote their opening pages to a prolonged circling about a crucial fact, the knowledge of which will give the reader important insight into the central character. The fact about Jim we learn finally from Jim's own lips, on page 111, "I had jumped . . ." and his evasive attitude toward it, "It seems." It takes Conrad over twice as long to reach the crucial fact about Flora's finding love in *Chance*. The reader learns of it from Flora on page 230. There we discover that Flora has met Anthony in the garden, and "he was gentleness itself."

Let us compare in some detail the structure of just these portions of the two novels. In the first 111 pages of *Lord Jim* there seem to be six distinct periods to Jim's history: (1) one moment in his early life, (2) the *Patna* incident, (3) the period immediately prior to the Inquiry, (4) the Inquiry, (5) the period after the Inquiry, (6) Jim's life as a water-clerk. In tracing the shifts of the narrative over these periods, we shall consider only those portions which describe *scenes* in Jim's life, and we shall omit the author's and Marlow's occasional *references* to events in Jim's life. The book begins from the author's point of view with an account of Jim as water-clerk (6), moves back to a scene from his early life, the training ship (1), then ahead to Jim aboard the *Patna* (2), then ahead to the Inquiry (4), back to Marlow's first view of Jim, prior to the Inquiry, and his visit to the mad chief engineer (3), ahead to Marlow's conversation with Brierly at the Inquiry (4), further ahead to Brierly's leap (5), back to Marlow's conversation with Brierly at the Inquiry and Marlow's first conversation with Jim (4), back to Jim's account of the disaster and his jump (2). This means that there are eight time shifts in the first 111 pages.

In the interests of simplification, we have omitted one segment of time, despite the fact that there are scenes in the novel during that time. This is the time present of Marlow's narration, "on a verandah draped in motionless foliage." As the book progresses and Marlow makes more and more references to the time when Jim became Tuan Jim, to the time when he was loved, the time present of Marlow's narration becomes more and more meaningful. For Marlow tells the first 337 pages of Jim's story in the light of Jim's current success in Patusan. The rest of Jim's story is told in a seventy-page communication from Marlow to the author, written in the light of Jim's death. Narrator's time present in the first part of *Lord Jim* would seem, then, to be more meaningful than narrator's time present in *Chance*, Part I, in which Marlow knows nothing of the eventual failure or success of the love affair.

The first part of *Chance* can be divided into four distinct segments of time: (1) Flora's childhood, (2) her visit to the Fynes and meeting with Captain Anthony, (3) the time of her disappearance, (4) her stay in London. (The first forty pages of *Chance,* the story of young Powell, must be viewed as, at best, introduction. They have almost no bearing upon the subject of Part I, "The Damsel." Only on the shakiest theoretical basis could one say that these pages illuminate Flora's story by opening up the theme of "chance" and by foreshadowing Flora's need for sympathy.) Flora's story begins with Marlow's initial view of her on his first visit to his cottage near the Fynes' (2), moves ahead to his second visit, her disappearance, and his hunt for her with Fyne (3), back to her childhood with an account of de Barral's disaster and the governess' cruelty (1), ahead to Marlow's teaparty for the Fynes (3), back to the hotel where Mrs. Fyne is comforting Flora after the governess episode (1), ahead to the teaparty (3), back to Flora's life with relatives and employers (1), ahead to the teaparty (3), further ahead to Marlow's conversation with Flora in London (4), back to her meeting with Anthony and their love affair at the Fynes' (2).

In the first 200 pages of *Chance,* then, there are nine time shifts. It will be readily observed that most of these are the result of Marlow's teaparty for the Fynes. While Marlow presumably acquires further information about Flora's childhood from Mrs. Fyne during the teaparty, he does not bother to distinguish between that information and what he learned from Fyne in the morning. He puts it all together to form the *consecutive* narrative of Flora's early life, a narrative broken only by essentially parenthetical scenes between Marlow and the Fynes at the teaparty. This means that in the first 230 pages of *Chance* there are only four major time shifts. The result is that the reader does not have a real sense of struggling toward an awareness of the crucial fact. In *Lord Jim* we actually have the sense of Jim's evasion of the fact, his difficulty in accepting it, because our own journey to reach that fact has been so arduous. It is also true that in *Chance* the fact per se ("He was gentleness itself") is something of an anticlimax. It lacks the clear outline of Jim's fact; it does not tell us anything important about Flora or Captain Anthony, and, as Douglas Hewitt says, it blunts "the edge of [the] perception of a possible darker side to Anthony's passion." [20]

Clearly, *Chance* is intrinsically much less complex than *Lord Jim* or *Nostromo*. Its apparatus of several narrators and seeming time shifts makes it superficially complex, but in fact, the machinery does little more than irritate the reader. It does not challenge him to ponder more deeply the meaning of the subject. Conrad has, probably deliberately, simplified his method. Why? Perhaps because he wishes to make his work more accessible to the mass of unenterprising readers. Perhaps because a simpler method will better express a new and simpler view of things. But probably also because he is no longer willing to devise a truly complex pattern.

Style as well as structure suffers from the later Conrad's view of the world. A convenient way of observing the effect of the later attitude upon the early, complex, rich style is to take a long passage from "The Rescuer" and compare it with what remains in *The Rescue*. The comparison should tell us two things: what the later Conrad likes in the early style and, of more interest, what the later Conrad feels capable of duplicating in the second, wholly new, half of *The Rescue*.

Conrad was faced with a very difficult problem in completing *The Rescue:* he had to write half of a novel in the same kind of prose that he had been writing more than twenty years before. Richard Curle, a young friend close to Conrad in his last years, feels that Conrad was successful in his attempt. He says that Conrad "recaptured the lyrical mood . . . but he also smoothed down the exuberance of the earlier chapters, and thus the book is, to some extent, a compromise between the earlier and the later Conrad." [21]

Before considering the passage from "The Rescuer," we should remind ourselves of some of the more important characteristics of the early style. We recall Conrad's famous dictum in the preface to *The Nigger of the "Narcissus"* that he considers his purpose, first of all, to make the reader *see.* This is really a two-fold purpose: to make the reader see striking images, and to make him understand their meaning. In short, the early Conrad's imagination is at once concrete and symbolic. Two other aspects of the early style are worthy of note. First, it is almost always ironic in tone, suggesting that the speaker is judging his subject. Second, its most characteristic feature is the overlong sentence, tending at its worst toward the mere mannerism which Conrad called "Conradese," but at its best suggesting that there is more meaning and more feeling to be expressed than language can quite contain.

The following passage from "The Rescuer" occurs very near the beginning of the manuscript. It is characteristic of the early Conrad in that, although purely descriptive, it is, like those descriptions of the sea and of the East in "Youth," something more than description. The passage shows Lingard's brig becalmed while on its last voyage to the hideout. Lingard expects soon to see the culmination of his dreams of reconquering Hassim's and Immada's country for them and establishing a new nation.

"The Rescuer"

As far as the eye could reach there was nothing but an oppressive immobility, an immobility so perfect as to become something distinct and appalling, something incomprehensible and solid, ringed in by the hard glitter of a cloudless horizon. Nothing moved on earth, on the waters, or above them in the unbroken lustre of the sky. Nothing but the sun that seemed to be slipping slowly, imperceptibly and helplessly down towards the sharp edge of the vast expanse of open water stretching to the westward. On the unruffled surface of the straits the brig floated tranquil and upright as if bolted solidly, keel to keel, with its own image reflected in the unframed and immense mirror of the sea. Both the vessel and its reflection preserved the stiff rigidity of their outlines upon the blue of the sky and the deeper blue of the water. To the south and east the double islands watched silently the double ship that seemed fixed amongst them for ever, as if destined for ever to remain within sight of their dark-green slopes — of their sombre and rocky shores: a hopeless captive of the calm in the wicked silence of burning days and of nights heavy-scented and poisonous that carry the perfumed breath of tropical lands to the angry and helpless prisoners of a narrow sea.

There was no stir in the brig's sails. The topsails sheeted right out and set up with taut leeches without a wrinkle in their surface, hung down, all of a piece resembling two smooth, thin and towering slabs of white marble; while under them the courses hauled up in their gear had the heavy aspect of those ornamental stone festoons that the commonplace hand suspends between the urns at the base of stolid monuments of mourning. The higher sails, also clewed up, were gathered motionless under the yards. Since midday, when the light and capricious airs of these seas had abandoned the little brig to its lingering fate, her head had swung round slowly to the westward and the end of her slender and polished jib-boom, projecting boldly beyond the graceful curve of the bow, seemed to point provokingly at [the] heart of the setting sun, like a spear poised high in the hand of an enemy. On the clear whiteness of the decks — ruled by straight lines of black pitch between the narrow planks — the shadows, that in a moving ship are always so restless and responsive to every slight balancing of the craft lay now clearly defined as if painted by a steady brush. There was no one visible on the main deck,

and the only sign of the presence of human beings was a pair of
black slippers standing at the door of the small galley forward.
The white paint of the bulwark dazzled the eyes in patches of
sunlight cut about by heavy coils of braces and running gear
hanging on the pins. In the profound stillness of the craft en-
closed by the larger silence of the sea the shuffle of feet on the
poop where the officer of the watch wandered aimlessly acquired
the importance of a startling discourse. Right aft . . .

The Rescue

As far as the eye could reach there was nothing but an impressive immobility. Nothing moved on earth, on the waters, and
above them in the unbroken lustre of the sky. On the unruffled
surface of the straits the brig floated tranquil and upright as if
bolted solidly, keel to keel, with its own image reflected in the
unframed and immense mirror of the sea. To the south and east
the double islands watched silently the double ship that seemed
fixed amongst them forever, a hopeless captive of the calm, a
helpless prisoner of the shallow sea.
[*The Rescue* moves immediately to what appears below.]
    Since midday, when the light and capricious airs of these seas
had abandoned the little brig to its lingering fate, her head had
swung slowly to the westward and the end of her slender and
polished jib-boom, projecting boldly beyond the graceful curve
of the bow, pointed at the setting sun, like a spear poised high
in the hand of an enemy. Right aft . . .

Before discussing these passages, we should make two
reservations. First, "The Rescuer" prose cannot be called a
great example of the early Conrad's style. It is very early, having been written in Lannion, Brittany, in March, 1896, several months before Conrad embarked upon his first artistic
success, *The Nigger of the "Narcissus"*; it is, moreover, an
absolutely unrevised first draft. Second, *The Rescue* passage represents a creditable piece of excision. It is coherent,
and it preserves from the original passage the information
necessary for the reader to understand the ensuing action.
    Conrad's method of revising this passage is typical of his

later handling of "The Rescuer." He cuts mostly, as here, in large swatches — whole sentences, rather than individual words. There is virtually no rewriting or even substitution of a new word for an old. One of Conrad's purposes in cutting this passage seems to be, simply, to shorten the book, and he succeeds in reducing the passage to about thirty per cent of its original length. Without question "The Rescuer" with the addition of the later and dictated half of *The Rescue* would have made too long a novel. Despite the pruning, *The Rescue* is longer than any of Conrad's novels except *Nostromo*. As his handling of this passage suggests, Conrad shortens the novel principally by cutting extensively from descriptive passages. He tends to take least from the dialogue, although it is undoubtedly the weakest aspect of the manuscript. But Conrad must match the old with the new, and dialogue seems to be the kind of prose that the later Conrad can most easily manage. In any case, dialogue dominates the later half of *The Rescue*.

Conrad's cuts from this passage are not random ones. He removes the most vivid and the most suggestive details, all those most likely to make the reader *see:* the blue of the sky, the darker blue of the sea, the dark green of the shore, the precise position of the sails, the lines of black pitch on the deck, the black slippers, and, perhaps most precise of all, the stillness of the ship's shadows that normally are in constant motion. Perhaps the later Conrad deletes these not only to save space but also because he knows he cannot match such images in the latter half of the book. Certainly there are few concrete details to be found there. Nevertheless, Paul L. Wiley, who admires the later Conrad's "visual effects," singles out for praise in *The Rescue* the "Delacroix-like panels of Lingard's parleys with the Malay chiefs in Part V." [22] An examination of these scenes from the new half of the novel reveals almost no visual images. The few that there are, the dress of the Mohammedans and the ornaments of the Illanun chiefs, seem to have originated in passages cut from the old manuscript.

Finally, Conrad cuts from "The Rescuer" passage portions that seem suggestive of added meaning, for instance, the comparison of the flat sails to marble slabs and the courses to ornamental stonework at the base of a monument. These details remind us that the graveyard imagery of *The Nigger of the "Narcissus,"* "Youth," and *Lord Jim* is one of the fine expressions of the early Conrad's symbolic imagination. Again, the later Conrad deprives us of richness by deleting the descriptions of the sea's immobility ("so perfect as to become something distinct and appalling, something incomprehensible and solid") and of the setting sun ("slipping slowly, imperceptibly and helplessly down towards the sharp edge of the vast expanse of open water"). To some readers, these details will seem well deserving of their fate. Yet though they partake of the pretentiousness and vagueness of early Conradese at its worst, they, together with the graveyard images, serve an important function in "The Rescuer" as it was originally conceived. Both act as ironic comments upon the situation. Lingard dreams of glory, but the sails, the sea, and the sun all show that dreams of glory are dreams of death. In short, these details prefigure the fundamental irony of "Youth" and *Lord Jim*.

If this interpretation is sound, the later Conrad either did not wish to or could not recover his early symbolic imagery and emotionally evocative prose. Most critics, however, tend to assert that in the last novels Conrad returned to his early style, a style they do not applaud.[23] Actually, it is doubtful whether the Conrad of 1919 could write with the suggestive power of even some of the poorer specimens of early Conradese. Throughout the later period there are clear examples of the later Conrad's ineffectual imitation of early Conradese. This is true of *Chance*, which belongs to the time when, according to some readers, Conrad has "purged" himself of the early style. The following passage can be seen as an attempt at self-imitation; its use of inversion and its stress upon the "incomprehensible" indicate its remote kinship with early Conradese:

> He stirred not; and Powell keeping near by did not dare speak to him, so enigmatical in its contemplation of the night did his figure appear to his young eyes: indistinct — and in its immobility staring into gloom, the prey of some incomprehensible grief, longing or regret.

Conrad's treatment of "The Rescuer" tends, then, to conform to our other evidence about the effect of the later attitude upon the range of Conrad's characters and upon his technique. His rejection of a concrete and suggestive style is of a piece with his altered view of the world and man's place in it. In his early work, he sternly judges those of his characters who try to evade responsibility and seek peace. Moreover, these characters go about their self-destruction with vigor of purpose and intensity of emotion. But in the later work, Conrad evades the question of moral responsibility and passively acknowledges peace as man's greatest good. If this is affirmation, it rises not out of serene old age but out of a desperate weariness.

The Exhaustion of Creative Energy
THE ARROW OF GOLD, THE ROVER, and SUSPENSE

The literary history of Conrad's very last years seems, on the surface, to be one of orderly continuation of old habits of mind and, at the same time, a development of new interests. Conrad's last two "Author's Notes," to *The Arrow of Gold* and *The Rescue*, certainly convey a sense of culmination and fulfillment. All his life he has waited for the right moment to render into art one of his most memorable personal experiences, his love affair with "Rita," and now the moment has come to give the public *The Arrow of Gold*. For twenty years *The Rescue* has awaited the appropriate time for its completion; that time is 1919. His French biographer, G. Jean-Aubry, tells us that Conrad had "dreamt over ever since 1907" a "Napoleonic romance" and that he was fulfilling this dream in the twenties with *The Rover* and the unfinished *Suspense*. M. Jean-Aubry concludes that Conrad's "imagination was still vitally active." [1] It is of course fitting that Conrad should die while at work on a novel, but Richard Curle finds its "tragic" that he did not finish *Suspense*, since even as a fragment it "will take its place among the recognized masterpieces of this remarkable man." [2] Even thirty years after Conrad's death, Mr. Paul L. Wiley shares this generous view of Conrad's final efforts. He finds that the "main thematic structure of Conrad's work [is] completed" in his last phase; moreover, although one does detect a change in tone, that change "is best accounted for by changing inspiration and not by declining energy." [3]

This chapter proposes, regretfully, to show that the productions of Conrad's last years are virtually without a redeeming feature. They reveal that Conrad has exhausted his creative energy. He has no longer anything to write about and must rework old materials, cling to someone's memoirs, or, in the case of *The Rover*, spin nearly three hundred pages out of almost nothing. Even more seriously, the last novels show that Conrad has finally lost control of the basic tools of his craft. He can no longer focus on his subject: the novels contain many beginnings but virtually no endings. The characters lack substance, and Conrad can only assert their emotions and ideas — he cannot dramatize them. The prose of the last works is very faulty. When Conrad tries his hardest to make a scene important, the prose drifts into thin, vague pretentiousness. Although Conrad writes awkwardly at times in all of his novels (least so perhaps in *Lord Jim* and the shorter sea pieces), the prose of the last novels stumbles on every page. Sometimes he cannot even execute a sentence. Besides the specific faults in technique, the last novels give a general feeling of weariness. All the characters, young and old, seem very tired, eager to sit or lie down. Moreover, the difficulty with which their creator manipulates them indicates clearly the source of their fatigue.

To demonstrate the weakness of the last period, we shall discuss the novels separately, dealing only with *The Arrow of Gold* (1919), *The Rover* (1923), and *Suspense* (1925). We shall omit *The Rescue* since its history is so complicated and since we have already discussed it at length. Yet all our comments on the other novels will apply with equal force to the dictated later half of *The Rescue* (Part IV, Chapter V, to the end). These will be brief because such dissection is essentially unpleasant and because any reader making a resolute effort to forget who wrote these books will immediately perceive that they are failures.

While external evidence suggests that *The Arrow of Gold*

contains only new material, a scrutiny of Conrad's early works reveals that its subject matter had been thoroughly exploited long before. From Conrad's note to *The Arrow of Gold* and his letters to his publisher, the source of that novel seems clear enough, a love affair in his early youth. In a letter to Doubleday, Conrad discusses the inner history of the novel. It "is a subject which I had in my mind for some eighteen years, but which I hesitated to take up till now." [4] Presumably Conrad is here thinking of his work over twenty years before on *The Sisters:* two of its main characters, Rita and her Uncle José Ortega, appear only slightly changed in *The Arrow of Gold*, and Stephen prefigures George. John D. Gordan comments appreciatively on Conrad's waiting all that time while the "material matured through the chemistry of the imagination." [5] Knowing the early Conrad's writing habits as well as Mr. Gordan does, he should be more suspicious of such a pat explanation of the history of *The Arrow of Gold*. Mr. Gordan shows in his account of Conrad's first years that he drew heavily from a few seminal experiences.[6] Five months sailing around Borneo on the *Vidar*, several memorable voyages to the East, the experience in the Congo — these Conrad exploited early in his career. M. Jean-Aubry stresses the importance of Conrad's Marseilles experiences, especially his friendship with Dominic Cervoni, whose presence he detects in Lingard [7] and who is, as Conrad himself admits in his introduction, the model for Nostromo. But why should Conrad have waited so long to write about his love for Rita, even granting that he failed with it in *The Sisters?* Mr. Gordan demonstrates Conrad's frugality with his material [8] and, as we have already noted, Conrad immediately worked some of the material of "The Rescuer" into *Lord Jim.* Is it really plausible, then, that Conrad deliberately saved the story of Rita and his exciting youth in Marseilles until the end of his career? Another look at *The Sisters* and a little detective work will show us that the materials of

The Arrow of Gold had been exploited long before 1917. Rita, of *The Sisters,* is an orphan, we recall, with two uncles, the Ortegas, brothers of her deceased mother. One uncle, a gloomy and fanatical priest, lives in the Basque country and works for the return of the Pretender, who he knows will be friendly to the Church. Rita lives with her other uncle, old José Ortega; a Legitimist like his brother, he lives in Paris, the very city where the Pretender holds court. Rita spends much of her time at the home of other Royalists, the Malagons, who are socially superior to the Ortegas. Mrs. Malagon, a little French woman much younger than her husband, is very fond of Rita and sometimes sends her landau to the Ortegas to pick her up. From time to time, old Ortega himself, dressed up in black, calls upon Mrs. Malagon, who always receives him with sweet patience. To him she looks like a princess, and he calls her an angel and always kisses her hands when leaving. Across the street from the Ortegas lives young Stephen, disillusioned, isolated, Bohemian, artistic, skeptical, longing for sincerity and, perhaps, for a girl like Rita.

These characters and their relationships must seem familiar to every Conradian; they appear in *Nostromo,* begun seven years after *The Sisters* was abandoned. Rita prefigures Antonia Avellanos, and her uncle, José Ortega, prefigures Antonia's father, Don José Avellanos. Rita's other uncle, the priest, recalls of course Antonia's fanatically religious uncle, Father Corbelàn. The refined little Mrs. Malagon seems to be a first version of Mrs. Gould, and Stephen foreshadows that Paris boulevardier, Martin Decoud. We do note some differences. Although José Ortega admires Señor Malagon and defers to him as readily as Don José Avellanos defers to Charles Gould, Malagon and Gould are clearly unlike. Yet part of Gould's name reminds us of the political background of *The Sisters.* The Spanish Legitimists support the Pretender, Don Carlos, "el Rey." The citizens of Cos taguana call Charles Gould, "Don Carlos," "Rey de Sulaco," and in one scene Conrad equates Gould with Charles IV by whose equestrian statue Gould ("the other Carlos") often rides. Thus Conrad comments ironically upon politics and business through the name Don Carlos Gould, half of it belonging to the romantic but anachronistic Spanish Pretender, the other half to American big business. *Nostromo* differs from *The Sisters* also in the seeming disappearance of Dolores Ortega, José's wife. Don José Avellanos, we recall, has lost his wife. Dolores of *The Sisters* is a termagant who shouts at her husband, "But look! Look! All these oranges. . . . Sanctissima. . . Look! You! José!" She is so noisy that Rita regrets going "into the atmosphere of scolding and garlic of her aunt's home." It looks very much as if Dolores becomes the scolding wife of old Viola in *Nostromo,* where the two keep an inn that smells of burnt onions.

The Sisters seems to follow Conrad's Marseilles experiences more closely than *Nostromo,* for what is surely the model for Señor Malagon appears in Conrad's nonfictional account of certain friends of those days. In *A Personal Record* Conrad mentions M. Delestang, a "frozen-up, mummified Royalist" banker whose young wife, "an imperious, handsome lady," he admired. They seem likely sources for the Malagons, and Mme. Delestang could also be present in the Mrs. Gould of *Nostromo.* Conrad's one vivid recollection of Mme. Delestang, letting him out of her carriage, leaning forward, holding his hand, and warning him not to waste his life, recalls the fine scene between Decoud and Mrs. Gould in her carriage after the departure of General Barrios.

While our quest for sources of *Nostromo* does little to illuminate that novel for us, it does tell us something of the dilemma facing Conrad as he tried to write *The Arrow of Gold.* Far from having waited all his life to draw upon his Marseilles experiences, he had used them thirteen years before, at the height of his artistic powers, in twenty months of the most intense creative effort of his career, on the broadest canvas he ever attempted. Conrad is not likely to have forgotten how much of the Marseilles days went into *Nostromo.* We know in fact that at the same time that he was embarking upon *The Arrow of Gold* (September, 1917)[9] he was also writing a preface to a new edition of *Nostromo* and making small alterations throughout the text. Perhaps Conrad deliberately used *Nostromo* in trying to refresh his mind about events now forty years past. It is difficult to tell whether the echoes of *Nostromo* in *The Arrow of Gold* come about because of a similar source or because of the influence of the early novel upon the later. Probably Conrad himself did not know whether he was writing about Costaguana or Marseilles. There are several verbal parallels which would suggest influence. The "comic effect" of Ortega's self-torture outside the door and his "distorted shape" afterwards, looking like a "shadow," remind us of the bitterly comic sufferings of Señor Hirsch and his unreal appearance after death. The utterly irrelevant Italian dancing master of *The Arrow of Gold,* with his two pretty daughters in their white stockings, reminds us of the patriarchal Viola of *Nostromo* and his daughters, Linda and Giselle. The dancing master, incidentally, exhibits a "patriarchal smile" through his great white beard.

Let us digress for a moment from *The Arrow of Gold* to note that self-imitation is typical of the later Conrad and a useful key to understanding his desperate lack of material. We have already mentioned in our discussion of love in *Victory* that the central situation, the arrival of Mr. Jones and his crew, bears resemblances to the last pages of *Lord Jim.* Again, in our discussion of *The Shadow Line* we observed many parallels with "The Secret Sharer." Moreover both stories rise out of the same autobiographical experience, Conrad's first command.[10] Conrad's decision to "finish"

"The Rescuer" has much in common with his decision to finish what he had started in *The Sisters*. In both instances, the early Conrad had had an important story to tell which he could not tell in the first attempt because of difficulty with the love affair. Shortly thereafter, he attacked the material again and out of these second attempts came his two greatest novels, *Lord Jim* and *Nostromo*. *The Rescue* and *The Arrow of Gold* represent, therefore, the completion of novels already completed; they are the dregs of fictional material long since thoroughly exploited.

In reading *The Arrow of Gold* we perhaps react first to its radical lack of form. It has virtually no center of interest, no basic conflict to be resolved, no climax toward which to move. Rather it has a series of possible narrative strands, each of which Conrad picks up, examines, speculates on, and drops. The novel begins with a long conversation among the young seaman, George, and two adventurers, Blunt and Mills, involved in the Carlist revolt in Spain. The latter do most of the talking, each telling what he knows about the mysterious Carlist patriot, Rita de Lastaola. Their ostensible purpose is to arouse George's interest to such an extent that he will join their conspiracy and smuggle guns to the revolutionists in Spain. Now this could be an effective means of engaging the reader's interest, except that Conrad seems not to have his purpose very firmly in mind. Most of the time the two older men are unaware of George's presence. Any possibilities inherent in a situation whereby George may be trapped into a dangerous assignment are lost in the ensuing scene, which describes the three men lunching with Rita. The dangerous work is not alluded to, except that the narrator (George) remarks after the lunch that "in those four hours since midday a complete change had come over me. For good or evil I left that house committed to an enterprise that could not be talked about. . ."

At this point in the novel we seem to have arrived at its

real center of interest, the love affair between George and Rita. Yet in truth little interest rises from it, since one senses few obstacles to be overcome. George does not slowly awaken to awareness of his feelings for Rita. Within a few minutes (and four pages) of his first meeting with her, we read:

That woman of whom I had heard these things I have set down with all the exactness of unfailing memory, that woman was revealed to me young, younger than anybody I had ever seen, as young as myself (and my sensation of my youth was then very acute); revealed with something peculiarly intimate in the conviction, as if she were young exactly in the same way in which I felt myself young; and that therefore no misunderstanding between us was possible and there could be nothing more for us to know about each other.

George's rapid intuition here proves to be perfectly justified by the action of the novel. Although George asserts that it takes a little time for Rita and himself to make "great progress in our intimacy," and although they have occasional childish and unimportant quarrels, they are obviously in love from the start. The only obstacle to their union is Rita's nameless fear that she will either lose her independence or control George too rigidly, a fear too vague to be of much interest. It cannot be resolved; Rita finally accepts George simply because her way out of the bedroom is blocked by her puritanical sister, Therese.

Conrad tries to create interest by giving George a rival, Blunt, with his accomplice, that "wonderful old woman," his mother. In what reads like a parody of Henry James, Conrad laboriously describes the battle of wits between the scheming mother and George, who appears to be a threat to her son's chances of winning Rita and, especially, Rita's fortune. Once again, Conrad does nothing with the situation. Rita rejects Blunt's proposal, without Blunt and George coming into any kind of conflict. Son and mother drop out of the novel on page 213. One hundred and thirty-three pages later, we are told in a few sentences that Blunt shot George in a duel. We must attribute this artless conclusion to what Mr. Guerard calls the "heavy hand of actuality." [11] Conrad's own Marseilles experience ended in his being wounded in a duel. Therefore the novel must end the same way, no matter how improbably.

Conrad focuses briefly on a final center of interest, the rivalry between George and Rita's childhood tormentor, José Ortega, but again he can develop no conflict. Ortega is a pitiful, shivering creature of whom George rightly has no fear. George knows that he can throw Ortega out bodily if necessary, and knows also that he and Rita are perfectly safe behind the locked doors of their bedroom. When he hears Ortega heading upstairs to expend his rage on Therese, he confidently unlocks the door and goes out to stop him.

Beyond these fumbling attempts to create interest in four undeveloped and in fact unrelated situations, Conrad focuses upon minor characters and seems to promise that significant future events will involve them. So George talks at length about his feelings of rapport with Mills, "that quiet man whom I admired, whom I trusted, and for whom I had already something resembling affection." Yet Mills drops out of the novel on page 105, not to return until page 348, when he nurses the wounded George back to health. Again, there is present in the lunch scene at Rita's a newspaperman whom Conrad describes in great detail. The man seems to be engaged in some secret work which might be dangerous to Rita, and George is suspicious when Blunt follows the journalist out of the room: "And it occurred to me, too, to wonder what sort of business Mr. Blunt could have had to transact with our odious visitor, of a nature so urgent as to make him run out after him into the hall?" Yet several sentences later George admits that the episode has no meaning: "As a matter of fact he was already far away;

and I may just as well say here that I never saw him again
in my life."

Presumably Conrad hoped to control his readers chiefly
through a sympathetic interest in the characters of Rita and
George. We have already seen with what difficulty Conrad
portrays women and particularly women for whom he wishes
to make special claims of distinction. Rita has little in common with the homeless waif; as the woman who has in her
something of "the women of all time," she remains only a
splendid and thinly clad body enclosing sporadically violent
and incomprehensible emotions. Conrad tries especially
hard, however, with George. He says in the preface that the
novel deals with "initiation (through an ordeal which required some resolution to face) into the life of passion."
Just what the ordeal is, never becomes clear. To be sure,
early in the novel George asserts his naïveté: "I listened
open-mouthed to these things into which my West-Indian
experiences could not have given me an insight." But his
immaturity does not seem at all shameful: "If I represented
anything it was a perfect freshness of sensations and a refresh-
ing ignorance." These statements about naïve simplicity
prove actually to be only assertions. Almost from his first
appearance, George speaks and acts with the assurance of
one to the manner born. We notice, for instance, how he
bests the great Mrs. Blunt:

And then for the first time during this conversation, for the
first time since I left Doña Rita the day before, for the first time
I laughed.
"Do you mean to hint, Madame, that Southern gentlemen are
dead shots? I am aware of that — from novels."
I spoke looking her straight in the face and I made that ex-
quisite, aristocratic old woman positively blink by my directness.
There was a faint flush on her delicate old cheeks but she didn't
move a muscle in her face. I made her a most respectful bow and
went out of the studio.

F. R. Leavis comments wryly upon *The Arrow of Gold:*

"It is a sophisticated piece of work, with a sophistication that elaborates and aggravates [a] deplorable kind of naïvety. . ."[12] With Rita, George maintains a suave and dignified air. When she asks him why he does not carry a weapon, we read, " 'Because if I am unconventionalized I am an old European,' I murmured gently. 'No, *excellentissima*, I shall go through life without as much as a switch in my hand.' "

Not only does George show himself to be a polished gentleman, he also proves himself a brilliant military strategist and a calm hero in action. In his conversation with one of the Pretender's chief lieutenants, George does not withhold from him his "young sagacity": "The matters we discussed were not of course of high policy, though from the point of view of the war in the South they were important enough. We agreed on certain things to be done. . ." When Ortega besieges the bedroom containing Rita and George, the latter acts perfectly. He remains calm; "with great presence of mind" he warns Rita to be quiet. Ortega's cries do not daunt him: "I really stood there smiling to myself, yet with a gloomy and uneasy heart." Though Rita is terrified, George recognizes the futility of Ortega's efforts; he comments: "He was terrifying, but he was not serious."

George thus takes his place in the new category of boy-hero, along with Powell, the young captain in *The Shadow Line,* the later Carter, and Cosmo. Each of these purportedly undergoes a maturing process, yet in fact shows no character development whatever.

The Arrow of Gold constantly overwhelms the reader with its pretentiousness. On almost every page, we see Conrad trying to convince us that what happens in his story is more important, more meaningful, than we might suppose. This pretentiousness appears most frequently in those passages proposing the infinity and eternity of the love between George and Rita.

A faint scent of violets filled the tragic emptiness of my head and it seemed impossible to me that I should not cry from sheer weakness. . . There was only the slight movement of her breathing that showed her to be alive; and with closed eyes I imagined her to be lost in thought, removed, by an incredible meditation while I clung to her, to an immense distance from the earth. The distance must have been immense because the silence was so perfect, the feeling as if of eternal stillness. I had a distinct impression of being in contact with an infinity that had the slightest possible rise and fall, was pervaded by a warm, delicate scent of violets and through which came a hand from somewhere to rest lightly on my head. Presently my ear caught the faint and regular pulsation of her heart, firm and quick, infinitely touching in its persistent mystery, disclosing itself into my very ear — and my felicity became complete.

What gives this passage its particular flavor is the juxtaposition of vague romantic effusion and a few specific, commonplace details. But a passage rich in specific detail carries no greater sense of reality:

She enchanted me. The ardent modulations of the sound, the slight play of the beautiful lips, the still, deep sapphire gleam in those long eyes inherited from the dawn of ages and that seemed always to watch unimaginable things, that underlying faint ripple of gaiety that played under all her moods as though it had been a gift from the high gods moved to pity for this lonely mortal, all this within the four walls and displayed for me alone gave me the sense of almost intolerable joy.

Here Conrad strings clauses together with some disregard for sense. It is not clear, for instance, why "all this" (lips, eyes, gaiety) should be "within four walls," rather than part of her person. Furthermore, the language of this passage has a very familiar ring: "beautiful lips," "sapphire gleam," "dawn of ages," "gift from the high gods," "this lonely mortal," and "intolerable joy" are the basic material of subliterary fiction. The passage is, simply, one huge cliché.

Let us glance, finally, at the climax to the love affair.

I only breathed deeply the faint scent of violets, her own particular fragrance enveloping my body, penetrating my very heart with an inconceivable intimacy, bringing me closer to her than the closest embrace, and yet so subtle that I sensed her existence in me only as a great, glowing, indeterminate tenderness, something like the evening light disclosing after the white passion of the day infinite depths in the colours of the sky and an unsuspected soul of peace in the protean forms of life.

Although this passage describes the most important moment in the love affair, it reveals principally that George feels no emotion at all and knows nothing of Rita. The one clear statement — that his response to Rita is as subtle as an evening sky — could mean anything — or nothing.

The pretentiousness of *The Arrow of Gold* appears in less obvious ways; through, for example, George's comments on some of the other characters. He frequently points out rather absurd occasions: Mills's eyes grow wider "than I had ever seen them before" (he has known Mills only a short time and this is their first real conversation together); Rita speaks "in a louder tone than I had ever heard her use before" (he has known her about one half hour, has heard her speak no more than a dozen sentences). George also conveys a sense of self-importance through his frequent assertions of powerful emotions. Within three pages, while George is listening to Blunt and Mills, he is "extremely embarrassed," "positively annoyed," "horribly vexed," and "suddenly extremely delighted." In his first meeting with Rita, George experiences "astonishment" at seeing her; two pages later he is equally "astonished" to see a newspaper man with white hair; at Blunt's departure he feels "extreme surprise." On learning that there are new roomers in the house he lives in, George experiences "intense surprise" and is "astonished," all within one sentence. The reader, incidentally, discovers ultimately that these new roomers have no bearing at all upon the plot.

The sympathetic reader will perceive fairly quickly that beneath the pretentiousness of *The Arrow of Gold's* rhetoric and beneath its vain assertion of unusual occurrences and powerful feelings lies Conrad's almost complete bafflement. He does not understand his characters as individuals, nor can he see relationships between them. We do not need to guess at his bafflement. He tells us of it through George explicitly on almost every page. Apparently attempting to suggest that the Blunts are mysteriously evil, Conrad succeeds only in telling us that they are incomprehensible. Blunt's personality, we learn early in the novel, is "not clearly definable." His "curiously flavoured" voice has an "indefinable," "peculiar" tone. The presence of the Blunts makes George "feel uncomfortable in a peculiar way" because of their "subtly different point of view."

Now we might grant Conrad the right to a pair of unfathomable characters in his novel, but we cannot help being confused when his narrator exhibits the same perplexity before Rita, particularly since he knows her completely upon first meeting and since he says of her "the real you . . . is in me." Nevertheless, George constantly finds Rita incomprehensible. She fascinates him "in an indefinable way"; her voice has an "even, mysterious quality" and an "undefinable tone"; she looks with a "profound unreadable stare"; her handclasp conveys a "unique sensation." Even her unsophisticated peasant sister, Therese, remains a mystery to George: "With her it was very difficult to distinguish between craft and innocence"; "there was something behind [her] attitude which I could not fathom." Finally, George tells us frequently that he cannot understand or verbalize his own feelings. When Blunt describes Rita, the effect on George is "more inward, a strange emotion." On his way to visit Rita, he experiences "an infinity of pangs too complex for analysis."

Perhaps the key word in *The Arrow of Gold* (and also in *The Rover* and *Suspense)* is "funny." It occurs with alarming frequency throughout the novel, usually meaning odd, strange, "indefinable," sometimes meaning amusing, sometimes used ambiguously. It is not what we think of as a characteristic Conradian word, and this suggests how atypical the last works are. Moreover, its frequent use indicates that Conrad is at a loss for a more precise word. We read that "women are funny," that Therese speaks in a "funnily compassionate tone," that Mrs. Blunt looks through "funny glasses," that Therese looks "funny" to Dominic, that Rita wears a "funny dress," speaks "funnily," and says "the funniest thing is," that José Ortega's whiskers are "funny," and his crashing into the door is "really funny," and that George's last visit to his house is a "funny experience."

The source of Conrad's bafflement in *The Arrow of Gold* is not far to seek. The sheer mechanical faultiness of the prose and the general exhaustion and despair of the characters betray fatigue too great for creativity. Inept prose ranges from simple clumsiness to downright gibberish. Sometimes the awkwardness results from a tangled arrangement of clauses: "she whom the quayside called Madame Léonore closed her outstretched hand before my face and opened it at once to show its emptiness *in illustration of her expressed opinion*." (The italics here and throughout this chapter are mine.) Much more frequently, however, the clumsiness seems directly the result of the older Conrad's difficulty in fusing two related ideas. In fact, one of the most characteristic constructions in the later prose is a complex sentence containing an "as to" clause:

> *As to* him whom we may regard as Mills' victim it is obvious that he has never harboured a single reproachful thought.

> I was feeling quite inanimate *as to* body and frightfully stimulated *as to* mind all the time.

> He advanced towards me, correct, supple, hollow-eyed, and smiling; and *as to* his costume ready to go out except for the old shooting jacket which he must have affectioned particularly, for he never lost any time in getting into it at every opportunity.

But *as to* the sound of the four magic letters of her name I was not very likely to hear it fall sweetly on my ear.

Conrad has some of the same difficulty with other connectives: "A waiter approached for orders and it was then, *in relation to* my order for coffee, that the absolutely first thing I learned of Captain Blunt was the fact that he was a sufferer from insomnia." At least once Conrad makes no attempt to provide a connection but simply puts two ideas side by side. This is a description of the carnival celebrants: "They were people of the poorer sort (white calico with red spots, costumes)." On another occasion his confusion appears in an ambiguous handling of pronouns:

But all the same the revelation turned many things into dust; and, amongst others, the sense of the careless freedom of my life. If that life ever had any purpose or any aim outside itself I would have said that *it* threw a shadow across *its* path. But *it* hadn't. There had been no path.

Some of the sentences in *The Arrow of Gold* simply break in half:

I only learned that for at least five mixed reasons, none of which impressed me profoundly, Doña Rita had started at a moment's notice from Paris with nothing but a dressing-bag, and pemitting Rose to go and visit her aged parents. . .

I shall never forget that grey dress with ample skirts and long corsage yet with infinite style, the ancient as if ghostly beauty of outlines, the black lace, the silver hair, the harmonious, restrained movements of those white, soft hands like the hands of a queen — or an abbess; and in the general fresh effect of her person the brilliant eyes like two stars with the calm reposeful way they had of moving on and off one, as if nothing in the world had the right to veil itself before their once sovereign beauty.

Sometimes the prose of *The Arrow of Gold* seems downright slovenly. We notice the redundancy of this sentence: "I felt suddenly the . . . whole woman go inanimate all over!" Slovenliness carries over into inattention to details. On page

286 we find "an eight-branched candelabra standing on a little table" (presumably borrowed from the climax of *Victory*); thirty pages later George overturns "the little table, bearing the six-branched candlestick." Clearly, at the time that Conrad needed him most, he had no one to furnish the kind of editorial assistance that Garnett had provided in the nineties.

Most novels contain a few slips in prose, but the pervasive faultiness of *The Arrow of Gold* indicates that we are reading not the Conrad we know but a very different and very tired writer. His fatigue appears not only in his style but in the weary actions of all his characters. Time and again we see them seated head in hand. During the long opening scene with Blunt and Mills, George lies on the divan and Blunt sits with his elbow on a table. In the next scene, the luncheon at Rita's, the whole party sits glumly at the table, Rita leaning on her elbow, her head on her hand. A later scene between Rita and Blunt takes place with Blunt leaning against the mantlepiece "on his elbow with his head in his hand." George talks to Rita "with my elbows on my knees and my head in my hands." The vigorous Madame Léonore can be seen "leaning with mature grace on her elbow," and Mrs. Blunt talks to George "leaning her elbow on the table and supporting her head on her old, impeccably shaped, white forearm." George discovers Rita in his bedroom "enveloped in the skins of wild beasts," with her "precious head repos[ing] in the palm of her hand."

Even more indicative of Conrad's own feelings of exhaustion and desperation are the descriptions of George's love pangs. George acts more like a sick old man than a young lover, in the first chapter of Part Four, despite the fact that Rita has preferred him to Blunt the night before and has clung to him dependently and sobbed upon his shoulder. When the chapter opens, George is waking up with "aching eyeballs":

In truth all that night had been the abomination of desolation to me. After wrestling with my thoughts, if the acute consciousness of a woman's existence may be called a thought, I had apparently dropped off to sleep only to go on wrestling with a nightmare, a senseless and terrifying dream of being in bonds which, even after waking, made me feel powerless in all my limbs. I lay still, suffering acutely from a renewed sense of existence, unable to lift an arm. . .

With painstaking care, Conrad follows George through all the steps of making his toilet:

Love for Rita . . . if it was love, I asked myself despairingly, while I brushed my hair before a glass. . . It is an illusion. Or perhaps mine was a physical state, some sort of disease akin to melancholia which is a form of insanity?

About the time I finished with my neck-tie I had done with life too. . . And now my toilet was finished, my occupation was gone. An immense distress descended upon me. . . "Why the devil don't I drop dead now?" I asked myself peevishly, taking a clean handkerchief out of the drawer and stuffing it in my pocket.

My five minutes' meditation in the middle of the bedroom came to an end without even a sigh. . . With measured steps I crossed the landing to my sitting-room.

George's physical lassitude continues throughout the following chapters. While talking with Mrs. Blunt he feels "like a very sick man." When he sits on the couch with Rita, he thinks in an unconscious joke: "All I was conscious of was the softness of the seat which seemed somehow to cause a relaxation of my stern mood." Another day during which George does nothing but watch his crew working on the ship leaves him so exhausted that he falls asleep in his chair: "Some time during the night I woke up chilled to the bone and in the dark. These were horrors and no mistake. I dragged myself upstairs to bed. . . The black-and-white hall was like an ice-house." Later, when George returns to his house, after the sinking of the ship, Therese helps him up the stairs and gives him hot milk. The next morning finds George again in despair:

I suppose an honourable bankrupt would know such an awakening: the sense of catastrophe, the shrinking from the necessity of beginning life again, the faint feeling that there are misfortunes which must be paid for by a hanging.

Conrad's close inspection of George's physical state is of a piece with his treatment of the other characters in the novel. We may guess that this partly expresses his own ill and exhausted condition. Yet the obsession with physical details also suggests a feeling of distance from his material. It is as if he must laboriously grope for his characters and describe their physical presences in order to believe in their existence. We notice, for example, repeated references to people's lips and mouths. Mills lets a remark "fall, gently, through his kindly lips." George admires Mr. Blunt's teeth; he finds Rita's even more impressive, despite their perplexing location: "At the last step she raised her eyelids, treated us to an exhibition of teeth as dazzling as Mr. Blunt's and looking even stronger." Rita's maid, Rose, shows "lips . . . compressed a little in a characteristic, capable manner." Therese, Rita's sister, also compresses her mouth:

The only gleam perhaps that one could find on her was that of her teeth, which one used to get between her dull lips unexpectedly, startlingly, and a little inexplicably, because it was never associated with a smile. She smiled with compressed mouth.

George is incongruously aware of his own mouth: "And with the words my life itself was being forced out through my lips."

These frequent detailed references to mouths of course weaken a reader's sense of belief. They suggest that Conrad is concentrating with difficulty, almost reading lips, trying to discover just what his characters are thinking and saying. On one occasion, while George waits for Rita to say something to him, he comments: "I expected it to come, but it didn't come. I must say, though, that I was swimming in my head and now and then had a noise as of the sea in my ears, so I might not have heard it." *The Arrow of Gold* makes precisely this impression. It reads as if it were taking place under water. Conrad seems continually to be guessing at what his characters look like, at the gestures they are making, and in particular at what they are saying. Rita appears "shadowy" to George's "bodily eyes." And in a conversation with Ortega, George says: "All my impressions were blurred; and even the promptings of my instinct were the haziest thing imaginable."

Imperfect as *The Arrow of Gold* is, it remains, nevertheless, the best executed of the last three novels. We need merely note briefly how generously *The Rover* and *Suspense* partake of the poor qualities of *The Arrow of Gold*. Both lack narrative focus and convincing characters. Both suffer from frequent passages of pretentious and essentially meaningless rhetoric and from extremely faulty prose. Finally, both reveal a gallery of exhausted and demoralized characters.

Like *The Arrow of Gold*, *The Rover* focuses briefly on several possible centers of interest but settles on none. In the first pages of the novel, Conrad draws our attention frequently to Peyrol's clumsiness and we shortly discover the cause: a money-belt full of gold. We then learn how Peyrol had got such loot, and we see him carefully hide it at the bottom of his sea chest at his new home, Escampobar Farm. The later Conrad then characteristically abandons the gold for 246 pages. (At the end of the book the Réals find the money in a well and turn it over to the French government.) In the early pages interest focuses, too, on Peyrol's strong feeling of communion with this portion of the south of France where he had been born but which he had left nearly fifty years before. Again the idea, which has real possibilities, remains undeveloped. Between Chapters Three and Four eight years pass and a nocturnal prowler becomes the new interest. We soon discover that he is a spy from an English corvette lying off-shore, and that he has been captured by Peyrol. The Englishman proves to be an old acquaintance of Peyrol's piratical days, whom Peyrol recognizes. This encounter arouses in Peyrol deep feelings of nostalgia for his old life as one of the "Brothers of the Coast." Yet he does not reveal his identity to the Englishman; he allows him to escape and never thinks of him again.

In addition to these three undeveloped fictional ideas, there are two more obvious subjects in *The Rover*: the rivalry between Peyrol and Réal over Arlette, and Réal's mission to trick the English navy by putting into their possession false French documents. The love story, like the George and Rita affair, does not inspire belief. Conrad, in fact, hardly attempts to dramatize the relationship between Arlette and Peyrol; he simply asserts at frequent intervals that violent and incomprehensible passions are engulfing one or all of the trio. Perhaps because of our recollections of the fine sea stories of the early period, we may respond more favorably to the account of Peyrol fulfilling Réal's mission by sailing his tartane, with the documents aboard, in such a way as to be caught by the English corvette. This story of three strangely assorted men in a small boat on a dangerous mission of political intrigue is, however, rather an old one. Twenty years before *The Rover*, Conrad told the story in *Nostromo*, about Nostromo, Decoud, and Hirsch. At about the same time, he described its autobiographical source in *The Mirror of the Sea*, where he tells of Dominic Cervoni, his traitorous, evil cousin, and himself aboard the *Tremolino* on an unsuccessful mission on behalf of the Carlists. In *The Arrow of Gold*, he mentions the story again and also, incidentally, "a money-belt full of gold." The version in *The Rover* probably depends heavily for its effectiveness upon the nostalgia of faithful Conradians. The account conveys little sense of action and conspicuously lacks the details of seamanship which so enrich the sea stories through "The Secret Sharer."

The Rover must stand or fall upon the credibility of its central character, old Peyrol. Conrad tries very hard to make him into a dignified and admirable figure. In fact, he uses some of the techniques that he had first employed with Singleton a quarter of a century before. He calls our attention frequently to Peyrol's "Roman" profile, and attempts to make him into something of a mythic figure with a face "like a carving of stone." His profile preserves the "immobility of a head struck on a medal." Yet Peyrol is *not* Singleton. Even though Singleton comes to understand that he is old and will die, the thought of retiring never enters his mind. It is unthinkable that a true Conradian seaman would spend eight years idling in a farmyard. Peyrol may have a Roman profile, he may look longingly at the sea, he may sneer at landsmen, yet the question remains: why did he give up? Why must he wait eight years before he suddenly feels the "longing for a great sea victory for [his] people?" The voyage on the tartane is, after all, a rather easy way out of a tedious and perplexing existence. The seamen of *The Nigger of the "Narcissus,"* "Youth," and *Typhoon* do not perform their heroic actions in a brief voyage on a lovely afternoon. And only such dubious heroes as Willems and Jim find their solution to life's problems in a quick and painless death by gunshot.

The prose of *The Rover* partakes of all the faults we have noticed in *The Arrow of Gold*. Since there are fewer and shorter love scenes, there are (happily) fewer and shorter passages of rhetoric about love. Yet we can easily find enough to know that Conrad has not really made any recovery:

> She dazzled him. Vitality streamed out of her eyes, her lips, her whole person, enveloped her like a halo and . . . yes, truly, the faintest possible flush had appeared on her cheeks, played on them faintly rosy like the light of a distant flame on the snow.

If the instances of love rhetoric diminish, the mechanical

faultiness becomes, if anything, more conspicious in *The Rover* than in *The Arrow of Gold*. We find the same difficulty with "as to," the same broken sentences:

But *as to* that, old Peyrol had made up his mind from the first to blow up his valuable charge — unemotionally, for such was his character, formed under the sun of the Indian Seas in lawless contests with his kind for a little loot that vanished as soon as grasped, but mainly for bare life almost as precarious to hold through its ups and downs, and which now had lasted for fifty-eight years.

As to what the farmer man had come for on board the tartane he had not the slightest doubt about it.

The possession of a common and momentous secret drawing men together, Peyrol condescended to explain.

Finally we find in *The Rover*, as in *The Arrow of Gold*, a pervading sense of weariness which infects all of the characters. It has perhaps a certain appropriateness in *The Rover* since the central figure and one of the important minor characters, Catherine, are both old. Nevertheless, their weariness results not only from age but also from despair. As in *The Arrow of Gold*, the most characteristic pose of the characters is seated, head in hand. At various points in the book we find Peyrol, Catherine, and Arlette in that position. More often, Peyrol and Réal sit facing each other with their arms folded on their chests. Young Réal habitually sits on a bench "with hardly a movement, for hours." When Peyrol and Réal are not sitting, they can be found leaning against a mast or a wall. The thirty-eight-year-old Scevola appears to be perpetually tired: "the patriot dragged his dirty clogs low-spiritedly in the fresh light of the young morning." He spends much of his time "lying open-eyed on his tumbled pallet in raging sulks about something." Sooner or later virtually every character despairs. The young lieutenant feels sick of life, "the desperation of a man under torture." Peyrol reaches "that depth of despondency" in which there is "nothing more before him but a black gulf into which his consciousness sank like a stone." Scevola resembles a "sick child," while Catherine, who tells Peyrol she is "tired of life," staggers under "the weight of her accumulated years." In short, *The Rover* hardly conveys the sense of serenity which its admirers have attributed to it.

Suspense, Conrad's unfinished last novel, represents that venture into historical fiction which he had contemplated since 1907. It is curious that Conrad had for so long aspired to write a historical novel, for his talent does not seem to point in that direction. The early Conrad deals with setting, costumes, manners, and public events not so much for their own sake as for their capacity to reveal what happens inside his characters. Even *The Nigger of the "Narcissus,"* which explicitly memorializes a passing phase of life dramatizes the *spirit* of that life more than its outward manifestations.

The early Conrad, nevertheless, does use history for his psychological purposes. We think, for example, of *Lord Jim*. John D. Gordan shows clearly that the Patusan portions of that book owe much to Conrad's reading in histories of Rajah Brooke of Sarawak. But Conrad there completely assimilated his sources. Mr. Gordan, in the light of his own painstaking study of all the books about Brooke available to Conrad, says that "it is impossible to tell exactly which he knew. He may have known them all equally well." [13]

Finding the source of *Suspense* has proved no such problem. Less than a year after its publication, Miss Mildred Atkinson, in a letter to the *Times Literary Supplement*,[14] showed that the source of *Suspense* is the *Memoirs of the Countess de Boigne*. Conrad does not, however, use the *Memoirs* as he does the history of Rajah Brooke, simply for hints about characters and events. Rather, the *Memoirs* furnish character relationships and even actual wording. Miss Miriam H. Woods quotes six passages from *Suspense*, some of paragraph length, one of almost a page, which follow the

Memoirs virtually word for word.[15] The *Memoirs*, in fact, supply practically all that is new in *Suspense*. We have already seen that *Suspense* tends to move in the same weary circle as the later love stories, complete with hero, heroine, and voyeur-villain. Some of the scenes appear to be faint echoes of Conrad's previous work: the salon scene, for example, seems to arise from a forty-five-year-old memory of the Carlist intrigue, filtered twice, through *Nostromo* and *The Arrow of Gold*. As history, *Suspense* gives us little sense of the past, and, except for the *Memoirs* material, it contains none but the most obvious historical details. In other words, Conrad, at the end of his career, was using history, not as an adventure into a new kind of writing, but as a crutch for exhausted creativity.

In his introduction to *Suspense*, Richard Curle indicates that Conrad himself, though he had written nearly 300 pages, did not really know where the center of interest would lie. He discussed *Suspense* with Curle the day before he died and told him: "I see five or six different lines of treatment." [16] Certainly, a reading of *Suspense* does not reveal any signs of a true subject emerging. Rather, as in *The Arrow of Gold* and *The Rover*, we find only a series of hints of emerging subjects, but no real development. Among the possible narrative "lines" we find these: the Count de Montevesso, Doctor Martel, and Cantelucci appear to be involved in a conspiracy to release Napoleon from Elba; Doctor Martel seems also to be in the service of the French Bourbons; the Count, out of jealousy over his wife, is plotting against Cosmo; the Count has a strangely paternal attitude toward his "niece," Clelia, which will need fuller explanation; and, finally, Cosmo is involved with Attilio in an adventure the nature of which is a complete mystery.

By far the most intriguing of *Suspense's* many subjects is the hint that Cosmo and his beloved Adèle are, unbeknownst to them, children of the same father. This would be the only time in Conrad's career in which he consciously dealt with incest, a subject which we have already seen lurking beneath the surface of a great many of his love stories. At any rate, Conrad has clearly prepared in *Suspense* for the revelation that Cosmo and Adèle are half-brother and -sister. Early in the novel we learn that Cosmo's father, Sir Charles Latham, had, as a young man touring Europe, gained "great social recognition in Paris and Versailles" but had "suddenly" left France for Italy. He spends "some months" in Florence, then "suddenly" determines to go home.

During a long, sleepless night which he spent pacing up and down in the agony of an internal struggle with himself in the magnificent rooms of his lodgings in Florence, he concluded that he would go home by sea. It was the easiest way of avoiding coming near Paris. He had heard not long before that the best friends he had made in the brilliant society he had frequented in France, the Marquis and the Marquise d'Armand, had a daughter born to them.

The daughter, of course, is Adèle, and there are hints of both her own and her mother's connection with Sir Charles several times in the early portions of the novel. During the French Revolution, Adèle and her parents seek refuge with the Lathams in England, where Sir Charles reacts more sympathetically to the Marquise's distress than does her husband. Adèle develops a "filial affection" for Sir Charles. When he looks at his own daughter, Henrietta, he has a "vision of another head, very different and very fair, by its side. It had been a part of his retired life and had had a large share of his affection." He understands Adèle "even better than he understood his own daughter." Cosmo furnishes perhaps the most convincing evidence after he has visited the grown up Adèle in Genoa. When he first sees her, he feels dimly that she is no stranger, that he has "seen her glory before." He does not connect this recognition with the little Adèle who had visited them during the Revolution. "And it had been in

Latham Hall — but not in a dream. . . She must have been foretold to him in some picture he had seen in Latham Hall. . ." "Terror-struck as if at the discovery of a crime," Cosmo leaps up and runs out of his hotel room. The use of a portrait to reveal the identity of an illegitimate child is hardly new in fiction. Dickens, for instance, exposes Lady Dedlock as the mother of Esther Summerson through the resemblance between Esther and a portrait in the Dedlock country house. What Conrad intended to do with the situation of Cosmo in love with his half-sister, Adèle, we shall never know. Our last view of Cosmo shows him headed out to sea with no suggestion that he will ever encounter her again.

Cosmo's characterization proves to be even less satisfactory than that of Peyrol or of George. He is the last in the new category of boy-heroes. Like the others, Cosmo appears to be moving from simple naïveté to complex maturity, but he in fact already evinces a kind of sophistication. Cosmo's most characteristic scene, a secret, "serious" conversation with Adèle, recalls scenes between George and Rita in the first half of *The Arrow of Gold*. While these scenes abound in sophisticated conversation with sexual overtones, they do not suggest maturity. Yet some critics of Conrad admire the later boy-heroes: Mr. Wiley finds that Conrad "establishes a basis of reference to the norm of conduct" through them.[17] We may agree that they are normal enough, but we would insist that it is important for their creator to recognize their immaturity. The early Conrad realizes that vulnerable heroes like Jim and Decoud are false; the later Conrad does not seem to understand that Powell, the young captain, George, Carter, and Cosmo remain throughout their stories rather talkative adolescents.

If Cosmo appears adolescent, he has, like George and Peyrol, little more physical and mental vigor than an ailing old man. Cosmo's every movement seems a tremendous effort. The novel abounds in staircases which Cosmo must toil "up and up." Like George, he has difficulty tying his neckcloth. He falls "heavily" into chairs and cannot endure the sound of a drum coming through his window. Up and about, he slips off into open-eyed sleep, but in bed, he sleeps fitfully. He has difficulty writing his sister a letter, and discovers, when he finally settles down to the task, that "it required all his courage to keep on, piling up words." He trembles with "doubts and apprehensions" when he wakes up in the morning and needs "keen, pure air" to rouse his "vitality." A feeling of immense depression constantly distracts him from the life about him, so that he loses the track of conversations with his beloved Adèle and with the fascinating Doctor Martel. The weary Cosmo scarcely hears the latter's talk of Talleyrand:

"The Prince?" repeated Cosmo, struggling to keep his head above the black waters of melancholia which seemed to lap about his very lips. "You have said the Prince, haven't you? What Prince?"

At the end of this day which has been full of hints of love and mystery, Cosmo can only ponder:

He had got through the day. Now there was the evening to get through somehow. But when it occurred to him that the evening would be followed by the hours of an endless night . . . the desolation of the prospect was so overpowering that he could only meet it with a bitter laugh.

These thoughts seem hardly appropriate to a youthful hero; they seem rather to be the author's personal musings, put down on the page untouched by imagination.

R. P. Blackmur, discussing Henry James's stories about artists, says that the artist "comes to life . . . only as he *fails* to be an artist, and he fails when the conditions of life overcome him at the expense of his art." [18] This statement applies to artists in life as well as in fiction. The failures of *The Arrow of Gold, The Rescue, The Rover,* and *Suspense* inevitably lead us to think not of Conrad the artist but of the man living out the last years of his life down in Kent.

The evidence from Conrad's biographers and from his letters indicates that the more than twenty years of very hard work, most of it under the stress of sickness (his own and his family's), much of it under severe economic pressures, at last took their toll. Jean-Aubry tells us that in the early part of 1916 "he was almost continuously ill." [19] In May, 1917, Conrad wrote to Garnett that he had "been gouty and almost continuously laid up since February." [20] A year later:

I can't think consecutively and the few distressed thoughts that are knocking about in my head I am totally unable to put into words. It's a most distressing and depressing state to be in. One marches staggering along the very edge of despair hour after hour, day after day, feeling that one will never get anywhere.[21]

New Year's Day, 1920:

I've done nothing for the last six weeks and I feel that I'll never do anything any more. Somehow I don't feel so happy about it as I ought to — for what could be more soothing than a sense of impotence? [22]

In 1922, he wrote Galsworthy:

Ever since finishing *The Rescue* (two years or more ago) I have had, in one way or another, a pretty bad time. The reaction from the war, anxiety about Jessie, the growing sense of my own deficiencies have combined to make anything but a bed of roses for my aging bones. My very soul is aching all over.[23]

And Mrs. Conrad speaks, in the twenties, of "his usual rather invalidish condition." [24]

Conrad's ill health unquestionably aged him early and it had perceptible effects upon his use of language. R. B. Cunninghame Graham, who had known Conrad since the earliest years of his writing career, noticed that although his flow of vigorous and idiomatic English never failed, and his vocabulary only grew richer as the years passed by, his accent (once slight) "became more marked, and certain turns of phrase appeared, that . . . were not English." [25] Ill health had still another effect upon Conrad's language; gout crippled his hand and wrist until he had to dictate his last novels. Doubtless that dictation added considerable strain to Conrad's creativity. When he was dictating *The Arrow of Gold*, his invalid wife could hear every word upstairs because the process so unnerved him that he shouted at his typist sitting only a few feet away.[26] He became wrought up over his difficulties with *Suspense* to the point of trying to write with a pen and dictate at the same time. Mrs. Conrad comments:

> The novel *Suspense* got itself written very slowly, and it was very plain to my anxious watching that the energy was out of everything for him. From my bedroom in the room above I could hear his voice strained to the top pitch. It was useless to attempt to get him to do only one or the other, either write or dictate. The more nervous he got . . . the more he used his strength in this trying fashion.[27]

It is difficult to assess the effect of dictation on style. The early style gives every indication of having been thought over with the greatest care. Its complexity would almost seem to require that the author think it out on paper. Moreover, the real break in Conrad's style occurs precisely at the point where he begins dictation. Though *Victory* has some fairly appalling purple passages, its style escapes the real faultiness of *The Arrow of Gold*. Conrad himself seems to have felt that dictation had a bad effect upon his expression. The letters of his last years contain a number of irritable remarks on the subject.[28] At the end of a long letter to Garnett trying to explain the weaknesses of *The Rover*, Conrad comments: "Had I been writing with pen and ink I would probably come nearer to expressing·myself." [29] Galsworthy, writing his reminiscences of Conrad immediately after his death, says of the dictation: "I cannot but believe that his work suffered from that necessity." [30]

While recognizing the effects of ill health upon the last works, we may also assume that these novels suffer from Conrad's relative isolation in Kent. After expending the rich materials of his early life in his work through *Nostromo*, Conrad did embark upon new subjects and settings in *The Secret Agent, Under Western Eyes,* and *Chance*. But from *Victory* on, he had recourse to early and already exploited material. Virginia Woolf, fortunate in the intellectual environment of her own art, gives a sympathetic and accurate account of Conrad's situation in her diary (she had just completed a destructive review of *The Rescue*):

> Wednesday, June 23rd, [1920]
> I was struggling, at this time, to say honestly that I don't think Conrad's last book a good one. I have said it. It is painful (a little) to find fault there, where almost solely, one respects. I can't help suspecting the truth to be that he never sees anyone who knows good writing from bad, and then being a foreigner, talking broken English, married to a lump of a wife, he withdraws more and more into what he once did well, only piles it on higher and higher, until what can one call it but stiff melodrama. I would not like to find *The Rescue* signed Virginia Woolf. But will anyone agree with this? [31]

Those recent critics who feel that Conrad's last novels are failures apparently assume that Conrad himself was totally unaware of his own decline.[32] Admittedly, Conrad, except in the 1897 preface to *The Nigger of the "Narcissus,"* rarely talks perceptively about his own work. But must we then believe that he considered his later work as good as the early? It is not likely that he would tell his readers in his prefaces that the later books are inferior. Moreover, the letters in which he purports to value his last work are chiefly to relative strangers.

The later letters to Galsworthy and Sanderson, whom Conrad first met aboard the *Torrens* in 1893, and to Edward Garnett, who "discovered" him in 1894, indicate that Conrad was continually haunted by an awareness of declining powers. If he had completely accepted this knowledge, he could not, of course, have written at all. But the knowledge was there. Upon the success of *Chance* he wrote to Galsworthy in 1914:

> *Chance* had a tremendous press. How I would have felt about it ten or eight years ago I can't say. Now I can't even pretend I am elated. If I had *Nostromo, The Nigger, Lord Jim,* in my desk or only in my head, I would feel differently no doubt.[33]

A letter to the Sandersons, written December 31, 1917, while he was working on *The Arrow of Gold,* indicates clearly the contempt and the shame he felt about his last novels:

> You can imagine what sort of stuff that is. No colour, no relief, no *tonality*; the thinnest possible squeaky bubble. And when I've finished with it, I shall go out and sell it in a market place for 20 times the money I had for the *Nigger,* 30 times the money I had for the *Mirror of the Sea.*
>
> It is a horrible prospect. And because I have not enough satanism in my nature I can't enjoy it. I am really a much more decent person than you would think. It's a great disadvantage.
>
> I don't know why I've told you all this; but I feel better for it.[34]

(This letter becomes even more meaningful when we remember the importance of the word "tonality" for Conrad. He uses it with particular emphasis in his 1917 preface to *Youth and Two Other Stories* where he tries to convey the symbolic richness, the resonance, of "Heart of Darkness.") If Conrad does not positively damn *The Rescue* and *The Rover,* his claims for them are very modest. He agrees, in 1919, with Garnett that his original impulse to drop "The Rescuer" in the nineties was right, but he adds:

> . . . I cannot say I regret the impulse which made me take it up again. I am settling my affairs in this world and I should not have liked to leave behind me this evidence of having bitten off more than I could chew.[35]

During the writing of *The Rover,* he wrote Garnett that the characters had gotten on his nerves in a way that had never happened before.[36] Richard Curle tells us "that Conrad, if not particularly pleased with [*The Rover*], was at any rate particularly pleased at having completed it." [37] In a letter to Galsworthy, Conrad called *Suspense* "a chase in a nightmare, — weird and exhausting." [38]

In the last years, then, Conrad the man appears to us more admirable than his work, more heroic than his characters. He had always looked upon writing as a career, a profession, just as he had earlier regarded the maritime service.[39] Unlike Peyrol, who chose to retire on the money he had acquired by luck, the later Conrad showed little inclination to stop writing. Like Singleton, Conrad had been caught by old age and ill health, and he was no longer the man he had been. Nevertheless, he, too, continued to pursue his career until time put an end to "the long record of his faithful work."

The principal concern of this study has not been, however, the man Conrad who died more than thirty years ago. While we cannot help responding to the tragedy of his last years, we neither honor him nor enlighten ourselves by trying to find some redeeming feature in his decline. From his earliest days as a writer, he had a terror of losing his imaginative powers; like the passing of youth, it happened "too soon — too soon."

Rather, our purpose has been to train ourselves to hear the authentic voice of the living Conrad which comes to us from the pages of his masterpieces. If we approach him without due awareness of his limitations and of the conflicting impulses that finally exhausted him, we shall confuse second-rate writing with the true Conrad. If we are not alert to his difficulty in dealing with love, we may, on the one hand, take Giselle seriously and yet, on the other, fail to appreciate the magnitude of his achievement with Emilia Gould. Much worse, we may actually persuade ourselves that Rita represents some sort of culmination to Conrad's work rather than one of the least convincing heroines in fiction.

If we are not conscious of the marked decline in the quality of his art after 1912, we may tend to mix indiscriminately in our minds early and late ideas and characters simply because of superficial resemblances. Explicit statements about self-recognition and initiation in *The Shadow Line* and *The Arrow of Gold*, about skepticism and romanticism in *Victory* and *Chance*, may lead us to believe that these novels embody the same profound perceptions as the great early works. Apparent resemblances between Anthony and Jim, Heyst and Decoud, Peyrol and Singleton, between the two young captains in *The Shadow Line* and "The Secret Sharer," may cause us to respond in much the same way to all of them. If this happens, it means that through insensitive reading we have deprived ourselves of the enjoyment and understanding which Jim, Decoud, and the other fine early characters can afford us. In the same way, imprecise attention to technique may lead us, as it has led a number of others, to think *Chance* the most complex of Conrad's novels, rather than the most cumbersome, and to read the opening pages of *The Arrow of Gold* as ingenious plotting rather than confused narration.

It is indeed difficult to conquer the impulse to find greatness in all the works of a man we sense to be great. Yet this impulse is pernicious. It has brought forth complicated mythical and allegorical interpretations of novels that probably ought not even to have been published. Such lack of discrimination is perhaps less reprehensible, however, than the approach that insists that literary greatness lies only in explicitly, unequivocally affirmative works. This approach has led to gross overrating of inferior Conrad and to dismissal of some of his best works as "minor." To fail to perceive the vast differences in his quality or to hunt for that quality in the wrong places means that one listens not to Conrad's voice but to one's own. And to be deaf to the true Conrad is to be deprived of one of the finest voices in our literature: pessimistic, skeptical, ironic — but also courageous, sympathetic, profoundly human.

Chronological List of Conrad's Significant Works

The list contains only those works of Conrad which are discussed in this book. It therefore omits the following: two volumes of short stories, *A Set of Six* (1908) and *Tales of Hearsay* (1925); two volumes of essays, *Notes on Life and Letters* (1921) and *Last Essays* (1926); two novels written in collaboration with Ford Madox Ford and containing very little by Conrad, *The Inheritors* (1901) and *The Nature of a Crime* (1924). The probable date of completion appears first, followed by the year of initial publication in book form. These dates come chiefly from Conrad's published letters, from Jean-Aubry's *Life and Letters*, and from Gordan's *Joseph Conrad: The Making of a Novelist*. All quotations from Conrad's works in this book are from the Doubleday, Page and Company "Canterbury Edition" (New York, 1924–26). This edition is identical to others published since by Doubleday and to the current Collected Edition of J. M. Dent and Sons Ltd., London. None of these editions contains *The Sisters*, published by Crosby Gaige (New York, 1928).

Almayer's Folly	May	1894	(1895)
An Outcast of the Islands	September	1895	(1896)
The Sisters (unfinished)	March	1896	(1928)
"The Idiots"	May	1896	(1898, in *Tales of Unrest*)
"An Outpost of Progress"	July	1896	(1898, in *Tales of Unrest*)
"The Lagoon"	August	1896	(1898, in *Tales of Unrest*)
The Nigger of the "Narcissus"	February	1897	(1897)
"Karain"	April	1897	(1898, in *Tales of Unrest*)
"The Return"	September	1897	(1898, in *Tales of Unrest*)

"Youth"	June	1898	(1902, in *Youth and Two Other Stories*)
["The Rescuer," Parts I–III]	December	1898	
"Heart of Darkness"	February	1899	(1902, in *Youth and Two Other Stories*)
Lord Jim	July	1900	(1900)
Typhoon	January	1901	(1902)
"Falk"	May	1901	(1903, in *Typhoon and Other Stories*)
"Amy Foster"	June	1901	(1903, in *Typhoon and Other Stories*)
Romance (with Ford Madox Ford)	March	1902	(1903)
"The End of the Tether"	October	1902	(1902, in *Youth and Two Other Stories*
Nostromo	September	1904	(1904)
The Mirror of the Sea	October	1905	(1906)
The Secret Agent	September	1906	(1907)
A Personal Record	June	1909	(1912)
"The Secret Sharer"	November	1909	(1912, in *'Twixt Land and Sea*)
Under Western Eyes	January	1910	(1911)
"A Smile of Fortune"	August	1910	(1912, in *'Twixt Land and Sea*)
"Freya of the Seven Isles"	Summer	1910	(1912, in *'Twixt Land and Sea*)
Chance	March	1912	(1913)
"The Planter of Malata"	Autumn	1913	(1915, in *Within the Tides*)
Victory	June	1914	(1915)
The Shadow Line	March	1915	(1917)
The Arrow of Gold	June	1918	(1919)
The Rescue	May	1919	(1920)
The Rover	July	1922	(1923)
Suspense (unfinished at his death, August 3, 1924)			(1925)

Notes

Introduction

1. M. C. Bradbrook, *Joseph Conrad: Poland's English Genius* (Cambridge, 1941).
2. F. R. Leavis, *The Great Tradition* (London, 1948), pp. 173–226.
3. Introduction by Morton D. Zabel to *The Portable Conrad* (New York, 1947), pp. 25–30.
4. Albert J. Guerard, *Joseph Conrad* (New York, 1947), pp. 55–56, 83.
5. *Ibid.*, pp. 27–30.
6. John Galsworthy, *Castles in Spain* (New York, 1927), pp. 109–110. (Galsworthy's memory played him false; "The Secret Sharer" was written several years before Conrad completed *Chance* and the first chapters of *The Rescue* were written in 1896.)
7. Douglas Hewitt, *Conrad: A Reassessment* (Cambridge, 1952), pp. 4–5.
8. Quoted by John V. Hagopian, "Minutes of the Sixth Annual Conference," *Literature and Psychology* 6:3 (1956).
9. Jessie Conrad, *Joseph Conrad as I Knew Him* (New York, 1926), p. 105.
10. *Ibid.*, p. 104.
11. *Ibid.*, p. 45.
12. Ford Madox Ford, *Joseph Conrad: A Personal Remembrance* (Boston, 1924), p. 119.
13. George H. Doran, *Chronicles of Barabbas: 1884–1934* (New York, 1935), p. 83.
14. Lionel Trilling, *The Liberal Imagination* (New York, 1953), p. 152.
15. Hewitt, p. 2.
16. *Ibid.*, pp. 16–30, 40–45.
17. Dorothy Van Ghent, *The English Novel: Form and Function* (New York, 1953), pp. 229–244.
18. *Joseph Conrad: Life and Letters*, by G. Jean-Aubry, 2 vols. (New York, 1927), II, 6. (Since three quarters of this work consists of Conrad's letters, it will be considered to be by Conrad and will hereafter be referred to as *Life and Letters*.)

Chapter I, The Early Conrad's Anatomy of Moral Failure (1895–1912)

1. Both Leavis and Zabel published articles on Conrad before their books, cited in the notes above.

2. *Conrad to a Friend: Letters from Joseph Conrad to Richard Curle,* ed. Richard Curle (New York, 1928), p. 147.

3. Introduction by Robert Penn Warren to *Nostromo* (New York, 1951), p. xxvii.

4. See, especially, Guerard, pp. 30–52.

5. See Introduction by Warren to *Nostromo*, pp. xxi–xxiii.

6. Quoted by Richard Curle, *The Last Twelve Years of Joseph Conrad* (New York, 1928), p. 83.

7. Joseph Warren Beach, *The Twentieth Century Novel: Studies in Technique* (New York, 1932), pp. 359–365.

8. Trilling, p. 215.

9. Leavis, p. 189.

10. Introduction by Zabel to *Portable Conrad*, p. 17.

Chapter II, The Uncongenial Subject: Love's Tangled Garden (1895–1924)

1. *Life and Letters*, II, 66. Conrad's italics. Actually, two stories of *A Set of Six*, "The Duel" and "Il Conde," are well worth the reader's time.

2. *Letters from Joseph Conrad, 1895–1924*, ed. with an introduction and notes by Edward Garnett (Indianapolis, 1928), p. 67.

3. Max Beerbohm, "The Feast, by J*s*ph C*nr*d," *A Christmas Garland* (London, 1912), pp. 123–130.

4. Vernon Young rightly castigates this passage as the "stubborn and overdressed misogyny that devitalizes much of Conrad's writing." "Lingard's Folly: The Lost Subject," *Kenyon Review* 15:529 (1953).

5. H. R. Lenormand, "Note sur un séjour de Conrad en Corse," *Hommage à Joseph Conrad, La Nouvelle Révue Française*, nouvelle série CXXXV (1924), 669.

6. This image recurs, of course, in the scene where little Nina's sigh topples Lingard's house of cards.

7. All information pertaining to the dating of Conrad's works from *Almayer's Folly* through *Lord Jim* comes from John D. Gordan's invaluable chapter, "A Chronicle of the Early Stories," in his *Joseph Conrad: The Making of a Novelist* (Cambridge, Mass., 1940), pp. 174–268.

8. Introduction by Ford Madox Ford to *The Sisters* (New York, 1928), pp. 1–16. Ford says that Stephen and Rita were to marry and that the story was to end violently, all of which the fragment certainly implies.

The novel was to have been primarily about incest, Ford goes on, and the final disaster was to have come about through Stephen's "incestuous" love for his sister-in-law, Therese. The text does not suggest this; it does hint that Ortega has incestuous feelings for his niece, Rita, but it seems unlikely that Conrad consciously intended this. Ford's speculations do not inspire confidence, especially when at one point in his introduction he confuses the older sister Therese, with the younger, Rita.

9. By August, 1897, Conrad had changed the title of the manuscript from "The Rescuer" to "The Rescue." In order, however, to distinguish the manuscript from the book, *The Rescue*, I have retained its original title. In so doing, I am following T. J. Wise, purchaser of the manuscript, who gave it the title "The Rescuer" despite the fact that the revised title occurs frequently in the manuscript after pt. I. (Brit. Mus. MS Ashley 4787.)

10. *Letters from Conrad*, p. 59.

11. In "The Rescuer" manuscript Conrad calls them Edith Travers, Mr. Travers, and Linares. Though Conrad's letters indicate that he first intended to call her Beatrix, her name is Edith throughout the manuscript. Linares becomes d'Alcacer in *The Rescue*, and both the author and Lingard speak of Edith as Mrs. Travers in *The Rescue*.

12. *Life and Letters*, I, 164, note.

13. *Letters from Conrad*, p. 61.

14. *Ibid.*, p. 63.

15. *Ibid.*, p. 141.

16. Twenty words of this appear in *The Rescue*, pt. III, chap. IX. The following quotations about Edith and Lingard from "The Rescuer" were retained virtually unchanged by the later Conrad in *The Rescue*, pt. III, chaps. VI, VII, and VIII.

17. *A Conrad Memorial Library*, ed. George T. Keating (New York, 1929), p. 62.

18. *Life and Letters*, I, 207.

19. *Letters from Conrad*, p. 111.

20. See Robert L. Morris, "Eliot's 'Game of Chess' and Conrad's 'The Return,'" *Modern Language Notes* 65:422–423 (1950).

21. Leavis, p. 181.

22. It is appropriate that the manuscript, "Tuan Jim: A Sketch," (Harvard College Library, MS Eng. 46.5), should contain a cryptic, one-sentence speech by Linares.

23. Gordan shows that "The Rescuer" and *Lord Jim* share the same "sources" from history and from Conrad's own life. Lingard's adventures in Borneo and Jim's in Patusan both owe much to Conrad's reading about Rajah James Brooke of Sarawak. The model for Tom Lingard was a trader of that name in Borneo; the model for Jim was his younger brother, Jim Lingard. Conrad met both while a mate on the *Vidar*. See Gordan, pp. 35–74, *passim*.

24. *Ibid.*, p. 53.

25. Leavis, p. 190.
26. Curle, *Last Twelve Years*, p. 84.
27. *Ibid.*, pp. 83–84.
28. *Letters from Conrad*, p. 171.
29. *Life and Letters*, II, 65.
30. *Ibid.*, II, 144.
31. *Letters from Conrad*, pp. 107, 243.
32. Love does not, perhaps, explain Conrad's other long, ambitious failure of this period, the uneconomical, sentimental "End of the Tether" (published in *Youth and Two Other Stories*, 1902). Nevertheless, hints of Captain Whalley's incestuous love for his daughter and of Massey's and Van Wyk's homosexual attraction to the old captain indicate that confusion about sexual material may have contributed to Conrad's difficulty with the story.
33. At the same time that he was working on "Falk," Conrad was collaborating with Ford Madox Ford (then Hueffer) on *Romance* (1903). Part IV (wholly by Conrad) reminds us of "Falk" in its handling of the lovers. Although hero and heroine have three long scenes together, they are virtually unable to talk to one another. In one they are vigorously chaperoned; in the other two, they are hiding from their enemy, Manuel-del-Popolo, who hovers so near they scarcely dare speak. Frankly an "entertainment," *Romance* has considerable vigor. Moreover, it foreshadows both *Nostromo* and *The Arrow of Gold*. The detailed description of Manuel's lingering death sounds two echoes: the drowsy eyes recall the memorable death of Señor Hirsch; the position of the broken body prefigures that of Señor Ortega lying wounded at the foot of the stairs.
34. Gordan, p. 90.
35. *Life and Letters*, II, 114.
36. *Letters from Conrad*, p. 15.
37. *Life and Letters*, II, 154.
38. Introduction by Morton D. Zabel to *Under Western Eyes* (New York, 1951), p. xiii.
39. Paul L. Wiley, *Conrad's Measure of Man* (Madison, 1954), pp. 132–198.
40. Introduction by Hugh Walpole to *Chance*, Memorial Edition (New York, 1925), p. viii.
41. Guerard, p. 24.
42. *Ibid.*
43. Hewitt, p. 98.
44. *Life and Letters*, II, 232.
45. Hewitt, p. 109.
46. *Letters from Conrad*, p. 299.
47. See Guerard, p. 23.
48. Wiley, p. 187.
49. Hewitt, p. 111.

50. Hewitt, p. 109.
51. See Wiley, p. 135.
52. See Edmund Wilson, *The Wound and the Bow* (New York, 1947),
pp. 237–240.
53. Wiley, pp. 135–136.
54. Hewitt, p. 96.

Chapter III, *The Later Conrad's "Affirmation"*

1. Bradbrook, pp. 75, 50–59, 67.
2. Leavis, pp. 187, 225, 209, 208.
3. Introduction by Zabel to *Portable Conrad*, p. 43.
4. Walter F. Wright, *Romance and Tragedy in Joseph Conrad* (Lincoln, Nebraska, 1949), p. 88.
5. Wiley, pp. 186, 198.
6. Introduction by Zabel to *Portable Conrad*, p. 19.
7. Jean-Aubry says Conrad finished *Victory* on June 28, 1914 (*Life and Letters*, II, 7).
8. *Chance* was completed March 25, 1912 (*Life and Letters*, II, 138).
9. See Wiley, pp. 158–162.
10. See *Letters from Conrad*, p. 246.
11. We must be cautious in handling "The Rescuer." Its pt. IV seems to belong almost wholly to 1916, when Conrad made an abortive attempt to finish the novel. Therefore only pts. I to III can be considered as authentic early work (1896–1898). We should be a little skeptical about minor differences between "The Rescuer" and *The Rescue* since these revisions could conceivably belong to the early period. When in 1918 Conrad sold "The Rescuer" to collector T. J. Wise, he told him that "several typed copies" had been made from it, "each introducing changes and alterations" (*Life and Letters*, II, 209). We do not know when these copies were made or how much they differ from "The Rescuer." Jean-Aubry indicates that one revision dates from early 1916 (*Life and Letters*, II, 165). In any case, the serial version, which appeared in *Land and Water* from January to July, 1919, retains essentially the language of the original although cuts have been made; only the new, second half represents the language of the later Conrad. The final revision was made between December 8, 1919, and January 24, 1920 (Gordan, p. 218); *The Rescue* appeared in book form a few months later.
12. See Wiley, pp. 173–187.
13. There are two sides to every question, including that of revision. Our bias has been that most revisions in "The Rescuer" are changes for the worse. Walter F. Wright holds a different view in "Conrad's *The Rescue* from Serial to Book," *Research Studies of the State College of Washington* 13:208 (1945). He has studied the changes that the later Conrad made when he prepared the serialized version of *The Rescue* for book publication. Mr. Wright apparently did not look at "The

Rescuer," so his discussion of revisions does not take into account the question of which prose in the serial belongs to 1896, which to 1919. In any case, Mr. Wright sees the changes in Travers and in all the characters as an improvement in the "emotional tone." For Mr. Wright, as for most students of revisions, every alteration is admirable. This is not necessarily a safe assumption; other writers, as well as Conrad — Pope and Wordsworth, for example — have been compulsive revisers, constantly tampering with manuscript, first edition, and collected edition, sometimes to revise brilliantly, sometimes to weaken a satisfactory passage.

14. See Leavis, pp. 201–209.

15. Beach, pp. 356–359.

16. Edward Crankshaw, *Joseph Conrad: Some Aspects of the Art of the Novel* (London, 1936), pp. 124–133, 173–177.

17. Leavis, p. 224.

18. Hewitt, pp. 2–3. My italics.

19. Introduction by Zabel to *Portable Conrad*, p. 16.

20. Hewitt, p. 94.

21. Curle, *Last Twelve Years*, p. 95.

22. Wiley, p. 173.

23. Vernon Young, although he has apparently not looked at "The Rescuer" manuscript, believes that Conrad does a good job of matching the old and new prose in *The Rescue*. Mr. Young, moreover, clearly disapproves of both the early and the late, preferring some middle prose; he writes of *The Rescue*: "The prose is of a piece with the unchecked illusionism of approach; it recovers the will to the mysterious which Conrad, between 1911 and 1917, had brought under control." Mr. Young goes on to quote two passages from *The Rescue* to demonstrate Conrad's recovery of the "will to the mysterious." He grants, however, that the new "illusionism" shown in his quotes is somewhat inferior to the old: "In these, and many other passages . . . the symbolic chiaroscuro which Conrad had used so deliberately in *The Nigger of the 'Narcissus'* has become a formula which confuses thought and observation alike." The two examples Mr. Young gives do seem to be a startling 1919 recovery of the style of the nineties, but unfortunately they were written in the nineties. Both quotations come from pt. III of "The Rescuer" and hence, on the basis of the available evidence, must have been written no later than a year after the publication of *The Nigger of the "Narcissus."* (See Young, pp. 537–538.)

Chapter IV, The Exhaustion of Creative Energy

1. *Life and Letters*, II, 166.

2. Introduction by Richard Curle to *Suspense* (New York, 1926), pp. vi–vii.

3. Wiley, pp. 132–133.

4. *Life and Letters*, II, 213.

5. Gordan, p. 33. Mr. Gordan thinks that Stephen foreshadows Henry Allègre, rather than George. But Stephen, though a disenchanted Bohemian, is certainly too young and too inexperienced in love to resemble that famous and mature artist. See Gordan, pp. 348–349, note.

6. *Ibid.*, pp. 35–60.

7. *Life and Letters*, I, 35–37.

8. Gordan, pp. 122, 125, 145–146, 164–165.

9. *Life and Letters*, II, 165.

10. *Life and Letters*, I, 108.

11. Guerard, p. 24.

12. Leavis, p. 182.

13. Gordan, p. 65.

14. Mildred Atkinson, *Times Literary Supplement*, no. 1,258 (Feb. 25, 1926), p. 142.

15. Miriam H. Woods, "A Source of Conrad's *Suspense*," *Modern Language Notes* 50:390–394 (1935).

16. Introduction by Curle to *Suspense*, p. vi.

17. Wiley, p. 198.

18. R. P. Blackmur, "In the Country of the Blue," *The Question of Henry James*, ed. F. W. Dupee (New York, 1945), p. 198.

19. *Life and Letters*, II, 165.

20. *Letters from Conrad*, p. 250.

21. *Ibid.*, p. 257.

22. *Ibid.*, p. 268.

23. *Life and Letters*, II, 274.

24. Jessie Conrad, *Joseph Conrad and His Circle* (New York, 1935), p. 230.

25. Preface by R. B. Cunninghame Graham to *Tales of Hearsay* (New York, 1926), p. ix.

26. R. L. Mégroz, *Joseph Conrad's Mind and Method* (London, 1931), p. 90.

27. Jessie Conrad, *Joseph Conrad and His Circle*, p. 267.

28. See *Letters from Conrad*, pp. 270, 283, and *Life and Letters*, II, 259, 318.

29. *Letters from Conrad*, p. 300.

30. Galsworthy, p. 117.

31. Virginia Woolf, *A Writer's Diary*, ed. Leonard Woolf (London, 1954), p. 27.

32. Discussing *The Rescue*, Vernon Young confidently asserts that Conrad "would not then have perceived" the irony inherent in making a glamorous and heroic figure out of the once foolish Lingard, "since he expressed no such violent dissatisfaction with *The Rescue* as he had with *An Outcast of the Islands*." (Young, p. 539.) Douglas Hewitt, on the basis of Conrad's letters, prefaces, and occasional writings, concludes

that Conrad, particularly in the later period, lacked self-knowledge. (Hewitt, pp. 118–128.)

33. *Life and Letters,* II, 152.
34. *Ibid.,* II, 198–199. (My italics.)
35. *Letters from Conrad,* p. 263.
36. *Ibid.,* p. 284.
37. Curle, *Last Twelve Years,* p. 96.
38. *Life and Letters,* II, 340.
39. Gordan, pp. 26–27.

Index of Titles and Characters

Characters are indexed under the name by which they are more commonly known; some are under first names and others under last names.

DATE DUE

MAR 15 '87			
APR 2 8 1995			
			•
GAYLORD			PRINTED IN U.S.A.